AMERICA'S JAILS

ALTERNATIVE CRIMINOLOGY

General Editor: Jeff Ferrell

America's Jails

The Search for Human Dignity in an
Age of Mass Incarceration

Derek S. Jeffreys

NEW YORK UNIVERSITY PRESS
New York

NEW YORK UNIVERSITY PRESS
New York
www.nyupress.org

References to Internet websites (URLs) were accurate at the time of writing. Neither the author nor New York University Press is responsible for URLs that may have expired or changed since the manuscript was prepared.

Library of Congress Cataloging-in-Publication Data
Names: Jeffreys, Derek S., 1964– author.
Title: America's jails : the search for human dignity in an
age of mass incarceration / Derek S. Jeffreys.
Other titles: Alternative criminology series.
Description: New York : New York University Press, [2018] |
Series: Alternative criminology | Also available as an ebook. |
Includes bibliographical references and index.
Identifiers: LCCN 2017034397 | ISBN 978-1-4798-3862-2 (cl ; alk. paper) |
ISBN 1-4798-3862-4 (cl ; alk. paper) | ISBN 978-1-4798-1482-4 (pb ; alk. paper) |
ISBN 1-4798-1482-2 (pb ; alk. paper)
Subjects: LCSH: Jails—United States. | Dignity. | Prisoners—Abuse of—United States. |
Prisoners—United States—Social conditions. | Prisoners—Mental health—United States. |
Stigma (Social psychology)—United States. | Imprisonment—Moral and ethical aspects—
United States. | Discrimination in criminal justice administration—United States.
Classification: LCC HV8746.U6 J44 2018 | DDC 365/.34—dc23
LC record available at https://lccn.loc.gov/2017034397

New York University Press books are printed on acid-free paper, and their binding materials are chosen for strength and durability. We strive to use environmentally responsible suppliers and materials to the greatest extent possible in publishing our books.

Manufactured in the United States of America

10 9 8 7 6 5 4 3 2 1

Also available as an ebook

For Zachariah and Caleb

CONTENTS

Introduction

But I have been trying to classify all prisoners and that is hardly possible. Real life is infinite in its variety in comparison with even the cleverest abstract generalization and it does not admit of sweeping distinctions. The tendency of real life is always toward greater and greater differentiation. We, too, had a life of our own sort and it was not a mere official existence but a real inner life of its own.
—Fyodor Dostoyevsky, *House of the Dead*[1]

In December 2014, Ismaaiyl Brinsley left Baltimore, Maryland, after shooting his girlfriend in her apartment. Arriving in New York City, he approached two police officers sitting in a patrol car in Brooklyn. Apparently angry at recent instances of police violence in Ferguson, Missouri, and New York City, Brinsley produced a handgun and fatally shot officers Wenjian Liu and Rafael Ramos. He then fled into a subway station and shot himself in the head. He was taken to a Brooklyn hospital and pronounced dead. The death of officers Liu and Ramos created a storm of controversy about policing. The head of the police union blamed New York City's mayor, Bill de Blasio, for inciting the police killing because he had expressed worries about his son and the police. The mayor responded by denying any causal connection between his remarks and the murder. A bitter dispute erupted between Mayor de Blasio and police officers.

These disagreements masked important facts about Ismaaiyl Brinsley. Initially, he seemed like a young man angry at police brutality. However, as journalists investigated his life they discovered a more complex picture. Born in Brooklyn but spending most of his life in Atlanta and Baltimore, Brinsley had a long and troubled history with the criminal justice system. He had been arrested twenty times, sometimes for petty crimes, other times for more violent ones. He failed to complete high school, had difficulties holding a steady job, and for a while lived a transient existence in different U.S. cities. Brinsley also seemed to suffer from mental illnesses that led to clashes with the police. He was alienated from family members, and came from households where he suffered from violence and sexual abuse. He frequently ranted on social media, revealing a grandiose sense of himself. He also served time in various jails, and had outstanding warrants and parole violations. In sum, he was a troubled person who cycled in and out of penal institutions.[2]

People who paid attention to this disturbing history responded in predictable ways. Those on the political right called for tougher law enforcement and greater restraint of those suffering from mental illness. Progressives and liberals condemned the police shootings, but also decried the broken condition of the U.S. mental health system and called for greater funding for it. All these facile responses ignored deep social problems. In particular, they disregarded the role that jails play in controlling people like Ismaaiyl Brinsley. They often go in and out of jails where they are dehumanized and degraded. They receive little or no help for their mental illness. Most are nonviolent, but some present a danger to themselves and others.

This is a book about U.S. jails that highlights the plight of inmates and considers philosophical questions about human dignity. Annually, millions of Americans have contact with jails. Those arrested for bar fighting, driving while intoxicated or without a license, parole revocations, drug use, domestic violence, and other law violations find themselves in jails. Those who can afford bail quickly exit them, but many wait months for a trial in horrific conditions. How do these experiences affect them? Do jails violate their dignity? How do these institutions deal with those with mental illness? What role does the contemporary jail play in controlling troubled people in the United States? What kind of power do jails exercise in U.S. society? Are they morally legitimate institutions? This book examines these questions primarily from a philosophical perspective that focuses on the dignity of the person.

Jails or Prisons?

In common parlance, people often use the terms "jail" and "prison" interchangeably, but the U.S. penal system distinguishes between them.[3]

A prison is a state or federal institution, and generally houses inmates who have been convicted of a crime. In contrast, local governments usually run jails, and most jail inmates have yet to be tried or sentenced. Others have received short sentences for relatively minor offenses, or are immigrants waiting for deportation hearings. Finally, some jail inmates are convicted, and are waiting to be transported to prison or are state prisoners being housed by the jail. Many Americans experience life in jail, but never find their way into a prison. Despite the powerful presence of jails in U.S. society, however, few scholars have explored life in them (except for sociologists like John Irwin). In fact, it was not until well into the twentieth century that in the United States we knew "the total jail population, annual committals, and even the number of jails" (McConville 1995, 312). Most scholars focus on prisons because in them they find a stable population that is easy to study. Jail populations are transient, with inmates coming and going. Life in a jail, particularly in a big one, can be disorderly and unstable, presenting safety challenges to researchers. Like prisons, jails are often secretive institutions that restrict access to visitors, scholars, and lawyers. For these reasons, we have little knowledge of what really happens in them.

Approaching the Jail

Scholars approach penal institutions in different ways. A few have been inmates or corrections officers, and have combined memoir with social-scientific research. Others have developed surveys they distributed to staff and inmates. Finally, some have performed participant observation, adhering to research methods for interviews while participating in the life of the jail or prison.[4] I am neither a sociologist nor a criminologist, and will therefore offer no original social-scientific research in this book. Instead, I am a professor of religion and philosophy who believes it's important to engage with social-scientific and historical approaches to punishment. Mass incarceration presents so many challenges that no academic discipline alone can understand all of them. This book is an attempt to encourage an interdisciplinary conversation about the jail.

I also think my experiences add something to discussions of the jail. For more than seven years, I gave volunteer philosophy and religion lectures in a maximum-security prison. I have offered similar lectures in a county jail for more than three years. I have spent hours teaching inmates, and have had wonderful discussions with them about religious and philosophical topics like evil, anger, and love. I have been a volunteer in the prison chapel, giving me time to talk to staff and inmates. I have also visited various prisons and jails in Wisconsin and overseas. For this book, I was granted access to the Cook County Jail by Sheriff Thomas J. Dart. I spent time in some of the jail's divisions, and freely talked to both inmates and staff. I have also spoken to advocacy groups in Chicago who work with inmates and who are involved in legal work on jail issues. I recognize the dangers of drawing on personal experience to generalize about jail conditions. However, I have learned a great deal from the inmates I have taught and known. I hope that what I have learned, when linked to research, will provide some insight into life in American jails.

This book differs from other approaches to penology because it focuses primarily on dignity. With good reason, contemporary thinkers often emphasize race, noting the deep racism that pervades our criminal justice system. African Americans are incarcerated at disproportionate levels throughout the United States, often because of policies going back decades. For example, my home state of Wisconsin incarcerates a higher proportion of African Americans than almost any state in the union. Throughout this book, I will highlight how race affects jail life, but will not make it central to my analysis. Other scholars have done this work better than I can, and I want my focus to remain on human dignity.[5]

Additionally, some contemporary scholars explore the inefficiency and wastefulness of our penal system.[6] In jails, we spend an extraordinary amount of money incarcerating hundreds of thousands of people for nonviolent offenses. In prisons, we impose exceptionally long sentences, and our incarceration system wreaks havoc on the lives of young people, their families, and their communities. We find a growing consensus on the U.S. political left and right that we need to back away from a counterproductive and damaging penal system. I endorse this idea entirely, and support it in this book. However, I will not focus particularly on economic issues. Instead, I will highlight the dignity of the person, and how our penal system degrades and damages it.

John Irwin and the Jail

To buttress my philosophical attention to dignity, I develop an argument that appeared in the work of the sociologist John Irwin. A self-styled "convict-sociologist," Irwin served prison time in California in the 1950s before earning a doctorate in sociology under Erving Goffman. He devoted a career to exploring jails, prisons, and the experiences of inmates. In his seminal book, *The Jail: Managing the Underclass in American Society* (originally published in 1985), Irwin defended the "rabble hypothesis" (Irwin 1985/2013). He maintained that the official purpose of the jail clashes with its basic purpose. Officially, the jail exists to hold dangerous people for trial or people who may pose a flight risk and never appear for trial. The basic purpose of the jail, Irwin maintained, is to control portions of the population that society deems unpleasant, undesirable, threatening, or different. These people, Irwin called, using an awkward phrase, "the rabble."

I don't endorse all Irwin's ideas, but in this book, I maintain that he was right in focusing on the jail's different purposes. Although jails "serve their historical purpose of detaining those awaiting trial or sentencing those who are either a danger to public safety or a flight risk, they have come to hold many who are neither. Underlying the behavior that lands someone in jail, there is often a history of substance abuse, mental illness, poverty, failure in school, and victimization" (Vera Institute 2015, 5). Jails hold hundreds of thousands of people who pose no danger to society, but cannot afford to pay the bail necessary for release. The collapse of our mental health care system has led to hundreds of thousands of people with mental illness cycling in and out of jail. For these reasons, I still find Irwin's "rabble hypothesis" illuminating. Rather than using the word "rabble," I employ the term "marginalized" to refer to those whom the jail targets. I use it in a moral and nonmoral sense to include a variety of people. It can refer to those who commit terrible crimes and evil acts that endanger others. Or it can denote those whom a community finds (with or without good reason) problematic, different, risky, or annoying.[7]

The contemporary jail targets marginalized people on a scale that was unimaginable when Irwin wrote his book. Since his day, we have become far more sophisticated in identifying people we think might commit a crime, and holding them in jail before trial. Thinkers like Jonathan Simon, Bernard Harcourt, and Issa Kohler-Hausmann have discussed techniques in criminal justice that aim at controlling large numbers of people and minimizing risk. The population of U.S. jails has skyrocketed in the past three decades. From 1983 to 2013, it grew from 6 to 11.7 million annual admissions (Vera Institute 2015, 7). The U.S. inaugurated a "war on drugs" that populated jails with drugs users and dealers. It enacted domestic violence and other legislation that mandated that jails handle a variety of crimes. Finally, in the 1960s and 1970s the United States closed many of its mental institutions, but failed to provide adequate mental health care for many citizens. Today, we have over three thousand jails operating in the United States that hold over seven hundred thousand people in them on any given day. Annually, there are close to twelve million jail admissions.[8] Although subject to federal oversight, jails are surprisingly decentralized, and depending on their location, citizens can find themselves under the power of either autocratic or benevolent officials.[9] Today's jails do incapacitate dangerous people and hold alleged offenders for trial. However, they also brutally control the lives of hundreds of thousands of people who are too poor or mentally ill to escape the jail's domination.

Demonizing the Captors

In this book, I highlight many disturbing abuses that occur in U.S. jails. When learning about them, people are tempted to seek a villain they can blame. Movies and television programs about jails reinforce this inclination by featuring sadistic wardens and malevolent corrections officers. Undoubtedly, the U.S. penal system contains no shortage of abusive personnel: corrupt judges, power-hungry sheriffs, pandering prosecutors, and violent and abusive corrections officers. However, I resist the temptation to demonize those working in corrections. Corrections officers have a very difficult job, and on daily basis deal with troubled and violent people. I have met many corrections personnel who struggle to make positive changes in a broken criminal justice system. In this book, I will feature people who accomplish remarkable things in horrible circumstances. They enable us to see the good people can do, but also point to the complexity of the problems confronting anyone trying to change our penal system.

Dignity, Values, and the Emotions

The central philosophical issue I discuss in this book is human dignity. Jails are dehumanizing, degrading places where inmates experience repeated assaults on their dignity. They often live in filthy and overcrowded conditions, are subjected to demeaning whole-body searches, and suffer violence and sexual assault from inmates and jail staff. Although they are often legally innocent, they may spend weeks or months in jail and are often assumed to be guilty by supervising staff. While sitting in jail, their financial situations can completely collapse because they lose their jobs, apartments, and familial ties. Finally, in captivity many inmates experience terrible despair, a sense of devaluation that leads them to engage in self-destructive behavior.

Although dignity seems to disappear in jails, what exactly is it? Contemporary historians, sociologists, and activists writing about mass incarceration employ ethical concepts like dignity, justice, and human rights. Yet, they often mistakenly presuppose that their meaning is clear or self-evident. When people morally condemn our society for its high level of incarceration, what principles of justice are they employing? When they maintain that jail and prison conditions violate human rights, how do they understand the controversial concept of a human right? Philosophers and theologians have discussed ethical and political concepts like human rights and justice for centuries, yet contemporary activists and historians of mass incarceration seem blissfully unaware of this rich debate. Too often, their discussions seem convincing only to those who share their unexamined philosophical ideas.[10]

To deepen the contemporary ethical conversation about mass incarceration, this book provides a philosophical analysis of the concept of dignity. Recently, scholars in philosophy and religion have vigorously debated its importance for ethics. Some see it as a useless idea that does little to help us think through ethical issues. Others maintain that dignity is an essential concept that we must continually affirm. Engaging this discussion, I maintain that all persons possess inherent dignity, dignity that exists simply by virtue of being a person. For this argument, I draw heavily on phenomenology of the Husserlian variety (Edmund Husserl, Max Scheler, and Dietrich von Hildebrand). Phenomenology is an approach to philosophy that originated in the twentieth century, and emphasizes careful analysis of our consciousness and experience. Many people associate it with the work of German philosopher Martin Heidegger, but in this book, I draw attention to a rich tradition of phenomenology that predates and differs from Heidegger's work.

This early phenomenological tradition emphasizes that we come to realize the dignity of other people through a personal encounter with them. Influenced by Husserl, phenomenologists like Max Scheler, Dietrich von Hildebrand, and Edith Stein write astutely about how reason and the emotions relate us to values, including the value of the person. For these thinkers, ethics involves both reason and emotion. Recent work in ethics from thinkers like Martha Nussbaum, Sara Ahmed, and Jesse Prinz has revived an interest in the emotions. They have moved away from a twentieth-century prejudice that emotions have no normative significance. However, contemporary philosophers often ignore the contribution of the early phenomenological tradition. By drawing attention to it, this book will emphasize the significance of what happens to us emotionally and cognitively when we encounter another person.

Dignity and Stigma

By focusing on the emotions, phenomenology also helps us understand why we deny that some people possess inherent dignity. For those who have been incarcerated, dignity relates closely to stigma. In the United States, those with criminal records receive public disapprobation; they are barred entirely from holding some jobs, often can't vote, face employment discrimination, and may be prohibited from receiving public assistance. Those suffering from mental illness face a double stigma from their illness and incarceration. They must answer harsh questions about their mental illness and their crimes. Unless a person commits a crime as a juvenile, her criminal record can remain with her throughout her entire life. In some states (like my own state of Wisconsin), this record is public, and easily available to anyone with access to the Internet. Thus, former inmates face a stigma that haunts them for years.

Yet, stigma is a puzzling phenomenon. How does it relate to dignity? If we grasp the dignity of others, why do we stigmatize them? Philosophers discussing dignity rarely consider stigma, assuming it is a topic best left to sociologists and psychologists. However, this is a mistake because stigma presents philosophical puzzles. I will explore them because they help us understand the experiences of inmates and former inmates.

One of the most famous accounts of stigma appears in the work of the American sociologist Erving Goffman. In the 1960s and 1970s, Goffman brilliantly analyzed how institutions like asylums and prisons shape their denizens' identities. He wrote an important book on stigma that has shaped many contemporary discussions of the idea. Critics have leveled sound criticisms of Goffman; he often disregarded biological contributions to mental illness, excessively celebrated those who deviated from social norms, and lacked an adequate conception of the human person. Nevertheless, I believe some of Goffman's insights remain important for understanding how stigma plagues the lives of jail inmates.

To explore how stigma blinds us to the dignity of inmates and ex-offenders, I focus on emotions like disgust, contempt, and fear. Following philosopher Dietrich von Hildebrand, I develop the concept of "value-blindness," the incapacity to perceive a value (in this case, the value of the person). We can fail to perceive values for many reasons, such as self-interest, an attachment to bad arguments, or pride. In this book, I show how disgust, contempt, and fear blind us to the person's dignity. We often use jails to house those we find disgusting, and the horrible conditions in these institutions can evoke further disgust among staff and the public. Disgust often breeds a contempt that further blinds us to the dignity of persons. Outside the jail, fear often distorts our response to other people, leading us to ignore their dignity. We fear certain kinds of people, and want them removed from our presence. The police take them to a jail, and we ask few questions about what happens once they have been removed. Public policies also promise to reduce our risk of encountering threatening people, thus reinforcing fears of whole classes of people. In recent decades, we have seen new approaches to risk assessment and crime that promise to reduce risk and completely incapacitate criminals. For example, we have developed a bail system that assumes the worst of people and incarcerates hundreds of thousands of poor people. In these policies, we see how disgust, contempt, and fear combine to produce a stigma that deeply damages the lives of jail inmates and ex-offenders.

The Jail and American History: A Different Narrative

Throughout this book, I will discuss the jail in the light of the long American practice of institutionalizing marginalized people in mental hospitals, jails, prisons, and other coercive institutions. Since the early part of the nineteenth century, we have segregated people in places where we have often tortured and abused them. Patterns of abuse and reform have characterized our penal and mental health systems since their inception. We have seen multiple attempts to apply evidence and data to change broken institutions. Some succeeded in bringing about short-term change, while others failed miserably to alleviate human suffering.

Because U.S. jails have rarely treated inmates humanely, studying them provides an opportunity to reevaluate some familiar narratives about U.S. penal history. We now imprison an extraordinary number of people in what has become known as mass incarceration. Over the past several decades, we have seen a growth in our inmate population that is truly astounding. This is a new development that departs in many ways from earlier approaches to crime and punishment. I will not contest this thesis in this book. However, too often scholars and activists fail to locate mass incarceration within a larger historical framework. For example, some contrast our current punitive system with an earlier era in which our society sought to rehabilitate inmates. I will suggest, however, that this thesis is far too simplistic. It ignores important regional differences in penal practices, often confuses rhetoric with the reality of the lived experience of inmates, and disregards our long history of using coercive institutions like mental health facilities to control people. I will draw attention to this history, emphasizing issues of powerlessness, vulnerability, and institutions that have often existed in U.S. history.

Reform or Abolition?

A final theme I explore in this book involves the limits of change in our jail system. I will propose policies to prevent the ongoing neglect and abuse of inmates in jails. Additionally, I will consider ways to reduce the size of our jail population, which has reached obscenely high levels. It is important to respond to the immediate crises we confront in our jail system, and I think the proposals I offer have a chance of gaining some political support.

However, as I will make clear in the conclusion, I see these reforms as short-term solutions to problems in a failed institution. Criminologists, sociologists, and activists sometimes adopt one of two approaches to penal institutions, a "reformist" model and an "abolitionist" approach.[11] Abolitionism is an umbrella concept that covers thinkers and activists with diverse and sometimes conflicting goals.[12] However, it unites those who think jails and prisons are not only unjust but also unreformable. Reformists agree about the injustice of our current penal system, but maintain that with proper reforms, we can make it just. Because I'm not a criminologist, I don't follow all the debates about reform and abolition, but I have learned a great deal from them. I don't call myself an "abolitionist" because I think we will likely need some institutions to contain violent people. However, I endorse much of the "abolitionist" agenda. Given our history of brutality toward marginalized people and the emotional dynamics the jail creates, the jail is unlikely to be a just institution. Given its power in our society, it will remain with us for some time. However, we can think about how to move away from it in the long run. I don't pretend to have a complete blueprint for replacing the jail, but will end the book by reflecting on what it might mean to reject its moral legitimacy.

The Book's Structure

In chapter 1 ("Degradation and Disorientation: A Glimpse into the Cook County Jail"), I provide an account of aspects of life in the Cook County Jail in Chicago. By considering this enormous jail, I will be able to identify problems confronting other U.S. jails. After discussing the jail's violent history, I describe how people end up confined there. I begin with the encounter between law enforcement officers and disruptive people or those who have allegedly committed crimes. I then describe the horrors inmates experience in the Cook County Jail. I highlight how committed but overworked mental health officials struggle to help inmates with mental illness. I demonstrate, however, that inmates suffer profound attacks on their dignity. This chapter provides a look at a large urban jail at a moment in time. I will also return to the Cook County Jail later in the book to explore how its officials have tried to improve its conditions.

In chapter 2 ("What Is the Purpose of a Jail?"), I consider the role jails play in U.S. society, exploring how they control the lives of millions of Americans. I devote much of this chapter to showing how jails throughout the United States often contain inmates in intolerable conditions. They live in repulsive environments, suffer brutality from staff and other inmates, and receive inadequate medical care. I then maintain that jails also house people who desperately need mental health care. I also explore how bail systems keep poor inmates in jail, and discuss how some county jails exploit them as a means of raising revenue. I conclude that jails exercise an extraordinary but often hidden power in our society.

In chapter 3 ("A Matter of Dignity"), I explore human dignity. After discussing ways to consider this topic, I distinguish between diverse kinds of dignity. I then examine contemporary thinkers who believe the concept is useless and unilluminating. Drawing on the work of early phenomenologists, I defend the idea that we possess inherent dignity because we exhibit both the capacity for self-transcendence and an individual nature. I also use Dietrich von Hildebrand's account of value perception to explain how we apprehend the person's dignity affectively. I then respond to arguments against dignity, maintaining that they are philosophically shallow. Finally, returning to the jail I describe general ways people denigrate inherent dignity in jails.

Chapter 4 ("Why Do We Stigmatize Inmates? Disgust, Contempt, and Fear in American Jails") examines why we often fail to perceive the dignity of others. Critically retrieving Goffman's idea of stigma as a "spoiled identity," I first describe its nature. I then turn to disgust, contempt, and fear, using philosopher Aurel Kolnai's work to carefully analyze their structure. I argue that these reactions can produce a value blindness to the dignity of the person. I then maintain that within the jail, disgust and contempt often blind staff to the person's dignity. Outside the jail, I show how fear contributes to narrow forms of risk assessment and a goal of total incapacitation of those accused of crimes. Finally, I consider the money bail system that dominates the U.S. penal system. I maintain that it reflects a fear of the risk of crime, and creates an unfair system that penalizes low-income citizens who cannot afford the money necessary for bail.

In chapter 5 ("What Can We Do? Responding to a Crisis"), I consider policy questions, proposing ways to minimally protect inmates and reduce the size of jail populations. I see these measures as short-term responses to emergencies, rather than as long-term reforms to the jail. I first note how decentralization of political power in the United States poses significant problems for improving jail conditions. I then recommend greater jail monitoring, more federal oversight of jails, investigative journalism, and legal challenges from organizations like the ACLU. I call for better mental health care and clear use of force policies within jails. I note that we won't be able to address the mental health crisis in our jails unless we deal with it in society. I then explore reforming the bond process, examining current attempts to make it more "evidence-based." These risk-assessment tools will likely reduce jail populations, but I express concern that they ignore individual dignity. I maintain that we would be better served by guaranteeing that all defendants have good legal counsel at bond hearings. Finally, I consider the moral transformation necessary for recognizing the dignity of inmates. I argue that we cannot directly control our affective responses, but can indirectly respond to them. In this way, we need not be trapped by disgust, contempt, and fear, and can try to treat inmates more humanely.

In the conclusion, I reflect on the long-term future of the jail. I maintain that anyone who cares about human dignity cannot defend the moral legitimacy of the contemporary jail. I then consider the prospect for long-term reform. I return to the Cook County Jail, highlighting its efforts to improve conditions for inmates. Under the leadership of Sheriff Thomas J. Dart, the jail has taken steps to reduce its population, decrease officer violence, and help those with mental illness. Although I commend these reform attempts, I argue they are precarious, and long-term attempts to make the jail more humane are unlikely to succeed. To support this claim, I describe failed attempts to reform the Cook County Jail in the 1920s. I reaffirm John Irwin's thesis that the American jail has often aimed to contain marginalized people. I then entertain the abolitionist thesis that jails cannot be reformed. I endorse the abolitionist call to find alternatives to the jail, but recognize the need to control violent offenders. I end the book with a call to inner change, featuring someone who exemplifies a commitment to enhancing human dignity.

1

Degradation and Disorientation

A Glimpse into the Cook County Jail

In the jail in Chicago, Illinois, the cells were dark, without ventilation and swarming with vermin. Some were so foul that, after a few minutes' stay in them, we felt a sickening sensation. Yet, in these close and filthy abodes human beings, crowded together, are confined for days, weeks, months even, many of whom are adjudged to be innocent. It is a crime against humanity to deprive anyone, however depraved, of the light and air of heaven, since, apart from the its essential injustice, such physical punishment invariably induces moral disorientation, and the individual subjected to it re-enters society a worse man than he left it. How great, then, must be the crime of such deprivation, when inflicted on the innocent.
—*Report on the Prisons and Reformatories of the United States*[1]

My first encounter with Chicago's Cook County Jail left me disoriented and confused. Located on the city's West Side, the jail encompasses more than ninety-six acres, and is one of the largest single-site jails in the United States. It holds anywhere from eight to ten thousand inmates, depending on the day and season. The jail has eleven divisions, most of which are surrounded by an old wall. On my first visit, I walked into one of the gates, and was immediately accosted by a corrections officer who barked, "Who are you? What are you doing here?" I explained that I was there to see the Sheriff's director of communications, who was going to show me around the jail. She called him, and he quickly arrived. He assured the officer that I was an authorized visitor, and soon ushered me into the jail.

We entered a maze of tunnels, and I immediately experienced sensory assault. I saw dozens of inmates in various parts of the jail. Some were in orange suits, and were being transported through the tunnels. Others were sitting on benches handcuffed and chained. As I walked, I was overwhelmed by unpleasant odors that I couldn't identify. I heard constant noise, produced primarily by corrections officers shouting at inmates. Occasionally, an officer would rudely inquire where I was going, and ask if I were a lawyer. I felt lost in a labyrinth, and was grateful that my host knew his way around the buildings. After spending the day in the jail, I was appalled at what I saw, and went away from the experience emotionally exhausted. In my subsequent visits to the jail, I never lost this sense of disorientation and confusion.

Because of its history and the work of its current sheriff, Thomas J. Dart, the Cook County Jail provides an opportunity to explore the limits and possibilities of change in our nation's jails. In this chapter, I describe some of the conditions that inmates experience in the Cook County Jail. First, I discuss the jail's recent history. Long a horrific place, it grew enormously in the 1980s and 1990s, and became the site of staff abuse, health hazards, and gang violence. Second, I describe some of the police encounters and crimes that land people in the Cook County Jail. Third, I discuss the journey of a person through the Cook County Jail. Hundreds of inmates pass through the jail daily in a degrading and frightening process, and those who cannot afford bail remain incarcerated. Fourth, I describe the terrible problem of mental illness at Cook County. Thousands of inmates suffer from mental illness, and confront a nightmarish existence. Finally, I describe how officials in the jail struggle to deal with these inmates, but lack adequate resources to address their needs. A large jail is no place for someone with mental illness, yet thousands of such people cycle in and out of the Cook County Jail annually.

A Brutal History

The history of the Cook County Jail is a brutal one. As I will note several times in this book, most people in jails are legally innocent. Although they are entitled to the presumption of innocence, for decades Cook County officials have assumed that inmates are criminals who deserve to be punished. Chicago had a jail for most of the nineteenth century, but built its House of Corrections in 1871. Because of significant overcrowding, Cook County opened the Cook County Jail in 1928. For several decades, the jail contained a death chamber where inmates were executed. Inmates were housed in horrible conditions, and routinely beaten by staff. The jail was poorly administered, and prominent criminals often operated as they pleased. The House of Corrections and the Cook County Jail were merged in 1969 (Olson 2012). In the 1960s and early 1970s, Cook County operated with the notorious "barn-boss system." Officials took a hands-off approach to managing the facility, allowing inmate gangs to control large sections of it. Because officials endorsed this system, inmates who were sexually assaulted or otherwise harmed had little recourse but to submit to the most powerful inmates in the jail. A series of lawsuits, arrests of corrupt officials, and tough administrators put an end to the barn-boss system.[2]

Because of the war on drugs and other policies, in the 1980s and 1990s the jail's population skyrocketed. Officials struggled to accommodate thousands of inmates, with many forced to sleep on the floor. Inmates brought lawsuits protesting these conditions, and Cook County entered a Consent Decree (a legal agreement between parties similar to a contract) with the U.S. Department of Justice. The agreement became official in 1980. It pledged to reduce overcrowding, and was named after one of the inmates who brought the suit (Dan Duran). The *Duran* Consent Decree, monitored by the John Howard Society, a prison reform organization, required every inmate to have access to a bed. It quickly became the subject of repeated court cases and lawsuits. Monitors reported that the jail often failed to meet the Consent Decree's requirements. County officials either denied these charges or proposed new ways to reduce jail overcrowding.[3] The *Duran* Consent Decree produced legal battles about conditions at the Cook County Jail that lasted for years.

As the jail population swelled in the 1980s and 1990s, officials experimented with different ways to alleviate overcrowding. These included releasing large numbers of inmates with bonds that required only their agreement to return to court, and a Day Reporting Center that offered services to those with addictions and other problems. For the most part, these measures served as Band-Aids that only temporarily addressed overcrowding crises. Moreover, they produced a massive growth in the physical facilities, as new units were added on to the original 1928 building. Gradually, the Cook County Jail became one of the largest single-site jails in the United States. Often operating at close to 100 percent capacity, it sometimes housed over ten thousand inmates.[4] It became a violent, frightening place with considerable inmate-on-inmate violence. Sophisticated gangs operated within the facility, and corrections officers faced dangerous and violent situations.[5]

The Strip-Search Cases

In these years (the 1980s and 1990s), inmates were routinely beaten by staff and lived in appalling conditions. To paint a picture of this hell, let me briefly focus on two cases involving the strip-searching of inmates. Jails have a legal right and obligation to search inmates upon their arrival in a facility. However, in the 1990s and early 2000s, the Cook County Jail conducted these searches in a deeply degrading manner. The details of the practice emerged in a class-action lawsuit in the 1990s. Courts found that upon entry to the jail, women would be ordered to remove their clothes. They would then be told to stand naked in large groups, so tightly packed that people touched each other. They would be forced to bend over, and be subjected to rectal searches. Corrections officers would shower abuse and ridicule on the inmates, and yell orders at them. Menstruating women would bleed on the floor, over-weight women would be derided by officers, some inmates would smell of excrement, and unmuzzled dogs would occasionally enter the search area. Women were often strip-searched twice, once while entering the jail and another time while exiting. In a key court ruling, judicial offi-cials demanded that the jail cease these abusive group searches. It also awarded monetary damages to tens of thousands of women who had been subjected to them.[6]

The Cook County Jail contested this court ruling, and dragged its feet in implementing change. Amazingly, it also continued to strip-search males in groups. Male inmates also brought a lawsuit, which revealed more terrible details. Males would be put in groups of fifty to seventy-five people. Naked and often forced up against each other, they would also be insulted with homophobic slurs and nasty comments about the size of their genitals. Dogs would also be employed, barking at them ag-gressively. In 2009, over a decade after the case related to women came to light, federal courts found that the Cook County Jail had violated the Eighth and Fourteenth Amendments of the U.S. Constitution. They awarded monetary damages to thousands of people.[7]

Before detailing additional history of the Cook County Jail, I want to pause a moment to consider the scale of the abuses I just described. Cook County processes anywhere from seventy-five to one hundred thousand inmates annually (Olson 2012, 2). This means that for the time covered by the strip-search cases, hundreds of thousands of people were forced to endure humiliating group body cavity searches. Many were guilty of only misdemeanor offenses and couldn't afford to pay the money for bail. Others were innocent of the crimes for which they were charged. Moreover, in this same period other big jails in the United States found technological ways of searching inmates that eliminated the need for group searches. Yet, for years the Cook County Jail stubbornly persisted with its brutal and unconstitutional policy. It's hard to fathom the kind of psychological damage this policy caused to many human beings.

The 2008 U.S. Department of Justice Intervention

The disputes over the *Duran* Consent Decree and other matters became very intense in 2008, when the U.S. Department of Justice (DOJ) released a scathing findings letter about conditions in Cook County Jail. Covering a host of areas including sanitation, staff behavior, and medical care, the letter stated,

> We find that CCJ [Cook County Jail] fails to adequately protect inmates from harm and serious risk of harm from staff and other inmates; fails to provide inmates with adequate medical and mental health care; fails to provide adequate suicide prevention; fails to provide adequate fire safety precautions; and fails to provide safe and sanitary environmental conditions. (U.S. DOJ, Civil Rights Division 2008a, sec. III)

In grim detail, the letter described extraordinary cruelty in the jail. Any sign of disagreement or questioning on the part of inmates was met with savage beatings. Groups of corrections officers would kick, stomp, and punch inmates, many of whom were handcuffed and helpless. Anyone who complained about such treatment could endure additional brutality.

Because of this treatment, inmates suffered serious injuries like concussions and broken limbs. Yet they had little recourse for responding to staff abuse. The DOJ found that the jail had a completely inadequate system for reporting use-of-force incidents. Corrections officers filled out forms in a vague manner, supervisors rarely read them, and a thick bureaucracy delayed their processing for months. The DOJ letter confirmed in detail what inmates and activists had known about the jail for decades: corrections officers used terrible violence with little or no accountability. Occasionally, they would be disciplined for excessive force and some were even fired for their behavior. Overall, however, officers knew that they could get away with violence with impunity. Cook County responded to lawsuits and outside monitoring with delaying tactics that enabled the officers to continue their cruelty. According to the DOJ, they managed a large and violent population with lawless violence (U.S. DOJ, Civil Rights Division 2008a, sec. IV, A).

In addition to staff abuse, the DOJ found a host of other horrors in the jail. It noted a major dysfunction related to health care, with two different chains of command unresponsive to each other. As

> a result of the administrative division between corrections and health care at CCJ communication between mental health staff and correctional staff is informal and often strained. Significant communication problems between custody and mental health staff result in a fragmented, uncoordinated system. (U.S. DOJ, Civil Rights Division 2008a, sec. III, C, 4)

Cermak, a private health care company with little accountability to the Cook County Sheriff's Department, provided health care to inmates. The DOJ letter found that because of this broken system, inmates received inadequate medical screening upon arrival at the jail. Many were on medications, but didn't receive them for weeks. In a particularly egregious case, an inmate told officials he was on the blood thinner, Coumadin, but received it only after waiting for three weeks. Others suffered from health problems that were never treated. In one case, an inmate had a limb amputated in what the letter called an unnecessary operation. The DOJ concluded that some inmates likely died after receiving inadequate health care (U.S. DOJ, Civil Rights Division 2008a, sec. III, B).

In a disturbing part of the DOJ letter, officials described how the jail was unprepared to control infectious diseases. Inmates with obvious skin rashes went untreated, raising the prospect of a tuberculosis outbreak. People handling food didn't wash their hands, and prepared it in ways that invited a disease outbreak. Cells and recreation areas were filthy, crawling with mice, flies, and cockroaches. Finally, inmates received washed clothes only once a week, and the laundry service failed to clean uniforms in a sanitary fashion (U.S. DOJ, Civil Rights Division 2008a, sec. II, B, 8).

The mental health care negligence at the Cook County Jail was appalling. According to the DOJ letter, incoming inmates were given a form to fill out regarding mental health needs and medications. They received inadequate mental health screening, often because of a shortage of qualified mental health care workers. Those treating inmates were often overwhelmed by the challenges they faced. Inmates often went weeks without psychotropic and other medications. Officials failed to monitor inmates who were suicidal. Finally, inmates with mental illness were often targeted for violence by staff and other inmates. Because they didn't understand or respond to orders quickly, officers would beat them until they complied (U.S. DOJ, Civil Rights Division 2008a, sec. II, C).

The 2008 DOJ letter described other problems at the Cook County Jail that I will not discuss (inadequate fire safety and decaying infrastructure). It offered a detailed look inside a large U.S. jail, and the picture wasn't a pretty one.

The 2010 Consent Decree

When the DOJ issues such a letter about a penal institution, it can result in a lawsuit against a county or municipality. Usually, however, authorities agree to make changes ordered by the DOJ. Sheriff Thomas J. Dart, a relative newcomer (and not sheriff for most of the period under investigation), entered negotiations with the DOJ. In a Consent Decree, the jail agreed to address all the concerns in the 2008 letter by making important changes.[8] These included better cooperation between Cermak and the jail, the hiring of additional correctional and medical staff, better use-of-force procedures, improved sanitation and fire safety, and better medical and mental health care. The parties to the Consent Decree also agreed on a monitoring system to ensure that these changes occurred. Monitors chosen by both parties would inspect the jail to ascertain if it complied with the Consent Decree. They would issue reports describing the jail's progress on key areas of concern. Sheriff Dart also initiated new policies to help those with mental illness. He appeared often on media programs like *CBS 60 Minutes* to sound the alarm about the crisis of mental illness in U.S. jails.

The MacArthur Center Lawsuit

Later in this book, I will discuss important and positive ways in which the Cook County Jail worked to remain in compliance with the 2010 Consent Decree. However, in 2014 the jail confronted a major lawsuit charging that it failed to correct the staff abuse charged in the 2008 DOJ investigation. The MacArthur Justice Center at Northwestern University's School of Law brought the lawsuit. This center does a range of legal advocacy work, including initiating lawsuits on behalf of inmates and those abused by the police. In dramatic fashion, its lawsuit maintained that "a culture of brutality and lawlessness infects the jail and forces these men [in the class], all of whom are awaiting trial, to live under a constant risk of life threatening violence."[9] It alleged that "the most recent monitor's report, filed in December 2013 (Doc. No. 211 in *United States v. Cook County*) and available to each of the Defendants, finds that the County is not in compliance with critical Consent Decree provisions related to protection from harm and excessive use of force."[10] According to the lawsuit, use-of-force reporting and prosecution of abusive officers improved only marginally.

The lawsuit alleged that corrections officers savagely beat inmates. Dozens of inmates reported to MacArthur Center investigators that they were harmed by staff. Officers would

> slam people to the floor, stomp, kick and punch them—often while the individuals are handcuffed and shackled. After beating shackled men until they lose consciousness, officers will drag them by their chains, banging their heads on steel doors or allowing their heads to slam into the concrete floor. Officers often violently attack people living with mental illness—generally for behaviors that are manifestations of mental illness

or in response to an individual's request for a mental health evaluation. People who appear to be in active psychosis are frequently brutalized by mobs of officers for alleged "non-compliance." Officers also order the men to attack, beat and stomp each other—instigating violence between the very individuals that they are supposed to protect.[11]

According to the lawsuit, staff members acted as if they were at war with the inmates. Moreover, they found ways around those who were monitoring them. For example, they would often take inmates for an "elevator ride." Inside an elevator and out of view of cameras or supervisors, officers would beat inmates into submission.[12] In other cases, while subduing inmates, corrections officers would yell "stop resisting" even when the inmates offered no resistance.[13] According to the lawsuit, officers were confident that they would avoid discipline for this behavior because the "State's Attorney rarely files criminal charges against officers who brutalize people housed in the jail."[14] Thus, despite the changes the jail made in response to the 2010 Consent Decree, the lawsuit alleged that officers continued to beat inmates with impunity.

The MacArthur lawsuit also maintained that officers fomented violence in the jail. If an inmate questioned an officer's order, he might be confronted by other inmates who assaulted him at an officer's bidding. Or inmates who were particularly adept at legal work might find themselves alone with gang members who attacked them. In an enormous institution like the Cook County Jail, it is difficult to ensure inmate safety. However, the MacArthur lawsuit alleged that officers deliberately encouraged inmates to assault others.[15]

Cook County responded ferociously to the MacArthur lawsuit's allegations. Sheriff Dart called the lawsuit a "fictitious novel," and vowed to fight it ("Lawsuit Accuses Cook County" 2014). He maintained that the violence the lawsuit alleged could not have occurred with the DOJ monitoring the jail. He also accused inmates of fabricating stories, and condemned the MacArthur Center for publicizing them. Long hearings ensued in which attorneys for Cook County challenged the expert testimony upon which the lawsuit relied.

The MacArthur Center lawyers asked for a preliminary injunction against the Cook County Jail to prevent officers from abusing inmates. Judge Virginia M. Kendall of the U.S. District Court of the Northern

District of Illinois rejected the call for a preliminary injunction.[16] She criticized the testimony of the MacArthur Center's use-of-force expert, and maintained the inmate testimony about jail violence was unreliable. The judge acknowledged that Cook County was a violent place, but held that authorities were not guilty of "deliberate indifference" toward the welfare of inmates.[17] Finally, Judge Kendall commended Sheriff Dart and DOJ authorities for working to reduce violence at the Cook County Jail. After this verdict, the MacArthur Center decided to no longer pursue its class-action lawsuit, although it continued to work on behalf of individual inmates at the jail.

For those interested in present issues in incarceration, my foray into history may seem like a waste of time. However, I will argue later in this book that the history of Cook County Jail and of jail incarceration in general is very important. It tells us a great deal about the difficulties and possibilities of positive change in jails. People of good will can work together to bring about change, but it will not come overnight. In the case of Cook County, officials face an uphill battle because of the jail's brutal history. Finally, I think it is important to briefly rehearse the history of this jail because we should understand how jails routinely degrade and abuse inmates. As I will show in the next chapter, many Americans in other jails endure similar degradation and assaults on their dignity.

Entering the Cook County Jail

With this history in mind, let me describe some aspects of an inmate's journey through the Cook County Jail. I visited the jail in 2013 and 2014, and it is a rapidly changing institution. I will return to recent developments later in the book, but want to provide readers with a snapshot of what I witnessed in the jail. I recognize the limitations that come from my status as an outsider to the jail, but think my experiences there can help us begin thinking about today's jails. Usually, a trip to Cook County Jail begins with an encounter with the police, prompted by a 911 call or a public incident. This encounter may be violent or nonviolent. The latest data we have about the Cook County Jail (2013) indicate that 29.10 percent of those entering it were arrested for violent offenses. Almost half of these involved domestic battery. The next largest categories of arrests included those for drug offenses (26.4 percent), property crimes

(18.3 percent), and DUI/traffic offenses (16.4 percent). The rest of those arrested committed a variety of other offenses (Olson and Huddle 2013).

Once someone is questioned and arrested, he will be placed in a police lockup, located at police stations distributed throughout Chicago and its suburbs.[18] Lockups are generally crowded, filthy places where the needs of those arrested receive little attention. People suffering from substance abuse withdrawals are often left to their own devices as alcohol or other substances leave their bodies. They may stay in the lockup overnight or even over the weekend if arrested after Friday night.

After the police lockup, people are transported to the Cook County Jail in vehicles that look like school buses with bars on the windows. Two large transportations occur daily, one from the city of Chicago and the other from the suburbs. Suspects are brought into a receiving area of the jail known as the Bullpen. This part of the jail receives up to two hundred inmates a day (sometimes more), the morning group from the city and the afternoon one from the suburbs. When I visited the Bullpen, I noticed dozens of men jammed into two small cells. Some were lying on the floor, others sitting on the one available bench. Most stood, waiting to be processed. Most of the men I saw were African American (in 2012, 67 percent of inmates in the jail were African American), with Latinos and a few white inmates (these groups represent 19 and 13 percent, respectively). The Bullpen reeked of sweat and other foul odors, inmates appeared sick and dirty, and I saw one inmate vomiting in one of the few toilets available outside the cells. Many in the crowd were young men, some of whom appeared frightened, others steely or confused. Older men also waited in the cells. Corrections officers barked out orders, shouted insults at individual inmates, and rudely responded to their questions.[19]

Outside the cells, several women approached the bars and called out names. For about five minutes, they interviewed individual inmates about their mental health history. These interviews, instituted by the Cook County Jail after the 2008 DOJ lawsuit, were held in public in front of other inmates. The inmate came to the bars of the cells, and reported his mental health history and which medications he took. This information was then reported to inmate lawyers and Pretrial Service authorities. I was surprised at how quickly the interviews ended. I spoke with the social workers doing them and expressed admiration for the

difficult job they were performing. They noted that many of those interviewed reported long histories of mental illness and currently exhibited
significant signs thereof. Those inmates with whom I spoke seemed confused. Some asked if I were a lawyer who could help them with problems. Others told me about their difficulties in finding mental health
care in Chicago. Still others discussed their crimes or told stories that
made little sense. Finally, some inmates could hardly speak at all; they
might have been suffering from withdrawal symptoms, been off pre-
scription medications, or been in need of medication. I later learned that
in the police lockups and at the jail, some inmates can go several days
without psychotropic and other mental health medicines.

Once an inmate receives a mental health screening, his name is
called for a brief meeting with Pretrial Service authorities (I will say
more about these services later in this book). These officials gather information that will be used in the bond hearing, including conviction
information and outstanding warrants. They are also responsible for
verifying this information, and filling out a risk-assessment form for
the judge to consider at the bond hearing. Pretrial Services don't exist
in all jails, and at Cook County they were initiated in 1990. I saw a bevy
of authorities sitting behind what seemed to be Plexiglas windows. They
appeared harried, and the inmates talking to them had no privacy. They
shouted out information, and the authorities responded through a mi-
crophone. The result was din of voices. The interviews were brief, and
the inmates then returned to another crammed cell to await the next
phase of processing.[20]

After a period of waiting, the inmate then goes to the Bond Court,
which is situated near the Cook County Jail. There, he will find out if
he will be required to post bail and how much it will be. A judge decides whether a defendant receives bail or will be released. He may be
released on an electronic monitoring program in which he must wear
an electronic device that monitors his movements. If he receives bail,
the judge decides on an amount. If the defendant receives a "D bond,"
he must come up with 10 percent of the bail's amount. Before appearing
in court, the defendant meets with his lawyer; if he cannot afford to pay
for one, he receives the services of a public defender. The lawyer has only
a brief time to look over his documents. Likewise, the judge has little
time to consider pretrial reports and other documents, and he examines

them quickly. Because of the sheer volume of people coming through the Bond Court, it operates rapidly. The judge hears from lawyers, and makes a bail determination. The proceedings for each person usually last anywhere from thirty seconds to two minutes.

One day, I sat through a morning of these bond hearings, and as an outsider to the judicial system I found the proceedings mind-numbing. Person after person was called before the judge, who seemed to repeat the same instructions over and over again. Lawyers made brief comments, and then a person would come from a holding cell after his or her name was called. Some charges were dismissed, and some people posted bail. In many cases, people were unable to post bail and were ordered to the Cook County Jail. I was surprised at how many people were charged with driving without a license. However, sometimes a person with a more serious crime would appear, and the proceedings took a little longer. Yet generally, they moved very quickly. I marveled at the capacity of the judge and other court officials to trudge through what seemed like a mindless task.

Classification

In the penal system, classification refers to how prisons and jails organize inmates. Since the early nineteenth century, prison authorities and reformers have sought to organize inmates according to the nature of their crime, their special needs, or safety considerations. After the bond hearing, those entering the Cook County Jail receive additional medical, mental health, and other screenings for classification purposes. They are then assigned to one of the jail's divisions. Those charged with dangerous crimes or who have a long criminal history may end up in maximum-security areas (Divisions I, X) or a supermaximum division (Division IX). The maximum units are generally the most dangerous areas of the jail, with gang activity and many incidents of violence and conflict between staff and inmates. Divisions II, III, and XI (a relatively new facility) hold minimum- and medium-security inmates, while Division IV holds the jail's female population. Medium- and minimum-security inmates in need of protective custody or serving disciplinary time end up in Division VI (Division V being the site of inmate intake). In 2014, Cermak opened a new medical facility to hold both male and female inmates suffering from mental illness, called the Residential Treatment Unit (RTU) ("President Preckwinkle Opens Medical Facility" 2014). Finally, Cermak also has a limited number of beds in secure parts of the John Stroger Hospital reserved for emergency cases.[21]

Although Division II houses minimum- and medium-security inmates, it presents the outsider with striking images. One large dormitory holds over three hundred men. A sea of cots appears as one enters the room. Some inmates are lying down, while others are standing. Many in the room are inmate workers in the kitchen and other parts of the jail. A small table serves as a locale for card-playing and other games, and several televisions are blaring. The room reverberates with a cacophony of voices. A small number of toilets, showers, and sinks are barely concealed behind partitions. Occasionally, an inmate mops the floor, but the bathroom areas are filthy. The inmates rarely leave the room for recreation, and receive lunch in the dormitory (I observed inmates eating cold sandwiches). After talking to inmates and staff, I was surprised to learn that this large room was connected to another one. I walked into it, only to discover that it also contained more than three hundred inmates. Inmates reported that these giant dormitories were much safer than the maximum-security divisions. The corrections officer in charge of other officers was an impressive, no-nonsense man who seemed to run a tight ship. However, only ten corrections officers per shift supervised over six hundred men, leaving plenty of possibility for clandestine activity and violence. The mass of humanity, lack of facilities, and other matters struck me as deeply degrading.

Mental Health Classification

The Cook County Jail houses an extraordinary number of people suffering from mental illness. Estimates range from two to three thousand who are officially diagnosed, and many others who escape detection. Dedicated but overwhelmed mental health staff struggle to help these inmates in some minimal way. Inmates entering the jail may have no access to mental health care and no medical records. If they take medication, they may be off it for days during arrest, booking, and classification. Finally, many inmates have self-medicated with alcohol or illegal substances. Health officials find that they suffer from both mental illness and substance abuse. After the Bond Court hearing, inmates receive a mental health examination, and are classified according to their condition and needs.[22]

I visited the Cook County Jail when it was undergoing a major transition in its mental health care system, and observed its old and new buildings. As I mentioned, in 2014 Cermak opened the new RTU mental health care facility within the jail. Costing over $86 million to build, it contains over nine hundred beds and houses males and females on different floors accessible by different elevators. Some inmates enter the jail in dire need of mental health care. They are assigned to the small Acute Care part of the facility. Others who suffer from severe but non-acute conditions get assigned to the Residential/Intermediate Care unit. Finally, other inmates receive outpatient care, sick call services, and suicide-prevention intervention.

Acute care inmates present major challenges to authorities. Some must be restrained or placed in cells where they can be observed. Others receive medications like Thorazine (an older antipsychotic with significant side effects and a controversial history of being used in prisons and other institutions) that numb and pacify them. Unless they present a danger to themselves or to others, inmates cannot be forced to take medication. Jail officials must get court authorization to medicate them if they refuse. This can involve a hearing that takes a day or longer, and requires staff members to go to court.

In this part of the jail, I met a dedicated young psychiatrist who worked with acute care patients. I admired his commitment and marveled at how he could work with patients all day. He spoke of the difficulties of dealing with a profoundly troubled group of people. Acute Care areas are small, and sometime lack enough beds for those in need. Sometimes, the jail places inmates in "boats," odd-looking structures on the ground that serve as makeshift beds. They began to be used after the *Duran* Consent Decree disputes. I noticed one boat that appeared to be urine-soaked. In the Acute Care unit, officials offer programs aimed at transitioning inmates into the Residential/Intermediate wing. Some inmates may never reach the stage where they can transition, and they await transfer to a mental institution. Beds in Illinois psychiatric institutions are scarce, however, and acute care patients may remain at Cook County for months before transfer.

The Residential/Intermediate Care unit houses most of the inmates with mental illness. They live in dormitories, each containing perhaps thirty to fifty people. The inmates occupy cots, and are brought their meals at specific times of the day. They receive a range of programming that includes cleanliness classes, expressive therapy, group and individual therapy, and occasional meetings with a psychologist and psychiatrist. Many receive medication, but the uncertainty of their condition creates considerable anxiety. When I entered a male dormitory one afternoon, numerous inmates suddenly surrounded me. Some thought I was a lawyer, and begged me to intervene to help them post bail. They were disappointed when they learned that I was a professor who couldn't offer them any legal aid. Others told me sad stories of being arrested for minor property theft or inappropriate public behavior. Initially, some inmates seemed rational, but then told strange and incoherent stories. When I visited the units housing women, I had similar experiences where people asked me for help and related their stories. I wanted to assist in some way, but all I could do was to listen.

Like all parts of the Cook County Jail, mental health care areas can be dangerous places for inmates and staff. For example, in 2014 Tony Purnell was murdered by other inmates, all of whom were receiving mental health care at the John Stroger Hospital. Serving a six-month term for contempt of court, Purnell was punched and knocked to the floor by an inmate. Another inmate then kicked him in the head. Although corrections officers arrived at the scene, Purnell had already been badly injured and he died a month after the incident. His family sued Cook County, alleging that overcrowding and staff neglect led to Purnell's death ("Inmate Tony Purrell Dies after Jail Fight" 2014).

In other cases, those suffering from mental illness commit suicide or engage in terrible forms of self-injury. For example, in 2014 an inmate charged with a parole violation was returned to Illinois from California. Suffering from schizophrenia, he gouged out one of his eyes while being transported. At the Cook County Jail, he gouged out his other eye and had to be rushed to the hospital. He was later returned to the jail, and placed in physical restraints to prevent further self-harm. Those who heard about this terrible act of self-mutilation expressed horror and dismay that such an episode could happen even when the jail knew about his history. Although this represents an extreme case, similar acts of self-mutilation occur at the Cook County Jail ("Chicago Inmate Gouges Out His Eyes" 2014).

To deal with this troubled population, Cook County employs only a small number of psychologists and psychiatrists. Psychiatrists come into the units, interview inmates for a few minutes, and then dispense medication. Some psychologists work with inmates full-time, and the jail also employs social workers. Finally, Cook County relies heavily on "mental health specialists" responsible for administering different kinds of therapy. Programming occurs in large groups, often because of staff shortages. A psychologist I met worked hard to help inmates, but described a caseload of several hundred patients. Additionally, he supervised new employees. He spoke about how he enjoyed his work and he was clearly dedicated to it. However, I couldn't imagine how he managed such an enormous burden.

In both the Residential/Intermediate and Acute Care wings, corrections officers confront a difficult task. Cook County has required its officers to undergo training on how to respond to mental illness. However, corrections officers are not medical professionals, and their primary responsibility is to provide security. When I talked to them, some acknowledged this fact, and lamented that the jail had become a large mental institution. Others seemed to genuinely care for those weakened by their illness. I noticed this concern particularly in the women's unit, where I met inmates in their sixties. Officers tried to help these women, who seemed completely lost and confused. Overall, custodial and therapeutic goals seemed to coexist awkwardly at the Cook County Jail.

A New Start?

County officials believe that the RTU constitutes a major improvement in mental health treatment, but its future success is unclear (I will consider this issue more fully in the conclusion). Officials promise a new array of services for inmates with mental illness. They note the large size of the new building, which they hope will reduce overcrowding. Finally, they have hired additional staff members who seem dedicated to helping inmates. However, given the challenges and structure of this new unit, only time will tell how much it will improve mental health care. Much depends on the population dynamics of the jail. They fluctuate widely, and this makes providing mental health care difficult. External factors shape the jail population. For example, in 2012 Chicago closed six of its twelve public mental health clinics, allegedly to save money (see Jaravsky 2012, 2013). These closures left many poor people with no place to get help with their mental health problems. Many ended up in the Cook County Jail.

Fiscal and hiring matters will also influence prospects for the RTU's success. Hiring additional staff costs Cook County money, and future budget crises in Illinois may reduce funding for staff. Additionally, Cook County cannot find qualified personnel easily. Working in correctional mental health care is an extremely difficult job. Personal safety worries alone deter people from working with inmates. Those who do work in penal institutions often burn out after their initial idealism and enthusiasm dissipate. Many medical professionals never bother to apply for jobs in corrections, preferring instead to go into private practice or to work in a hospital setting. All these factors will determine if the RTU will succeed in its attempt to improve mental health care.

In my visit to the RTU, I noticed several areas of concern. Despite its newness, the structure itself is ugly, a huge building with concrete walls. Disturbingly, the RTU contains a bank of video screens for visitations. Many of its inmates no longer have face-to-face visitations with relatives but must talk to loved ones who are in another building, and they can only see them on a screen. When I inquired about this change, I was informed that it occurred for cost and convenience reasons. However, I was approached by several women begging me and my guide to return them to a part of the facility where they could see their children. I, of course, could say nothing, but my guide told these women that there was nothing that could be done. They had been determined to have mental illness, and must remain in the new unit. One woman angrily denied that she was mentally ill, and became so upset that we had to retreat from her. Although I understood the need to save money, I couldn't fathom how the jail could help people recover from mental illness by denying them close contact with family.[23]

Languishing in the Jail

In addition to enduring miserable conditions and brutal staff treatment, inmates also languish in the Cook County Jail. Because of the seriousness of their crimes, some inmates receive no bail. Cook County cannot risk releasing them, and they remain in the jail throughout their trials. However, thousands of other inmates remain for days, weeks, or months in the jail because they cannot afford to pay the 10 percent of their bail required for release. Analyses of inmate bond hearings from 2010 to 2012 indicate that in "2010, roughly 30.6% of defendants posted bond, followed by 33% in 2011, and 32% in 2012" (Illinois Supreme Court, Administrative Office of the Illinois Courts 2014, 28). Some inmates spend a few days or a week in jail before posting bond. Others remain for six months to a year until their trial ends (Chicago Appleseed Fund for Justice 2013). In 2012, the average stay for those who couldn't post bail was fifty-seven days (Olson and Huddle 2013, 7).

Disturbingly, many inmates who remain in the jail have relatively low bail requirements and have been accused of minor crimes. For example, if a judge sets bail at $6,000, a defendant must post a bond of $600. If a judge requires bail of $25,000, a defendant must come up with $2,500. These amounts are simply beyond the reach of many poor people in Chicago. They wait for weeks or months in the jail until their cases are resolved. Many sit in the jail, only to receive probation or some other kind of supervision. The courts found them safe enough to be released to the community, although they had to endure the hell of the Cook County Jail for weeks or months.

Still more problematic, in 2011 over eleven thousand inmates served an average of twenty-five days only to have their cases dismissed (Olson and Huddle 2013, 8). Cook County detains a high number people for misdemeanor charges, but later drops the charges. Between 2006 and 2012, "eight out of 10 misdemeanor cases" were dismissed (Caputo 2013). This dismissal rate is "among the highest in the nation" (Caputo 2013). These dismissed cases include offenses like drinking in public and getting into fights. In many cases, they involve minor property crimes like shoplifting. Arresting officers may never show up to court, forcing the charges to be dismissed. In other cases, prosecutors decide to dismiss charges. Either way, thousands of people languish in the Cook County Jail for minor offenses that are ultimately dismissed.

Recognizing that this system is unfair and inefficient, the sheriff's office and some Chicago politicians have called for its overhaul. For example, Sherriff Dart commented that minor offenders "are the guys who stay [in the jail] for five days, 20 days," and noted that they are "gumming up the system" (Caputo 2013). Cook County Board President Toni Preckwinkle has repeatedly sought to change bond requirements. I will be exploring the efforts of these officials to make positive changes later in this book. However, according to critics of the bond system, it is "a result of a wink-and-nod agreement between police and prosecutors that goes like this: Police make petty arrests to get people off the streets to deter more violent crimes, and prosecutors or city attorneys run with the charges with few questions asked. It's an exercise of justice that's more show than substance: Defendants spend days, weeks or even months in the system where odds are their cases will ultimately be dismissed" (Caputo 2013). Many of those who find themselves in the Cook County Jail represent little or no threat to others. Instead, they endure its degradations and brutality because they are too poor to post bail.

These problems are exacerbated by miscommunications and dysfunctions in the pretrial process. Pretrial investigators interview inmates very briefly.[24] They forward pretrial documents to judges who don't trust them to do good work or to verify the information inmates provide them. The bond hearings are so short that judges cannot be expected to make detailed judgments about defendants. Defendants with private attorneys who spend time on their cases may receive lower bails. Most defendants, however, work with overworked public defenders who can devote little time to each case. Consequently, many people find themselves sitting in the Cook County Jail for weeks or months.

Recidivism and Mental Illness

A final challenge confronting the Cook County Jail involves recidivism and mental illness. Many inmates released from the jail find their way back. For example, from 2007 to 2012, out of a total of over 501,432 inmates admitted, 156,631 were admitted only once, 50,173 twice, 45,162 three to five times, 9,865 six to ten times, and 903 more than eleven times (Olson and Huddle 2013, 4).

Some who repeatedly return are violent offenders who represent a significant danger to others. For example, Chicago's recent explosion of gun violence has often reflected a deeply disturbing disregard for human life. Some of the people coming to the jail have been accused of killing people or of committing other terrible crimes. However, as I have already discussed, many others come in and out of the jail because of mental illness. Corrections officers, social workers, and psychologists with whom I spoke lamented this cycle of arrests and rearrests. Sheriff Dart has appeared on multiple media outlets to decry it, and has instituted policies to help those with mental illness transition out of the jail. However, the problem of mental illness at the Cook County Jail seems overwhelming. The jail has only a few social workers to help the hundreds of inmates who exit every week. Those on medication receive a small dose when they leave, and are advised about where they might find mental health care. However, authorities cannot ensure that people take their medication. Moreover, outside the jail public mental health services are in such disarray that many former inmates cannot find help. If they do, they discover that they may have to wait weeks or months for it.

Predictably, many people who suffer from mental illness and leave the Cook County Jail either don't take their medication or run out of it quickly. Symptoms of their illness reappear, they commit minor crimes or become a public nuisance, and they find themselves rearrested by the police. Sometimes, these arrests result from minor property crimes. I spoke with inmates who broke into stores or shoplifted small items. Other arrests come from disruptive public behavior like defecating in public or accosting strangers on the street. Like other big U.S. cities, Chicago has undergone major changes to its downtown areas, now designed to attract upper-income residents and tourists. Police patrolling these areas are often intolerant of what they think is disruptive public behavior. In Chicago, it often comes from those who are homeless or mentally ill. When they disturb public order, police rapidly remove them, and they end up in the Cook County Jail. They reappear on the streets after a few months, and once again the vicious cycle of arrest and incarceration begins.

Conclusion

The Cook County Jail is a brutal, overcrowded, confusing, and filthy place. From the moment people enter the Bullpen, they are verbally and physically accosted. They find themselves in conditions that most people would find revolting. Crowded in with a mass of humanity, they lose all privacy. They face the constant threat of violence from other inmates. Medical care is substandard, and inmates often cannot convince the authorities that they need it. They often don't know when their hellish experience will end, and have little idea about when they can resume something of a normal life outside the jail.

These conditions are particularly trying for the thousands of people who suffer from mental illness and often must live without their medication for days. Their conditions can worsen when they enter the jail. Or they receive perfunctory medical care designed to stabilize their condition and pacify them. Given the extraordinary caseloads they carry, mental health care workers can learn little about individuals' needs and histories. They work hard to help the inmates, but confront a herculean task. Those who succeed in helping an inmate do so in the face of extraordinary odds. In a penal setting, the demand for order often supersedes the task of responding to an inmate's mental health care needs. The treatment of mental illness at the Cook County Jail is little more than a small bandage over a gaping wound. It leaves suffering inmates frightened, confused, angry, and sick. Sadly, they are often treated briefly, are discharged, and find themselves once again within the walls of the Cook County Jail.

Because of its size and history, the Cook County Jail confronts special problems that don't exist in all U.S. jails. However, we find similar problems in jails in Los Angeles, New York, and other large urban areas. Moreover, some of Cook County's problems do appear in other jails, including staff brutality, poor sanitation, and the influx of inmates with mental illness. Therefore, I have spent considerable time depicting this jail, and will use it as a reference point throughout this book. More than anything else, what occurs in this jail shows that many people experience jail as a degrading place that assaults their dignity. If this is the case, why do we have such an institution in our society? To answer this question, we need to carefully consider other jails and the role they play in U.S. society.

2

What Is the Purpose of a Jail?

It is clear that punishment is overdetermined by utilities of
all kinds.
—Friedrich Nietzsche, *On the Genealogy of Morals*[1]

For millennia, philosophers and theologians have discussed the purpose of punishment. Punishment inflicts deprivation on someone, and
thoughtful people recognize that we should give some ethical justification for this behavior. Some maintain that it looks to the future, seeking
to deter individuals and groups from harming others. Others hold that
punishment is backward-looking, providing retribution for a harm a
person has committed. Some philosophers insist that it annuls the harm
done or expresses a value to the offender. For still others, punishment
seeks to rehabilitate an offender, bringing him back to good standing in
a political community. Some Christian theologians have linked atone-
ment, repentance, and punishment. Finally, some philosophers conclude
that punishment aims only at incapacitation, and has no purpose beyond
stopping evil people from committing evil acts.[2]

These philosophical and theological debates shape how we approach
incarceration, and citizens should think hard about punishment's purpose. However, currently the U.S. penal system confronts a chasm between theory and reality. Few of the standard philosophical justifications
of punishment come anywhere close to legitimizing the contemporary
penal system. Many Americans gave up on rehabilitation decades ago,
concluding that "nothing works" or that rehabilitation is too soft on
criminals. Contemporary punishment expresses few positive values to
offenders, instead sending them the message they are worthless garbage.
Some inmates receive the retribution they deserve, while others face disproportionate sentences for their crimes. The U.S. penal system fails to
fulfil most of the criteria of deterrence theories. Currently, incapacitation seems to be the only plausible candidate for a justification for pun-

ishment in the United States. Anyone who looks rationally at the U.S. criminal justice system can conclude only that it bears little resemblance to any other ideal of justice.

Additionally, as philosopher Friedrich Nietzsche notes, even if punishment can serve a moral purpose (as I believe it can), it simultaneously performs diverse social purposes.[3] In this chapter, I buttress this argument by looking at the function jails perform in contemporary U.S. society. I update John Irwin's thesis that they exist partly to control those we consider marginalized in society. Although they incapacitate dangerous people and hold those who present a flight risk for trial, jails also brutally restrain people suffering from mental illnesses, the poor, and those who cannot conform to social norms. First, returning to the Cook County Jail, I note that some of its problems exist in other large jails. Like Cook County, Rikers Island in New York City and the Los Angeles County Jail face difficulties in managing large numbers of inmates. Second, however, I identify challenges most U.S. jails confront: controlling staff and inmate violence, maintaining sanitary conditions, and dealing with those suffering from physical and mental illness. Third, after briefly describing source material, I maintain that many U.S. jails have failed miserably to meet these challenges in a way that respects human dignity. Throughout the United States, we find patterns of brutality and horrible conditions in jails of all sizes. Jails that manage to avoid these difficulties confront problems of mental illness and overcrowding. Fourth, I turn away from specific conditions and consider several functions that jails serve in U.S. society. I identify three: responding to those with mental illness, controlling poor people who cannot afford bail, and generating revenue for cash-strapped municipalities. Fifth, I reflect on the conditions of jails in light of narratives about rehabilitation. Although mass incarceration has brought an increasingly punitive set of attitudes and practices, I resist the idea that we have departed from an earlier commitment to rehabilitation. Instead, I suggest that jail problems relate to issues about powerlessness and institutions that have existed throughout U.S. history. I conclude the chapter by noting that U.S. jails are often degrading institutions that show little respect for human dignity.

The Challenges of a Big Jail

Cook County is one of the largest single-site jails in the United States, but its problems appear in large jails elsewhere. New York City, Los Angeles, Houston, Dallas, Miami, and other cities all have large jails. They process hundreds of thousands of people annually. Large U.S. jails incarcerate a significant percentage of the U.S. jail population. The "largest jails (those with an average daily population (ADP) of 1,000 or more inmates) held 48% of the inmate population at midyear 2013, but accounted for 6% of all jail jurisdictions nationwide" (Minton and Goloinelli 2014). The sheer volume of people coming and going from these facilities creates management and information problems. Those at the top of the organization may be unaware of what happens at the ground level. Keeping big buildings clean is an enormous task, particularly when inmates routinely damage property. Well-entrenched bureaucracies like facilities management react slowly to property damage and frequently impede change. Finally, population dynamics deeply affect large jails. Administrators may know little about exactly how many inmates will enter their facility. Riots, spikes in crime, policy changes, and other events bring sudden and unexpected surges in jail populations that create logistical problems.

In addition to these difficulties, large jails must deal with political tensions and multiple constituencies. For example, Cook County has a sheriff, a County Board, and elected judges. Often, they clash on key issues, stifling important changes. Additionally, the Cook County Jail has a strong union representing its corrections officers. It protects employees, some of whom may need to be disciplined or fired. Rikers Island confronts a similar problem. Its union leadership has fiercely resisted making changes to solitary confinement policies for adolescents, maintaining that they would endanger staff. Union leaders have frequently and publicly clashed with New York City's mayor.[4]

To see how Cook County's problems appear in other large jails, let me note some recent events at Rikers Island and the Los Angeles County Jail. The latter jail houses close to fifteen thousand inmates. In 2013, eighteen of its deputies were indicted for brutalizing inmates. Media investigations, an ACLU lawsuit, and a Department of Justice investigation revealed a long-standing pattern of extreme violence toward inmates.

Deputies belonged to gangs that sported their own tattoos. They adopted point systems for breaking inmates' bones, fomented violence between inmates, and intimidated officers unwilling to engage in violence. Deputies savagely beat, sexually humiliated, and raped inmates. They particularly targeted those with mental illness, at one point reportedly beating a man in a wheelchair. This brutality continued for years, but things came to a head when sheriff's deputies tried to intimidate an FBI agent investigating conditions at the jail. Federal indictments and convictions followed soon afterward.[5]

New York City's Rikers Island prison complex, with an average daily population of fourteen thousand inmates, has a long history of brutalizing inmates, but its abuses have recently garnered publicity. A Department of Justice investigation and multiple investigations by the *New York Times* revealed terrible violence at the jail. A 2014 DOJ investigation passionately concluded that

> for adolescents, Rikers Island is a broken institution. It is a place where brute force is the first impulse rather than the last resort; where verbal insults are repaid with physical injuries; where beatings are routine while accountability is rare; and where a culture of violence endures even while a code of silence prevails. The adolescents in Rikers are walled off from the public, but they are not walled off from the Constitution. Indeed, most of these young men are pre-trial detainees who are innocent until proven guilty, but whether they are pre-trial or convicted, they are entitled to be detained safely and in accordance with their Constitutional rights—not consigned to a corrections crucible that seems more inspired by Lord of the Flies than any legitimate philosophy of humane detention. These young men, automatically charged as adults despite their age under New York law, may be on an island and out of sight, but they can no longer remain out of mind. Attention must be paid immediately to their rights, their safety, and their mental well-being, and in the wake of this report we will make sure that happens one way or another. (U.S. Attorney's Office, Southern District of New York 2014)

The DOJ discovered extraordinary rates of violence against helpless youth. It also found a code of silence among officers and medical staff that enabled abuse. It presented a sickening picture of how corrections officials devalued the lives of young people.

The situations in New York City and Los Angeles illustrate how large jails confront significant difficulties controlling staff and inmate violence. Large populations of troubled, violent, and unruly people inhabit them. Those guarding them can also be violent and abusive, and commit terrible acts with a sense of impunity. The result is an environment where inmates constantly fear staff and other inmates. Often, staff violence occurs with full public knowledge. For example, for years the *Los Angeles Times* wrote about deputy violence in the Los Angeles County Jail. An apathetic public paid little attention, officials found ways to stall legal action, and unions protected abusive personnel. Sadly, we find similar dynamics in other large cities in the United States.

Issues Confronting Many Jails

We can identify problems these large institutions also share with smaller and medium-size jails. Minimally, all jails must prevent inmates from escaping, incapacitate them from committing crimes in the community and hold them if they are awaiting trial. However, beyond these basic functions, today's jails must also control inmate and officer violence, provide basic sanitation in their facilities, offer minimal health care, and help those with mental illness stabilize their conditions.

To consider how well jails perform these tasks, I have relied on several sources of information. First, I examined documents available from the U.S. Department of Justice (DOJ). The DOJ's Civil Rights Division (established in 1957) through its Special Litigation Section conducts investigations of prisons and jails (as it did with Cook County).[6] It makes its reports publicly available, and its investigations follow a general pattern. The DOJ notifies a county or state that it plans to investigate a penal institution. It then investigates, using correctional experts to examine diverse features of the jail or prison. Afterward, it sends a letter to county or state officials detailing its findings. In some cases, the DOJ pursues a lawsuit against the jail or prison. However, in most cases (again, like that of Cook County), the parties reach a Consent Agreement about how to ameliorate conditions. They appoint monitors, people specially trained to watch for problems. These monitors periodically visit the penal institution and issue reports. After an agreed period, the DOJ may announce that the jail or prison has met the terms of the Consent Agreement. Or it may continue monitoring the institution, initiate a new investigation, or file a lawsuit.

Another important source of my information is documents from organizations like the American Civil Liberties Union (ACLU). The ACLU issues multiple reports on jail and prison conditions, and initiates lawsuits against institutions. In some cases, these lawsuits end up in protracted legal disputes that go on for years. In others, jails settle lawsuits, agreeing to make changes to avoid legal difficulties. Either way, ACLU documents provide a valuable look at jail conditions.

Investigative journalism provides another important source of information about jail and prison conditions. In particular, print publications possess the resources and access to penal institutions needed to do long investigations. For example, the *New York Times* published multiple articles about conditions at Rikers Island. The *Miami Herald* offered a long series about inmates who were tortured to death in Florida prisons.[7] The *Los Angeles Times* published stories about abuses at the Los Angeles County Jail. These media investigations reveal hidden aspects of jails and prisons.

Finally, inmate lawsuits in federal courts can be windows into what happens in jails. Because of bureaucratic and legal barriers, inmates face difficulties filing suit against jails and prisons. However, public interest groups learn about their complaints and initiate lawsuits. Depositions, witness testimony, and court findings reveal conditions in jails. Sometimes, lawsuits result in protracted legal battles. In other cases, counties and states settle them quickly and agree to make changes to their facilities. The legal documents in these cases help us understand how jails function.

Profound Failures

If we read the sources I have mentioned, we find numerous jails that fail to operate humanely. Multiple investigations and lawsuits describe how inmates live in abysmal sanitary conditions, suffer violence from staff and fellow inmates, and receive little medical and mental health care. In some cases, jails have completely failed to care for inmates at all. For example, the Orleans Parish Prison (OPP, a jail rather than a prison) is a huge jail (about 8,500 inmates) in New Orleans with a long history of inmate and staff brutality. During Hurricane Katrina in 2005, corrections officials completely abandoned inmates. When the storm approached, corrections officers used violence and chemical agents to force inmates into cells. They then locked them in, and didn't return for several days. During this period,

> thousands of men, women, and children were abandoned at OPP. As floodwaters rose in the OPP buildings, power was lost, and entire buildings were plunged into darkness. Deputies left their posts wholesale, leaving behind prisoners in locked cells, some standing in sewage-tainted water up to their chests. Over the next few days, without food, water, or ventilation, prisoners broke windows in order to get air, and carved holes in the jail's walls in an effort to get to safety. (ACLU 2006)

After a few days, officials returned to the jail to open cell doors. Then, inmates

> were bused to receiving facilities around the state, where, for some, conditions only got worse. At the Elayn Hunt Correctional Center, thousands of OPP evacuees spent several days on a large outdoor field, where prisoner-on-prisoner violence was rampant and went unchecked by correctional officers. From there, prisoners went to other facilities, where some were subjected to systematic abuse and racially motivated assaults by prison guards. (ACLU 2006, 9)

In their rush to abandon inmates, authorities disregarded any attempt to classify them. They mixed juveniles with adults and inmates accused of violent crimes with those jailed for minor offenses. Among those living with adults were children ages ten to thirteen. Subsequent investigations of the scandal at OPP showed that New Orleans had no serious evacuation plans for its jail inmates. It thus completely failed to treat them with any sense of humanity.

Jail Sanitation

Jail officials rarely abandon inmates in this way, but instead treat them inhumanely. Let me begin with sanitation, which in many investigations and lawsuits emerges as a serious problem. Jails are often filthy places filled with vermin and insects. Plumbing, heating, and cooling work inadequately, and inmates prepare food in unsanitary conditions. Food is left cold for long periods or is exposed to insects, rats, and mice. Laundry facilities are deficient, with clothes cleaned in unsanitary ways maybe once a week. These conditions create an environment that breeds and spreads disease.

To illustrate difficulties with sanitation, let me describe the case of the Suffolk County Correctional Facility (SCCF) on New York's Long Island. In 2012, the New York Civil Liberties Union filed a lawsuit on behalf of inmates in this jail. Suffolk County is a relatively affluent part of Long Island, but its jail long had problems that it didn't fix. Although its capacity was eleven hundred inmates, it often held up to fourteen hundred people. The ACLU maintained that the men

> detained in the SCCF lack access to clean drinking water and safe food, as well as basic necessities such as sanitary and properly functioning sinks, toilets, and showers. Rodents and insects invade their living areas and contaminate their food. In the winter, the men sleep in freezing cells, made colder still by leaking water that drips into their sleeping quarters. They attempt to stave off the cold with a single worn blanket. These conditions, independently and through their mutually reinforcing effects, produce a serious deprivation of basic human needs.[8]

Most appallingly, toilets in this jail frequently malfunctioned, flooding the cells with sewage. Individual cells contained a toilet that sat two to three feet away from the individual's bed. Flushing a toilet in an adjoining or nearby cell caused sewage to burst up in another's toilet.[9] Inmates would announce to others when they were flushing so as not to cause too much overflow. However, at night the toilets would flood, and inmates woke up with raw sewage in their cells. Sewage also burst into shower areas, making it impossible for inmates to clean their bodies completely. The jail lacked adequate cleaning supplies, so inmates were forced to constantly live in sewage. Suffolk County knew about this revolting situation for years, but did nothing to remedy it. Finally, jail officials promised to make some changes. Although this case represents a particularly egregious example of poor sanitation, we find similar situations in jails throughout the United States.[10]

Staff Violence

We have already seen how large jails have difficulties controlling staff violence, but this problem also plagues medium-sized and smaller jails. Throughout the country, we have reports of corrections officers who beat inmates into submission. They will take them beyond the range of surveillance cameras, and punch and kick him. Officers will then threaten them with further violence if they complain. For example, the Passaic County Jail (PCJ) in New Jersey has been subjected to lawsuits alleging brutality against inmates. Designed to hold eight hundred inmates, in 2005 it housed two thousand, most of whom lived in large dormitories with triple bunks. Some of the inmates came from outside of Passaic County because the county raised revenue by accepting inmates from other counties.

In 2008, the ACLU filed a lawsuit against Passaic County because of the conditions in its jail. In addition to describing grossly unsanitary conditions, it detailed how corrections officers conducted "beat downs" where they would punch, kick, and stomp inmates (*Angel Colon v Passaic County* 2008, 131–142).[11] The lawsuit also alleged that "dogs are routinely permitted to bark ferociously, growl, snarl, and lunge at PCJ inmates. There have also been instances in which PCJ inmates have been bitten and required hospital treatment" (*Angel Colon v Passaic County* 2008, 128).[12] At one point, an attorney visiting a client described how a dog barked and lunged at him. In 2012, the ACLU reached a proposed settlement with the PCJ to make major use-of-force and sanitary policy changes.

In 2010, documents from a class-action federal lawsuit told a horrifying story about brutality in the Franklin County Corrections Center in Columbus, Ohio. The facility held between 250 and 350 inmates. The lawsuit charged a pattern of unconstitutional use of Tasers in the jail. This practice is carried out through the frequent and gratuitous use of Tasers to inflict pain, fear, corporal punishment and humiliation. Tasers operate in two different modes. One mode is designed to subdue a person at a distance by firing two darts or probes that strike and attach to the person. The second is "drive stun" mode, or the "pain compliance option." Drive stun mode produces a continuous extremely painful electrical shock useful for an officer engaged in close hand contact with a resisting subject.[13]

The lawsuit charged that when processing people into the jail, officers used Tasers in their "pain compliance option" to quell even the slightest sign of disagreement or dissent. Often,

> when an arrestee voices a verbal objection to having to remove his or her clothes, or otherwise shows any lack of cooperation during the booking process, such as failing to answer routine medical questions from a nurse, a team of deputies takes the person into a side table, forcibly strips the individual without telling the person why they are being "dressed out," and tases the person being stripped.[14]

Male deputies were sometimes present while female inmates were stripped of their clothes and tased. In one case, deputies tased an inmate in his cell fourteen times. In others, they tased inmates who were completely restrained, and tased a pregnant woman for failing to remove her tongue ring quickly enough.

One incident at the Franklin County Corrections Center illustrates how people can suddenly find themselves in a jail dominated by brutal staff. Because of a traumatic brain injury from a motorcycle accident, Michael Reed suffered from seizures. One day while walking in the street he had a seizure, and when emergency medical personnel arrived he allegedly acted aggressively. He was arrested for assaulting a peace officer, and was incarcerated in the Franklin County Corrections Center. A judge determined that he was not guilty of a crime because of his condition, and ordered him placed in a psychiatric facility. However, due to overcrowding in the only available psychiatric hospital, he remained in the jail. Officials were fully aware of his medical condition and history. One day, he suffered a seizure and needed immediate medical attention. Officers opened his cell door, and Reed resisted their attempts to handcuff him. They tased him twice, and transported him to the hospital. While in the hospital, he allegedly acted belligerently, and was again tased. Strangely, the U.S. Sixth Circuit Court of Appeals ruled that Reed's treatment did not constitute an Eighth Amendment (prohibiting cruel and unusual punishment) violation because it was not done "maliciously and sadistically for the very purpose of causing harm."[15] The court therefore affirmed the summary judgment dismissing Reed's demand that he receive individual monetary damages. However, the class-action lawsuit against the Franklin County Corrections Center was settled in 2011 and the county changed its tasing policy.

One final example from York County Prison (a jail) in Pennsylvania illustrates how jail inmates can endure capricious staff violence. In 2015, inmates brought lawsuits against the prison, which has a maximum capacity of twenty-four hundred beds. They alleged that corrections officers staged "fight clubs" where inmates were forced to fight each other. Officers also held "retard olympics" in which inmates with disabilities were forced to engage in humiliating activities like drinking milk until they vomited and eating food laced with pepper foam. Several officers were later convicted of crimes in these cases.[16]

Staff Sexual Assault

Staff sexual assault of inmates also occurs in U.S. jails. We find it particularly in juvenile facilities, where officers take advantage of troubled youth.[17] For example, in 2011 in the Terrebonne Parish Juvenile Detention Center in Houma, Louisiana (inmate population forty to sixty, with seven thousand people passing through its doors since 1998), DOJ investigators discovered a pattern of sexual assault on young people. Allegations "of sexual misconduct have led to criminal charges against seven staff members."[18] Additionally, DOJ investigators reported that

> we found that staff did not receive minimally adequate training, and that existing policies and procedures are inadequate to ensure: that minimally necessary force is used to control youth; that chemicals are used safely; or that youth are protected from sexual or physical abuse. In addition, we found that the facility lacks adequate staff and that the staffing pattern places youth at risk of harm because of fatigue, reduced accountability,

overreliance on seclusion, and inadequate supervision. (U.S. DOJ, Civil
Rights Division 2011d, 2)

In many other cases in U.S. jails, staff members sexually assault vulnerable inmates. They then intimidate them into silence, or claim that
inmates are liars who can't be trusted. Institutions enable this behavior by failing to provide adequate grievance procedures and refusing to
discipline sexual predators. In 2014, the U.S. Bureau of Justice Statistics
released a study revealing an appalling level of both staff and inmate
sexual assault in jails and prisons. Of cases of sexual assault or harass-
ment, 49 percent involved staff members. Many inmates are unwilling to
come forward with sexual assault allegations and have difficulties sub-
stantiating them. Therefore, experts suspect that studies underestimate
the numbers of those assaulted (Rantala, Rexroat, and Beck 2014).

Controlling Inmate-on-Inmate Violence

Jails of all sizes experience difficulties controlling inmate-on-inmate
violence. Often, overcrowding, dated physical structures, and understaffing prevent them from adequately monitoring inmates. They may
be unable to patrol cellblocks frequently or may leave inmates in day-
rooms without supervision. This failure to supervise provides inmates
with opportunities to assault each other. This is particularly true when
a jail has gangs who coordinate violent attacks. Although endemic to
larger jails, gang presence also plagues medium-sized and smaller jails.
In many cases, officers leave gangs to their own devices rather than
intervening to prevent inmate assault. Finally, in some jails correctional
officers foment inmate-on-inmate violence by pitting groups against
each other. Or they use violent inmates to maintain order in the jail.

For example, in a 2013 DOJ investigation of the Escambia County
Jail in northern Florida (population fourteen hundred), federal officials
discovered that the sheriff deliberately segregated black inmates. When
asked why he adopted this policy, the sheriff explained that his jail had
always had it, and claimed that segregation reduced inmate violence.
However, DOJ investigators found the opposite to be the case. Official
racial segregation not only is unconstitutional, but also often produces
deep antagonism between different groups. As the DOJ noted, the "Jail's

practice of segregating on the basis of race has clearly contributed toward the perception held by many prisoners that some in the Jail are intent on discriminating against African-Americans. This perception leads to racial tensions at the Facility and, along with staffing shortages and a failure to adequately monitor violence, creates a combustible situation that poses a serious and significant threat to the safety of both prisoners and staff" (U.S. DOJ, Civil Rights Division 2013a, sec. IV, a, 4). In Escambia, official segregation combined with unsafe physical facilities and understaffing produced considerable inmate-on-inmate violence. After the DOJ investigation, the Escambia County Jail abandoned its racial segregation policy and attempted to reduce inmate-on-inmate violence.

In 2011 in the Miami-Dade County Jail (population seven thousand inmates), DOJ investigators discovered that corrections officials used violent inmates to control other inmates. Juvenile inmates "selected as 'trustees' are often involved in incidents of violence. Trustees assisted in the jail operations by cleaning the units and delivering food trays and hygiene supplies. The Trustee program is dangerous and contributes to unconstitutional conditions" (U.S. DOJ, Civil Rights Division 2011b, sec. IV, c).[19] Following the orders of corrections officers, juvenile trustees would often mete out violent punishment. DOJ investigators noted that "most of the juvenile prisoners we interviewed spoke about the practice of 'taxing,' an unauthorized and undocumented method of discipline in which corrections officers will lock down a juvenile prisoner in his cell for rule violations and force another prisoner (or prisoners) to inflict physical punishment on the locked-down prisoner. The juveniles reported that a 'tax' also can result in extended lockdowns, sometimes lasting up to three days" (U.S. DOJ, Civil Rights Division 2011b, sec. IV, c). In this case, inmate-on-inmate violence resulted from a deliberate policy of using juvenile trustees.

Many of the jails in major U.S. cities suffer from dangerous levels of inmate-on-inmate violence. For years, Baltimore, San Francisco, Philadelphia, Detroit, and other cities have operated jails where inmates often assaulted and raped each other. Authorities knew about these dangers, but offered inadequate protection from harm.[20]

Medical Care

People entering a jail bring with them a variety of medical conditions and needs. Some require immediate attention to remain alive or well. Reports on jail conditions group these medical needs under the category of "acute care." Other medical conditions call for sustained attention and are classified under the category of "chronic care." With health care, jails must also pay close attention to infectious diseases. Inmates may bring them into the institution, and diseases can easily spread in the close quarters and unsanitary conditions. Finally, jails must carefully monitor inmates with the risk of suicide. Some may be mentally ill, but others may take their own lives out of despair. In either case, jails must adopt procedures for preventing inmates from killing themselves.

In all these aspects of medical care, many U.S. jails have a miserable record. First, many fail to medically screen inmates properly when they arrive. Sometimes, inmates receive no medical screening at all. For example, in 2011 the DOJ issued a report about the Leflore County Juvenile Detention Center in Greenwood, Mississippi. Although a small institution (thirty beds), in its existence this jail had held hundreds of young people ages ten to seventeen. The DOJ report found that although the facility claimed to offer health assessment upon entry, officials often skipped such examinations. The jail provided documentation attesting to health screening but "upon close examination, that same documentation noted that four youth entered the facility at 12:23 p.m. on November 10, 2009 and that medical screening for each of the four youth was also completed at 12:23 p.m. that same day. It is not credible that all four youth were admitted and medically screened within the space of one minute" (U.S. DOJ, Civil Rights Division 2011a, 5, a). At Leflore, officials wrote confusing records citing health screenings that never occurred.

In other cases, intake screenings are wholly deficient, and officials miss medical conditions they should easily discern. In the Dallas County Jail in 2006, corrections officers without medical training performed medical intakes (U.S. DOJ, Civil Rights Division 2006a, sec. III, a). The DOJ speculated that inmates may have died because of serious medical conditions that went undetected. In other cases, qualified medical personnel collect poor information about incoming inmates. For example, in 2005 the DOJ issued a report about the Grant County Detention Facility in Williamstown, Kentucky. The facility had a capacity of three hundred male and female inmates. For this population, the jail employed one full-time nurse who was assisted with patient care by corrections officers. A physician came into the facility for two to three hours a week. While the jail used an intake assessment, it did not "mandate the collection of sufficient information to ensure that serious medical issues" were addressed (U.S. DOJ, Civil Rights Division 2005, sec. III, a). Sometimes, it took the facility twelve days to perform a medical assessment. DOJ investigators found many inmates suffering from medical problems that went undetected by the jail. Grant County later reached an agreement with the DOJ to make major improvements in health care.

For acute care, jails often fail to respond to health emergencies. For example, in 2009 the DOJ issued a report on the Mobile County Metro Jail in Birmingham, Alabama (maximum capacity of over eight hundred inmates). The jail failed to provide timely and appropriate responses to the acute medical needs of inmates (U.S. DOJ, Civil Rights Division 2009c, sec. III, a). Consequently, an inmate died of cardiac arrest because her "deep vein thrombosis was not timely recognized or treated."[21] Another inmate arrived at the jail "with an acute trauma to his left eye and a paralysis of the right side of his face" (U.S. DOJ, Civil Rights Division 2009c, sec. III, a). He received little medical attention and was placed in general population. His condition worsened, and he died of a heart valve infection. Such failures to respond promptly and properly to inmate health problems plague many U.S. jails.

Those with manageable, but chronic diseases also receive poor medical attention in many U.S. jails. Understaffing certainly accounts for some of this neglect, but it sometimes occurs because of the demand that inmates pay for medical services. Indigent inmates rarely have the resources to pay for medical care, but some jails charge them anyway. For example, at the Sebastian County Adult Detention Center in Fort Smith, Arkansas (between three and four hundred inmates), a 2006 DOJ investigation found that a fee structure prevented many inmates from receiving medical care (U.S. DOJ, Civil Rights Division 2006b, sec. II, a). For a nurse call, inmates had to pay ten dollars, for medications three dollars, and for a physician consultation sixty dollars. In the list of fees, one item appeared truly bizarre. For inmates to be removed from suicide watch (a highly restrictive form of confinement), they needed to pay ten dollars! Many inmates who either were unemployed before incarceration or lost their jobs while jailed couldn't pay for medical services. Consequently, they simply suffered, sometimes from serious conditions that could have led to long-term physical damage or death.

With poor acute and chronic care, jails often take in inmates without detecting medical issues. For example, the 2009 DOJ report about the Mobile County Metro Jail found that officials failed to provide all incoming inmates with a tuberculosis (TB) test, and tested only 10 percent of them for syphilis. Those whose TB was discovered later received improper medical care. DOJ investigators found an outbreak of an unknown skin disease that jail authorities failed to identify, with inmates displaying strange boils on their skin (U.S. DOJ, Civil Rights Division 2009c, sec. III, a). DOJ reports about the Cook County Jail, the Oklahoma County Jail and Jail Annex, the Dallas County Jail, and others have highlighted similar failures to control infectious diseases.[22]

Mental Health Care

Some of the most egregious failures in jails involve mental health care. I have already discussed the challenges Cook County faces in caring for those with mental illness. Throughout the United States, many jails are completely unprepared to deal with mental illness. Inmates receive little or no medical attention and often commit suicide. They are victimized by staff and other inmates who take advantage of their vulnerable condition. Their conditions often worsen, and once they are released, they engage in behavior that brings them right back into a penal institution. This is the fate of tens of thousands of Americans.

We have already seen how medical intake procedures in jails can be completely inadequate. For inmates with mental illness, this failure often proves disastrous. Officials learn little about their condition, and provide no medication. Once they are in the jail, it may take weeks for them to receive medication. In the meantime, their conditions worsen, particularly because suddenly going off certain medications can produce serious side effects. Many inmates with mental illness find ways to withdraw from people, but others become disoriented. They fail to follow orders from corrections officers, and may be physically abused by them. In 2015, Human Rights Watch produced a report describing numerous cases of staff abuse against inmates who suffer from mental illness in jails and prisons. It is not a blanket condemnation of all corrections personnel or an accusation that all officers are monsters. Nevertheless, it provides evidence that "the misuse of force against prisoners with mental health problems is widespread and may be increasing."[23] In addition to suffering from staff abuse, those with mental illness often end up in solitary confinement; jail segregation units are filled with people with serious mental illness.[24]

Investigations into how jails treat those with mental illness reveal massive failures. Almost all the DOJ reports I have read include scathing indictments of mental health care. For example, in 2008 the DOJ reported on conditions in the Oklahoma County Jail and Annex in Oklahoma City (although designed to hold 1,250 detainees, it held 2,543). Shockingly, at the time of the investigation the DOJ reported that other "than medicating detainees with Thorazine (which is an older anti-psychotic medication with serious potential side-effects), the Jail offers essentially no mental health services to its seriously mentally ill" (U.S. DOJ, Civil Rights Division 2008b, sec. B, 2). Because of this negligence, the report speculated that some inmates might have died. Certainly, many suffered and created disorder in the institution. Other jails medicate inmates minimally, but isolate them in solitary confinement. Some use the euphemism "therapeutic lockdown" to describe locking those with mental illness in their cells for long periods of time.[25] In other cases, jails administer psychotropic drugs poorly.[26] They fail to properly check the identities of those receiving medication.[27] They keep poor medical records or sometimes have no records at all.[28] Inmates receiving medication may receive no therapy or blood work to monitor their conditions.[29] Inmates seeking help may wait weeks before they see a nurse or doctor.[30]

Tragically, because jails often fail to care for those with mental illness, they see high rates of inmate self-harm and suicide. The experience of jail shocks many people who first experience it. The degradation, the change in their lifestyle, perhaps the loss of a job and shame can incline people toward suicide. For those with mental illness, the shock of incarceration can be even greater. They are suddenly subject to foreign stimuli, abuse, constant orders, close contact with other people, and violence. All these factors may lead them to kill themselves. Because of this possibility, jails are supposed to be attentive to those who might take their own life, and devise procedures to help them.

Yet, jails often fail to identify or help those in danger of suicide. They are inattentive to inmates who are clearly crying out for help. Jails often lack procedures for monitoring those known to be suicidal. If they have policies, corrections officers may disregard them, leaving inmates alone when they should be watched. When inmates attempt to take their own life, officers may fail to react in time to save them. Or in some terrible cases, they simply allow inmates to continue their suicide attempt without opening cell doors. Those identified as suicidal may receive medication, but no follow-up appointment to monitor their condition. Finally, those with mental illness who end up in solitary confinement live in extreme circumstances that exacerbate their illness. Jails see many cases of inmate suicide in segregation units.

Let me offer one example to illustrate how jails fail to help those who might commit suicide. In 2009, the DOJ investigated the Lake County Jail in Crown Point, Indiana (an institution with a population of 1,053 at the time of the investigation). In this jail, unqualified, nonmedical health clinicians performed suicide screening during intake. No licensed medical personnel reviewed their screenings. Assessments were poorly conducted, often lacked a basic history, and were plagued with errors. Some inmates who didn't need to be were placed on suicide watch, while others desperately needed help and received none. Those on suicide watch were not checked properly, and officers made little use of the cameras designed to watch them. When confronted with inmates harming themselves, corrections officers didn't know what to do. Finally, inmates receiving psychiatric medications obtained all their daily medications in one dose, thus increasing the danger of overdose. The results of these multiple failures were sadly predictable. At the time of the DOJ investigation, staff "reported that there have been seven completed suicides in the past four years. Five completed suicides occurred in the past two years, a rate which is more than five times the national average" (U.S. DOJ, Civil Rights Division 2009b, sec. II, a). The DOJ eventually reached an agreement with the Lake County Jail to improve its mental health care and help inmates in danger of committing suicide.[31]

The Tip of the Iceberg

I have detailed staff brutality, failures to protect inmates from violence at the hands of other inmates, horrible sanitary conditions, negligent medical and mental health care, and poor suicide-prevention policies. I want to emphasize that not all U.S. jails suffer from all these abuses. Some perform safety and health functions relatively well. Nevertheless, the cases I have considered are only a small sample, the tip of a large iceberg. For obvious reasons, inmates are reluctant to complain about abuse or other failures out of fear of retaliation. For example, DOJ investigators at the Los Angeles County Jail and Rikers Island found that staff often threatened inmates with abuse if they complained to authorities. Additionally, filing a lawsuit against a penal institution is far more difficult than many people think. In 1996, the U.S. Congress passed the Prison Litigation Reform Act. It created numerous legal, financial, and bureaucratic hurdles for inmates who want to file suit against jails and prisons. Before filing, they must exhaust all administrative grievance procedures. They must also pay for some of the legal documents required for initiating a lawsuit. For all these reasons, inmates in U.S. jails probably experience more problems than we currently realize, but they can't complain about them.

Jails as Mental Institutions?

Considering the terrible conditions in many jails, what purpose do they serve in U.S. society? Obviously, they incapacitate some people who pose a threat to others. For example, laws prohibiting domestic violence rely heavily on the prospect of jail time for offenders. Others who are accused of sexual offenses or particularly heinous crimes must also be incapacitated from doing further harm. Jails also hold those who are unlikely to appear for trial if released on their own recognizance.

However, as John Irwin argued, beyond their official purposes jails play a much larger role in U.S. society. As we have seen in the case of Cook County, they function as the place of last resort for many people with mental illness. When scholars and journalists discuss this phenomenon, they often employ the term "deinstitutionalization," and blame one political party or the other for closing mental institutions and turning jails into asylums. However, this is far too simple an explanation. Scholars locate the beginnings of a move away from large mental institutions in the late 1940s and 1950s. In 1955, the United States confined over 559,000 people in state mental institutions.[32] Some were senior citizens who were no longer taken care of by their families, and many others were forcibly committed by their families or the state. For many reasons, by the 1980s the United States had drastically reduced the size of its state mental institutions. These included federal policies encouraging community care, the desire of states to save money, changes in civil commitment laws, developments in pharmacology, and activism on the part of the disabled and those with mental illness.[33]

With the failures of some community care settings and reduced bed space in psychiatric institutions, the jail superseded the mental hospital as a place to control the behavior of some people with mental illness. Some have used the term "transinstitutionalization" to describe the move from mental hospitals to jails and prisons.[34] It is a complex phenomenon, and scholars warn that we cannot simplistically conclude that those who left mental institutions in the 1970s ended up in jails and prisons. However, clearly, an extraordinary number of people now need psychiatric care, and jails have become the means to control them when they present problems for a community. Nationally, "serious mental illness, which includes bipolar disorder, schizophrenia, and major depression, affects an estimated 14.5 percent of men and 31 percent of women in jails—rates that are four to six times higher than in the general population" (Vera Institute 2015, 12). These are averages, and studies have demonstrated that in some jails rates of mental illness can be much higher. If we include less serious cases of mental illness, the percentages of inmates suffering from at least one of them increase substantially. In 2005, over 64 percent of jail inmates had a recent history of some mental health problem as diagnosed or treated by a mental health professional (James and Glaze 2006, 1). With jails' poor intake procedures, we can expect that many inmates with serious mental illness go undetected.

As the case of Cook County illustrates, jails often provide temporary custody for those who commit "public nuisance" crimes, minor robberies, or violent offenses. Cook County struggles to provide minimal mental health care to stabilize inmates, but as I have noted, many other jails leave those with mental illness entirely to themselves. A 2006 study indicated that only 15 percent of those in jails with mental illness reported receiving any medication (James and Glaze 2006, 9). Without care and in an environment inhospitable to getting better, their conditions often worsen. As I have already noted, those with mental illness frequently violate institutional rules, and find themselves in segregation. They end up in fights or disobey orders in far greater numbers than do inmates without mental illness (James and Glaze 2006, 8).

Multiple factors conspire to lead people with mental illness to return to jail. A recent Vera Institute study notes, "seventeen percent of people with mental illness in jail were homeless in the year before their arrest" (Vera Institute 2015, 17). Police may arrest homeless people for trespassing or vagrancy. Almost a third of inmates with mental illness were unemployed a month before their incarceration, and "thirty-four percent of people with mental illness in jail were using drugs at the time of their arrest compared to 20 percent of the rest of the jail population. Fifteen percent of people with mental illness were using both drugs and alcohol at the time of their arrest compared to seven percent of the rest of the jail population" (Vera Institute 2015, 17). Laws targeting drug offenders will likely result in arrests of many people with mental illness and substance abuse problems. Doris J. James and Laurent Glaze concluded in their 2006 study of jail and prison inmates who had mental health problems that "an estimated 23% had received treatment during the year before their arrest: 17% had used medication, 12% had received professional therapy, and 7% had stayed overnight in a hospital because of a mental or emotional problem" (James and Glaze 2006, 9).[35] These statistics reveal just how little mental health care jail inmates receive before their incarceration. Many live disorganized lives, leading them back to jail repeatedly.

Bail and Social Control

In addition to containing those with mental illness, jails also hold hundreds of thousands of poor people simply because they cannot afford to pay their relatively minor bail. In places like Cook County, inmates must come up with 10 percent of their bail, while in other municipalities (like Brown County, Wisconsin), they must pay the entire amount. In some cases, judges hold accused criminals without bail. In others, they release people on their own recognizance. In most others, the U.S. criminal justice system combines bonds with forms of supervision.[36] Money bond arrangements include a cash bond, where the person pays for the bond up front; a deposit bond, where she pays a percentage of the bond; a commercial bail bond, where she uses an outside service like a bail bondsman; and a property bond, where she pledges property as collateral to be forfeited if she fails to appear for trial (Justice Policy Institute 2012, 9). If a person cannot come up with the money for these arrangements or if her county doesn't offer them, she will be held in jail until her trial ends.

From 1992 to 2006, the trend in the United States has been to release fewer inmates on their own recognizance and to demand bail. In 2006, over 70 percent of inmates had to pay bail. Additionally, "a Bureau of Justice Statistics survey of felony cases in the 75 most populous counties of the U.S. showed that average bail amounts have increased by over $30,000 between 1992 and 2006" (Justice Policy Institute 2012, 10). These statistics show that the past few decades have seen an increasingly punitive approach to those accused of crimes.

These trends combine to make it difficult for poor defendants to post bail. If someone must post 10 percent of a relatively low bail, she may have to come up with six hundred to a thousand dollars, which many people simply don't have available. Tens of thousands of people also have their charges dismissed or are granted probation after they spend time in jail. Jail time and the need to come up with bail money put considerable financial pressure on a person's family. The situation worsens for those who lose their jobs or apartments while in jail. Often, inmates may be willing to plea-bargain rather than remain in jail waiting for a trial or the dismissal of their case. In fact, over 90 percent of defendants in criminal cases in the United States never go to trial, choosing instead to work out a plea agreement. In some cases, the terrible conditions in jail incline them to plea-bargain rather than stay in jail.[37]

This may be a rational decision because in some states, the longer a person remains in jail the worse her prospects may become. For example, the Arnold Foundation conducted a large study of the relationship between pretrial detention and sentencing in Kentucky. It found that the longer a person stays in jail, the more likely it is that she will be sentenced to jail or prison. It also found that those who remained in jail for lengthy periods received longer sentences. These findings were particularly disturbing because they applied primarily to low-risk offenders. Many were simply too poor to pay for bail, and their indigence cost them dearly when it came time to be sentenced.[38]

This system enables judicial authorities to control the lives of large numbers of poor people, particularly those who are young and are for some reason considered a threat or problem. One of the most important studies of the bail system found that "in many of the largest U.S. jurisdictions, around half of those kept in jail would have been less likely to be rearrested than those who had been released" (Justice Policy Institute 2012, 17).[39] This was a large-scale study and the researchers examined over a hundred thousand pretrial records. It reinforced older research that cast doubt on the capacities of judicial authorities to predict future violence. The study noted a historical trend from the 1980s to the present toward allowing judicial authorities leeway to consider vague definitions of "dangerousness" in considering bail amounts. Throughout the United States, judges include all kinds of elements in their calculation of dangerousness that have little predictive value (family background, employment history, finances, character and reputation, treatment of animals).[40] These calculations about dangerousness contribute to the enormous numbers of those confined before trial.

As we saw in Cook County, courts also make poor use of the information they do possess. Bail hearings occur so fast that judges can't possibly consider the details of individual cases. A thirty-second bond hearing cannot suffice for the court to discover anything significant about a person's financial situation or flight risk. Cook County is not alone in conducting rushed bail hearings. In many municipalities, they last for very short periods. Judges make quick decisions based on the nature of the crime or a prosecutor's recommendation. Public defenders representing indigent defendants have little time to understand the details of their clients' lives. Consequently, thousands of people end up in local jails because they cannot afford their bail.

A good example of this unfair bond system exists in Montana. In 2015, the ACLU issued a report on jails in Montana. In addition to finding multiple problems with violence, physical structure, sanitation, and medical and mental health care in jails, the ACLU noted difficulties with pretrial services. It found that Montana's bail system "disproportionately affects the indigent, who lack the financial resources to make bail and so remain incarcerated regardless of their innocence or guilt" (ACLU 2015, 5). Montana's jails were overcrowded and dirty, often because they housed many inmates who committed minor offenses but could not afford bail.

Inmates as a Source of Revenue

In some municipalities, jails also perform the function of collecting revenue from poor defendants. For example, some jails in Wisconsin charge inmates over twenty dollars a day for their incarceration. Once released they receive a bill. If they cannot pay it, their bill passes to a collection agency in Madison. If they can't make payments, their credit rating can be damaged, affecting their future employment and capacity to receive loans. Even if someone is acquitted at trial, it can take him years to pay off his debt to the state of Wisconsin.

In other cases, inmates can be jailed again if they fail to pay legal and jail costs. A report by the ACLU ("In for a Penny: The Rise of America's New Debtors' Prisons") drew attention to this troubling phenomenon. It found that counties in Louisiana, Georgia, Ohio, Washington, and Michigan relied on the criminal justice system to enhance county revenues. County courts assessed and collected legal financial obligations (LFOs), fees and fines associated with criminal sentences (ACLU 2010, 5). Those unable to pay them were sent to county jails, and often assessed additional fines. Once released, they were forced to work out payment plans to meet these financial obligations. When they failed to make payments, they were jailed again. Rather than charging them with failure to pay a debt (which courts have rejected as a legal justification for incarceration), judges used contempt of court or other charges to jail people.

Let me illustrate this financial nightmare with the example of New Orleans. For a long time, it fined inmates for minor offenses, and then entrapped them in a system of payment and incarceration.[41] Criminal defendants who were charged fees for public defenders faced "fines, court costs, and a host of fees that fund the operation of the justice system" (ACLU 2010, 17). Those unable to make payments were assigned late fees, and if they couldn't meet them, they could be jailed in the OPP.

The ACLU report described how some people were ordered to drug or alcohol treatment programs, but were required to pay for them. When they failed to do so because they couldn't afford payments, the program expelled them, and the court found that they violated their rules of supervision. This yielded additional jail time and more fines.

In the New Orleans case, the ACLU found that the costs of incarceration and the LFOs far exceeded the original fines levied. Cases began with minor traffic violations, begging citations, or drug violations, and the bills from court costs mounted and mounted. Courts mandated fines without considering the capacity of people to pay them. Those with felony records often couldn't find jobs, and when they did work they received low wages. Yet, courts still demanded they pay huge fines that grew into a mountain of debt. Taxpayers ended up footing the bill for incarceration, while the person in debt found himself in an impossible financial situation. Yet, this irrational cycle continued to function because various parties financially benefitted from it.

People caught in the debt cycle can end up in truly horrifying conditions. This is certainly true for those who get sent to the OPP, which for years after Katrina remained an unsafe and unsanitary facility. Several DOJ investigations, one in 2009 and another in 2012, found that the OPP continued to suffer from staff abuse, inmate violence, and sickening sanitary conditions (U.S. DOJ, Civil Rights Division 2009d). In 2016, OPP had become so troubled that the federal judiciary took over operations from local authorities.[42] Thus, for minor offenses people incurred debts that led them to be incarcerated multiple times in a hellish environment.

These practices came to national and international prominence in 2015 after the DOJ issued a report about Ferguson, Missouri. In 2014, Ferguson police officer Darren Wilson shot and killed a young man, Michael Brown. Protesters clashed with police for weeks, maintaining that Brown died because of the actions of a violent police officer working for a violent police department. However, Wilson was never indicted for killing Brown, and the DOJ declined to pursue a civil rights violation case against him.

Along with its finding about Wilson, the DOJ issued a report that revealed that the City of Ferguson supported its criminal justice system through fines and incarceration. City officials, the police chief, the

jail, and other actors united to enact heavy financial penalties on African Americans. The DOJ report found that Ferguson's "law enforcement practices are shaped by the City's focus on revenue rather than
by public safety needs" (U.S. DOJ, Civil Rights Division 2015a, I). Ferguson "budgets for sizeable increases in municipal fines and fees each
year, exhorts police and court staff to deliver those revenue increases,
and closely monitors whether those increases are achieved" (U.S. DOJ,
Civil Rights Division 2015a, I). Police targeted African Americans as a
means of raising revenues, levying multiple citations on them for minor
offenses. Courts issued thousands of warrants for minor charges, and
when arrested people would be jailed for failing to pay citations. This
would lead to further fines and costs, all of which had devastating consequences for Ferguson's poor citizens.[43]

People found the Ferguson case shocking because officials acted bra-
zenly to create what amounted to debtors' prisons. They would communicate the need to increase revenue through more citations, arrests,
and jail time. Police officers openly expressed racist stereotypes that influenced how they interacted with African Americans. Sadly, Ferguson
is not alone in creating a system that traps thousands of poor Americans
in a cycle of incarceration and entanglement with authorities.

Disturbingly, some counties enlist private debt companies to aid them
in extracting fees from inmates and ex-offenders. Often, misdemeanor
offenders receive probation (a form of supervision where the offender
is subject to rules and must report to a probation officer). However,
counties often cannot afford to fund probation services, and therefore
contract them out to private companies. In 2013, Human Rights Watch
issued a report detailing how private companies agree to collect LFOs
for counties:

> Every year, U.S. courts sentence several hundred thousand people to pro-
> bation and place them under the supervision of for-profit companies for
> months or years at a time. They then require probationers to pay these
> companies for their services. Many of these offenders are only guilty
> of minor traffic violations like speeding or driving without proof of in-
> surance. Others have shoplifted, been cited for public drunkenness, or
> committed other misdemeanor crimes. Many of these offenses carry no
> real threat of jail time in and of themselves, yet each month, courts issue

thousands of arrest warrants for offenders who fail to make adequate payments towards fines and probation company fees. (Human Rights Watch 2013, 1)

In grim detail, this report described how private companies offer courts probation services free of charge, and then hound people to pay them fees. Because the courts support the companies by jailing those who cannot pay, they give private companies considerable coercive power. By threatening people with jail time, probation agents can extort substantial fees from those desperate to remain out of jail. Some courts even link the length of probation time to a fee payment. They then delegate debt collection responsibility to a private company that adds additional fees to the original LFO. People can thus remain on probation for years while they struggle to pay growing debts. Human Rights Watch estimated that in some states, private probation companies generate tens of millions of dollars in revenue by supervising ex-offenders. They often keep their financial records hidden, so we can't know exactly how much they earn. Nevertheless, they clearly have a strong financial incentive to keep people on probation. In these cases, we have a distorted combination of state coercion and the market that deeply damages people's lives.

Human Rights Watch and the ACLU have investigated private probation companies in only select states like Georgia, Ohio, Mississippi, Alabama, Ohio, Louisiana, and Washington. However, LFOs exist throughout the United States. Hundreds of thousands of Americans live with legal debts to courts. They fear having their lives upended by a stint in the local county jail. Their families suffer from financial deprivation. Yet, we rarely hear their stories and don't consider how our local jail functions to perpetuate an unjust and irrational system.[44]

The Jail and Narratives about U.S. Punishment

When reading about this system, we might be tempted to trace its cause to recent developments in the U.S. penal system. Mass incarceration has brought unprecedented numbers of people into our prisons and jails. In the past few decades, we have seen an extraordinary prison and jail construction boom. We have also abandoned any commitment to rehabilitation, adopting an increasingly punitive attitude toward inmates.

Scholars struggle to explain these changes, offering competing explanations (the "New Jim Crow," the power of prosecutors, a conservative political backlash, liberal policies in the "War on Poverty," and the prison-industrial complex). Perhaps we have moved from an earlier commitment in rehabilitation to a harsher, punitive approach to inmates.

As a teacher in prisons and jails, I am sometimes tempted to adopt this narrative. Wistfully, I hear stories from older professors who taught in prisons in the 1970s and 1980s when inmates could earn college degrees. Today such educational opportunities rarely exist, having died in the 1990s when the U.S. Congress eliminated the Pell Grant program for prison inmates. County jails and state prisons often have little or no programming for inmates. Gone are theater and music initiatives that brought some light into the lives of inmates in the 1960s and 1970s. Finally, life for ex-offenders has becoming increasingly harsh. After serving extraordinarily long sentences, they come out of prisons confronting numerous restrictions on their lives that inmates in the past didn't face. Thinking of all these developments, we can easily believe that our current jail conditions represent an aberration from an earlier American commitment to rehabilitation.

Nevertheless, for a variety of reasons I resist this comforting narrative. I don't deny the general thesis that in the past few decades we have become more punitive. In fact, I have written about how since the 1980s, U.S. penal authorities have developed solitary confinement as a powerful tool to control inmates (Jeffreys 2013). However, the contrast to an earlier, better era often gains its power from uninformed and unsophisticated comparisons with the past. In the twentieth century, a penal system's commitment to rehabilitation often depended on regional differences. For example, as Robert Perkinson shows in his masterful study of the Texas system, *Texas Tough: The Rise of America's Prison Empire*, Texas had little commitment to rehabilitation for most of the twentieth century (Perkinson 2010). Instead, the state worked inmates on large farms, and savagely beat and tortured them into submission. Arkansas, Louisiana, Georgia, and Florida ran equally brutal penal systems. In these states, jails supporting these prisons showed a similar disinterest in rehabilitating inmates.

Sometimes scholars maintain that prisons and jails in other parts of the United States displayed a greater commitment to rehabilitation, but we ought to distinguish between rhetoric and reality. Often, institutions gave formal commitment to rehabilitating inmates, and sponsored rehabilitative programs. However, reality often differed from official images. We see this particularly when we read case studies of individual institutions. Some years ago, Alexander W. Pisciotta wrote an excellent book on the Elmira Reformatory in New York State, one of most famous facilities for young offenders in the early part of the twentieth century (Pisciotta 1996). Its world-famous superintendent, Zebulon Brockway, trumpeted a new noncoercive approach to juvenile justice that would depart from physical brutality. Yet, he administered severe corporal punishment to thousands of young men during his tenure. In a more recent book, Joseph Spillane tells the story of Coxsackie, a youth reformatory in New York State. He reveals that although it officially announced its commitment to rehabilitation, life in the institution was often brutal and harsh. African American and Latino inmates were excluded from the circle of those who could be rehabilitated (Spillane 2014). For so many juveniles in U.S. jails and prisons, life before mass incarceration was hardly an era of enlightened rehabilitation. Historians have written other excellent studies of penal systems and specific institutions that reveal the horrible history of U.S. punishment.[45]

An additional reason I refuse to harken back to an earlier era of rehabilitation involves mental illness and institutions. As I have already noted, mental illness represents one of the serious challenges confronting jails today. However, those writing about mass incarceration rarely consider our long history of mistreating those with mental illness. People with money in the United States have always had access to some decent mental health care (although even they were often subjected to brutal treatment). Those without resources and unable to function were shunted into terrible institutions where they received little treatment. Many couldn't leave of their own free will, and were patients in name only. If we consider today's problems in light of this history, our sense of an early era's commitment to rehabilitation changes considerably.

A final reason I resist the urge to recall a better age of rehabilitation is philosophical. Scholars and activists in the 1960s and 1970s raised important questions about the nature of rehabilitation. For example, what exactly does it mean for someone to be rehabilitated? Is coerced participation in therapy and other forms of rehabilitation morally justifiable? Why should rehabilitation be the aim of punishment at all? Rehabilitation is neither a simple nor an uncontroversial concept, and we shouldn't accept narratives that ask us to return to a golden age when we practiced it.[46]

Later in this book, I will present a narrative that links abuses in our jails to questions about institutions, powerlessness, dignity, and emotions. Historically, the United States has long embraced practices of institutionalizing people. Dealing with institutionalized people confronts us with a host of moral issues that we (and those in other countries) have always struggled to address. Mass incarceration has exacerbated them, but I think problems in our jails offer opportunities to explore historical continuities as well as discontinuities.

Conclusion

Not all U.S. jails are mismanaged hellholes. Some compassionate sheriffs and staff work hard to prevent violence and maintain minimally decent health care and sanitation. I want to emphasize again that I'm not condemning all corrections personnel. I have taught in a jail where I have met fine officers. In the conclusion, I will describe how Sheriff Dart at the Cook County Jail has introduced positive changes. However, in this chapter I am identifying systemic issues that confront the contemporary jail. Many U.S. jails fail miserably in performing the tasks assigned to them. They allow corrections officers to brutalize inmates, fail to control inmate violence, provide completely inadequate physical and mental health care, and allow inmates to languish in squalor. As John Irwin argued years ago, jails perform functions other than their stated ones of keeping the community safe from harm and holding defendants until their trials. They serve as institutions that control those with mental illness. Often, families can no longer effectively help their loved ones with mental illness. Sometimes, people have no family to rely on. When those with mental illness commit petty crimes, act violently, or become a "public nuisance," police take them to the county jail. They may remain in jail for weeks or months, are released, and once again find themselves in the same trouble they encountered before incarceration.

If our goal is to violently control people with mental illness and keep them out of our sight, perhaps we should empower U.S. jails to better perform this task. Over the past decades, many large U.S. cities have seen major renewals to their downtowns. Young people with higher incomes have moved to expensive urban apartments. They crave a stable, clean environment with multiple amenities. People with mental illness who create public disturbances don't fit into their image of a renewed central city. When an offensive person appears, police arrive to quickly remove her. For example, those who create a public nuisance on Chicago's Magnificent Mile may soon find themselves in the Cook County Jail, where shoppers no longer need to think about them.[47]

In addition to housing those with mental illness, jails also control the lives of hundreds of thousands of people who cannot afford to pay for bail. Some are accused of committing minor crimes and pose little threat to public safety. Others are charged with acts of violence. Regardless, they languish in horrible places like the Cook County Jail. Some see their charges eventually dropped, while others plea-bargain their way to lesser sentences. In the process, hundreds of thousands of poor people are dominated by an abusive criminal justice system.

Finally, some municipalities use jails to force people into a cycle of paying fines and fees. Cash-strapped counties entrap people into a life where they must continually pay legal fees. When they are unable to do so, they are jailed. They may lose their job, be unable to parent their children, and lose their housing and health insurance. However, they provide revenue to counties that relentlessly pursue them as a means of paying bills.

We can see the utility of the jail vividly in ordinances cities pass to discourage homelessness. The National Coalition for the Homeless has published numerous reports describing this phenomenon (National Coalition for the Homeless and National Law Center on Homelessness and Poverty 2006, 2009; National Coalition for the Homeless 2016). Throughout the United States, cities have passed ordinances criminalizing encampments, begging, feeding the homeless, and a variety of other activities. They often legitimize aggressive policing that leads to the arrest and jailing of homeless people. In 2005, Los Angeles Police Chief William Bratton expressed the ethos of this form of policing well: "If the behavior is aberrant, in the sense that it breaks the law, then there are city ordinances. . . . You arrest them, prosecute them. Put them in jail. And if they do it again, you arrest them, prosecute them, and put them

WHAT IS THE PURPOSE OF A JAIL?

in jail. It's that simple" (quoted in National Coalition for the Homeless and National Law Center on Homelessness and Poverty 2006, 41). This kind of attitude toward policing, often supported by merchants and citizens, results in sending poor citizens to their local jail for minor "public nuisance" offenses.

The United States currently has a broken jail system. Even the best-run facilities struggle to deal with mentally ill inmates. Even those that deal compassionately with inmates may be enforcing a senseless and irrational policy of harassing poor people for revenue. In reading documents, I am struck by how capricious the U.S. jail system really is. If someone is accused of a crime in one county, she may be transported to a jail that performs its stated function in a minimally humane fashion. However, if she lives in another county (or is passing through it!), she can be racially segregated, tased, beaten, assaulted, raped by other inmates, deprived of medical care, and forced to live in raw sewage. The quality of justice in this system thus depends entirely on where you happen to live.

A few years ago, a man came to my house in Green Bay, Wisconsin, and sat on my porch. He held his head in his hands and didn't move. When I tried to speak to him, he said nothing. I called the police, and when they arrived, they took him away, informing me that he had an outstanding warrant for some law violation. I never saw the man again, but wondered what happened to him. Like many other citizens, I knew nothing about how he fared in our county jail.

Why, however, should we bother to find out what happens to those in our jails? If a person isn't poor or mentally ill, he likely won't find himself in jail. If he gets in a bar fight or gets caught smoking marijuana, things will change. However, if he has the financial resources, he can avoid spending any time in jail. For most Americans, the jail provides a Hobbesian bargain, perceived public safety in exchange for allowing jails to brutalize offensive and dangerous people. Many people are happy to make this bargain without asking any questions. However, is it a compact that respects human dignity? Why should we even care about human dignity? Why should we believe that jail inmates have it at all? To these questions I now turn.

3

A Matter of Dignity

Prisoners receive much more than treatment required to in-
troduce them to the jail and hold them there. They are im-
personally and systematically degraded by every step in the
criminal justice process, from arrest through detention to
court appearance. They are also degraded personally by the
hostility and contempt directed at them by police officers,
deputies, and other criminal justice functionaries.
—John Irwin, *The Jail*[1]

In the past decade, the United States has seen explosive growth in public
and private jails that hold undocumented immigrants. Millions of people
have been arrested, and have found themselves in immigration jails waiting to find out if they will be deported. Some have committed crimes, but
many others are incarcerated because they have entered the United States
without proper documentation. Counties have often contracted with
federal authorities to house them. Two corporations, the Corrections
Corporation of America (CCA) and the GEO Group, Inc. have profited
enormously from building private immigration jails. Often, they locate
them in remote areas, which prevents immigrants from obtaining legal
and familial assistance. People arrested in one state can be transported
hundreds or thousands of miles away. Under President Obama, several
million undocumented immigrants were deported. The U.S. government
has often contracted with private jail companies to construct facilities for
holding those it seeks to deport. Yet, jails housing immigrants face little
federal oversight, and consequently inmates suffer from a host of abuses.
They are sexually assaulted by staff and other inmates, beaten by corrections officers, and forced to live in unsanitary conditions. Because they
are in a highly vulnerable position, they can do little to report abuse.

For example, in 2008 the ACLU and other organizations brought a
lawsuit against Los Angeles County. It charged that undocumented im-

migrants were housed in a facility called B-18. At the time of the lawsuit, the ACLU reported that this facility "does not provide soap or a change of clothes to detainees and routinely denies menstruating women sanitary napkins. Detention under such conditions is not only unlawful, but also downright cruel. While in B-18, detainees are crowded into a cell with as many as 50 other people. In the cell, there is a single phone, a bench and one or two exposed toilets, but no soap or drinking water. Detainees are often forced to sleep on the floor. Menstruating women who ask for sanitary napkins are routinely ignored. And there is no access to medical attention. On some occasions, it has taken ICE [U.S. Immigration and Customs Enforcement] officials more than a day to fix a clogged toilet" (American Civil Liberties Union 2009).[2] Inmates in B-18 could do little to protest these conditions, and feared the consequences if they complained. Rather than contesting the lawsuit, officials in Los Angeles promised to change their practices. This case revealed only one of many instances in which immigration jails subject inmates to degrading and brutal treatment.

Some people say that treating human beings this way is unconstitutional. Others appeal to human rights, holding that people have a right to live in minimally sanitary conditions. However, these approaches miss something fundamental about our moral responses to injustice. When I describe unsanitary conditions in jails, people respond with revulsion and a sense that human beings simply shouldn't be treated this way. Forcing people to live in sewage and menstrual blood seems inappropriate to their status as human beings. These conditions violate a sense of how we should treat others, and seem undignified in some fundamental sense.

In this chapter, I explore the concept of human dignity, and argue that jail inmates possess an inherent dignity that should govern how we treat them. First, I consider different ways of approaching dignity. Second, I distinguish between kinds of dignity, focusing on inherent dignity, dignity as status, and imputed dignity. Third, I turn to some contemporary attacks on the concept of dignity, exploring philosopher Michael Rosen's sustained assault on it. Fourth, responding to this attack, I describe how our affective response to values reveals self-transcendence, a key basis for affirming our inherent dignity. I also retrieve Max Scheler's idea of individuality as a ground for recognizing the inherent dignity of the person. Fifth, I consider how we discover dignity affectively when we encounter other people. Sixth, returning to dignity's detractors, I consider some general but flawed ways people deny that we possess inherent dignity. I then return to Rosen's arguments, showing how they are philosophically impoverished, and describe how we can relate kinds of dignity. Finally, I illustrate how the practices I described in chapter 2 (inmate and staff violence, unsanitary conditions, and inadequate medical and mental health care) denigrate human dignity.

Approaches to Dignity

I will approach dignity philosophically, but before doing so I want to note other ways of thinking about it. In the past decade, dignity has emerged as a topic of considerable interest in ethics and legal scholarship. Some scholars approach it historically, debating the meaning and origins of dignity in diverse historical contexts. For example, they often see the Roman statesman and philosopher Cicero as an important source for the idea of dignity as a form of status. Or they focus on the Renaissance philosopher Pico della Mirandola as an early proponent of ideas about dignity and human freedom. The philosopher Immanuel Kant frequently appears in contemporary ethics as the most important modern defender of the inherent dignity of the person. Finally, Christian scholars maintain that the biblical concept of the image of God is a key historical source for ideas about dignity.[3]

An important debate has also developed about dignity's recent history. Most scholars recognize that it gained prominence in the twentieth century, but construct different narratives about its origins. Often, they maintain that an emphasis on dignity emerged from the ashes of World War II. The Nazi Holocaust and other horrors led many people to construct institutions that would protect human dignity. Famously, the preamble to the 1948 United Nations Universal Declaration of Human Rights states that the "recognition of the inherent dignity and of the equal and inalienable rights of all members of the human family is the foundation of freedom, justice and peace in the world" (United Nations 1948, preamble). The Constitution of the Federal Republic of Germany also emphasized dignity. Some scholars, however, maintain that World War II had little to do with dignity's importance in the twentieth century.

Instead, they argue that it originated in Catholic and Kantian concep-tions in Germany and elsewhere.[4] Both sides of this debate agree, how-ever, that dignity became an important ethical idea in the past century.

Other scholars approach dignity legally, taking as their starting point state constitutions and international law. Philosopher Jeremy Waldron goes as far as to claim that the law is the proper home for dignity. Others take a more modest stance, limiting their inquiry to exploring consti-tutional and legal documents. They consider the role dignity plays in different constitutions, discuss its links to human rights law, and debate how governments incorporate dignity in judicial decisions and legal in-stitutions. Generally, these scholars take legal frameworks for granted rather than exploring deeper philosophical questions.[5]

Finally, contemporary scholars focus on dignity philosophically and theologically, considering its conceptual justification. Some insist (as I will) that dignity is inherent in the person. In contrast, others argue that it is a social construct that originates in agreements or practices. Some theologians maintain that we can defend dignity only by appealing to something transcendent in all persons. Others reject this idea, arguing that an ethics of dignity must be independent of any religious ideas. In sum, the contemporary discussion of dignity is rich and variegated, with philosophical, theological, legal, and historical dimensions.

Introducing Kinds of Dignity

Contemporary discussions of dignity are sometimes confusing because they involve alternative conceptions of it. Historically, thinkers have used different words in different languages, some of which point to dig-nity without specifically using the word. We can distinguish at least three ways of understanding dignity. We can talk about it as a *status*; someone has dignity because she occupies a specific place in the universe or soci-ety or behaves in a particular way. We can also discuss *inherent dignity*, which a person possesses simply because she is a person. Finally, we can describe *imputed dignity*, which a person has because other people ascribe it to her for social or political reasons.[6]

Dignity as status takes diverse forms, some based on our place in the cosmos and others on our social status. For example, Thomas Aquinas attributes dignity to human beings because they live on the horizon of the spiritual and the physical. They bring together these aspects of the universe in a way that no other being does. Pico della Mirandola also grounds dignity in the person's place in the cosmos. Human beings have dignity because they enjoy no fixed status in the universe, and can move either toward higher spiritual realities or toward the lower material world. Pico and Aquinas both insist that human beings possess dignity because they occupy a specific place in a hierarchy of beings with diverse natures.[7]

Some thinkers defend dignity as a status without appealing to our position in a cosmic hierarchy. Instead, they consider how people respond to adversity and suffering. Those who bear it in special ways exhibit dignity, and therefore should enjoy a high status in society. They show a gravitas in the face of injustice or suffering. For example, in a famous moment in the U.S. civil rights movement in 1960, a group of African American students sat down at a segregated Woolworth's lunch counter in Greensboro, North Carolina. The restaurant refused them service, but the students continued to sit at the counter. These actions sparked other lunch counter protests throughout the nation. A 1963 photograph captures one protest at a Woolworth's in Jackson, Mississippi, where a white mob responded to the sit-in with jeers and violence, pouring condiments on the protesters' heads. Rather than responding violently, the protesters sat silently at the lunch counter. The Jackson protesters exhibited a dignity that we can all recognize as a remarkable response to adversity and injustice. For this reason, we should grant the protesters an exalted status in society.[8]

Most frequently, we find dignity as status linked to social position. In many societies, only certain people possessed it, be they nobles, kings, monks, or parents.[9] Often, a society sees this dignity as a natural part of a hierarchy that we should all accept. Societies reinforce the hierarchy through rituals and social expectations on the part of both those with and those without dignity. When I consider this kind of dignity, I often think about the monarch of Thailand, a country where I taught for much of a year. Traditionally, the Thai king has had an extraordinarily high dignity buttressed by law and custom. In turn, he and his family are expected to behave in certain ways. Royal status confers dignity on those who hold it and demands recognition from those who lack it. In many societies if a status changes, the person's dignity changes accordingly. For example, someone may lose dignity upon conviction of a crime. Russian novelist Fyodor Dostoyevsky reflected deeply on this phenomenon. In the nineteenth century, he was arrested and imprisoned in Siberia for sedition against the czar. He wrote about what it was like be a member of an upper class who found himself thrown in with convicts from a lower class. In a class-conscious society like czarist Russia, Dostoyevsky's experience in prison was deeply unpleasant (Dostoyevsky 2004).

I will say a great deal about inherent dignity shortly, but a few preliminary comments are in order. First, because of the United Nations Universal Declaration of Human Rights and other human rights documents, legal discussions have often accepted it as a given. Second, inherent dignity means that no individual, society, custom, or government can accord or remove it. Third, the person possesses inherent dignity regardless of her behavior. She may be the worst criminal, but retains a dignity that makes ethical demands on us.

Imputed dignity involves how other people assess someone in local or customary ways. For example, a high school teacher I once met acted like a teenager, adopting the behaviors and language of his students. He took to social media via Facebook, posting multiple messages and talking about school events. Some parents felt that he acted in an undignified manner that was incongruous with his place at the school. Others said that the teacher was only trying to teach more effectively, and dismissed claims about dignity as mere prejudice. In this case, local social norms and attitudes came into play. No one mentioned our place in the universe or our response to suffering. No one insisted on the teacher's inherent dignity. Instead, people appealed to their own life experience or the way things had always been done in the community. We find this kind of dignity in most societies and historical periods.

Sometimes we find imputed dignity and dignity as a status in the work of the same thinker, an example appearing in Cicero's *On Obligation*. Drawing on Stoic and other philosophical sources, Cicero discusses the unique status of humanity in the cosmos. Humans are the only creatures capable of directing their lives by reason, and therefore have a unique place among beings in the universe. However, Cicero also seems to maintain that the wise man has greater value or dignity than the fool, and draws distinctions in value based on Roman conceptions of the good person. In his work, two kinds of dignity sit together uneasily.[10]

A complete account of dignity should relate imputed, inherent, and status kinds. As theologian Gilbert Meilaender notes (when discussing two kinds of dignity), forms of dignity should not simply be placed "side by side" (Meilaender 2009, 7). Otherwise, we risk confusions and cannot account for the rich diversity of ways dignity appears historically and linguistically. Before relating kinds of dignity, we should consider why so many people reject the ethical significance of dignity altogether.

The Attack on Dignity

Philosopher Michael Rosen notes that in the mid-twentieth century, a consensus emerged about the importance of human dignity. The end of World War II, new human rights documents, and the development of the United Nations all reflected a commitment to dignity. Rosen thinks this postwar consensus was "a product of a very particular confluence of ideas (and a willingness to make political compromises) on the part of different groups and interests in an unusual, exceptionally important point in history. In my view that time has passed" (Rosen 2012, 80). We no longer enjoy this consensus, Rosen maintains, because contemporary debates about abortion, torture, war, and embryonic stem cell research often devolve into contentious disagreements about dignity's origins and to whom we should accord it.

This debate became particularly acrimonious in the early 2000s in the United States. In 2001, President George W. Bush appointed Leon R. Kass (one of my undergraduate teachers) to head the President's Council on Bioethics. This body was charged with considering bioethical issues and producing reports about them. Kass assembled a group of professors, researchers, and others in Washington, D.C., to deliberate on issues like stem cell research and therapy and enhancement in biotechnology. Many on the panel were considered politically conservative, and the council produced reports that relied heavily on the concept of dignity.

In some circles, a furious dispute about dignity erupted. Bioethicist Ruth Macklin penned an article maintaining that dignity is a "useless" concept. She argued that it is nothing more than an appeal to autonomy, informed consent, and respect for persons. For Macklin, dignity constitutes a vague concept and a lazy slogan supporting pet political projects. Linguist Stephen Pinker went further, arguing in the public journal the

New Republic that the idea of dignity is "stupid." He asserted that it is a subjective preference masquerading as an objective value. For Pinker, dignity is also fungible because people use it for diverse political and social purposes. For example, some think physician-assisted suicide enables us to die with dignity, while others see this practice as an affront to dignity. Pinker believes dignity, because of its fungible and relative character, to be a harmful concept, too often used to limit technical progress and curtail human freedom (see Macklin 2003 and Pinker 2008).

Since Pinker published his article, scholars have argued that both he and Macklin provide only shallow criticisms of dignity. Legal scholars maintain that contra Macklin, dignity serves a greater purpose than simply affirming autonomy. For example, South African judge Edwin Cameron writes about how dignity in South African law condemned subordination, and activists and judges later used it to support equal rights for gay people (Cameron 2014). Similarly, Pinker's claim that dignity is relative requires more argument than he provides. It amounts to a simplistic assertion of ethical subjectivism without philosophical argument. At one point, Pinker cautiously affirms dignity's importance, claiming that it is a form of perception drawing our attention to a person's attractive features. However, considering the long history of philosophical reflection on perception and values, his analysis appears remarkably impoverished.[11]

A Powerful Critique of Dignity

Since the Pinker/Macklin attack on dignity, however, a few philosophers have provided serious critiques of it. In particular, Rosen has written extensively on dignity. In *Dignity: Its History and Meaning*, he discusses the history of the idea, and distinguishes different types of dignity. Rosen examines dignity as a status in a hierarchy, intrinsic dignity, and grace and dignity. He provides an intriguing analysis of the German thinker Friedrich Schiller, who links dignity to grace. Rosen also considers European legal cases where dignity was contested (most notably a French dispute over whether dwarf-throwing contests violate human dignity even when dwarves choose to participate in them). Finally, he explores the symbolic function of dignity and its relationship to human rights and autonomy.

In an essay he wrote after publishing his book ("Dignity: The Case Against"), Rosen presents his misgivings about dignity systematically (Rosen 2014). First, he maintains that it presents a "deceptive façade" (Rosen 2014, 143). Dignity appears as something grand and important, but hides facts about inequality and mass slaughter. Twentieth-century uses of the idea coincided with unprecedented brutality and injustice, revealing a mismatch between ideals and reality. Second, dignity denotes nothing beyond a social agreement to behave in certain ways. Rosen analogizes it to chess, in which beyond a rule, "there is no acceptance that underlies the chess piece with a horse's head being entitled to move in an 'L' shape" (Rosen 2014, 145). Historically, as a social convention dignity distinguished human beings in a hierarchy of virtue. However, today it has been transposed to everyone, robbing it of its original purpose of making important social distinctions.

In a third criticism of dignity, Rosen maintains that it simply doesn't exist in the person. People assert that it is based on an "inner transcendental kernel" in someone (Rosen 2014, 146). Yet, Rosen thinks that we cannot establish that such a value exists. Moreover, he holds that even if we could, inherent dignity provides no guidance for how we should treat people. If they have it, how can any treatment destroy it? For example, if jail inmates possess inherent dignity, forcing them to live in raw sewage cannot remove it. Thus, the concept of inherent dignity is both pragmatically useless and philosophically baseless.

Rosen also links inherent dignity to religious arguments, charging that it constitutes a "Trojan horse for religiously inspired attacks on equality" (Rosen 2014, 147). He is particularly concerned with Roman Catholic conceptions of dignity, which played a role in the development of some modern state constitutions. For him, the Catholic tradition has historically supported a hierarchical and undemocratic view of society. After World War II, it embraced the idea of inherent dignity, but this departs from the Catholic emphasis on social hierarchies. Rosen suspects that the hierarchical view has reemerged in debates involving bioethics, creating an opening for dangerous religious ideas.

Additionally, Rosen maintains that the idea of inherent dignity undermines autonomy. For him, autonomy means that "the self is sovereign—it is, in that sense, a law unto itself" (Rosen 2014, 150). Autonomous persons have a right to do as they choose, obviously while respecting the rights of others. However, the concept of dignity allows the state to override people's choices if they undermine dignity. Rosen notes how dignity has appeared in legal cases denying people the right to autonomously choose to take their own lives. He returns to the dwarf-tossing contest he features in his book. In it, a "dwarf" named M. Manuel Waneheim was prohibited from earning a living by participating in dwarf-tossing events. Waneheim insisted that he autonomously chose to participate and didn't feel the contests attacked his dignity. However, courts ruled that they violated human dignity, thus overriding his autonomous choice.

Finally, Rosen argues that the concept of dignity gives license to disregard democratic decisions. Because it's based on controversial metaphysical and epistemological assumptions, courts cannot legitimately use dignity to override democratic choices. Pluralistic societies contain many ethical ideas other than dignity, and courts should allow people to democratically embrace their own ethical views. To illustrate the dangers of this position, Rosen discusses several cases where German courts used dignity to override democratic decisions in the biomedical area (Rosen 2014, 152–153).

I have taken the time to examine Rosen's argument carefully because he provides extensive support for the idea that dignity is a useless and dangerous concept. Although he doesn't call for us to jettison it completely, he maintains that when dignity appears in ethical and legal arguments, we should carefully scrutinize it.

The Philosophical Ground of Inherent Dignity

In responding to Rosen, one can take two philosophical approaches, only one of which I will pursue in this book. The first follows the lead of Cicero, Pico della Mirandola, Thomas Aquinas, and others who present a metaphysical defense of human dignity. It provides an account of the most general features of reality and the nature of the human being who possesses dignity. The second approach proceeds phenomenologically, considering how we grasp that people possess dignity through our encounter with them. This is the approach taken by Max Scheler, Edith Stein, Emmanuel Levinas, and other twentieth-century thinkers. The phenomenological and metaphysical approaches need not conflict and can and I believe should complement each other. However, here I concentrate only on a phenomenological one.

Scheler and other phenomenologists use a philosophical approach inspired by Husserl. In it, we seek to identify the essence of a phenomenon.[12] We put aside what science or metaphysics teach, and focus instead on our awareness of objects and their properties.[13] We seek to discover what they essentially are, meaning that we identify properties without which they would not be what they are. For example, my awareness of dignity relates to changes in my brain. They may precede or accompany my experience, and we should study them carefully. However, they tell me little about exactly what dignity is (unless we arbitrarily assume that conscious states are simply brain events). How do we define it? Does it have certain properties? To consider these questions, we must carefully analyze how we experience dignity.[14]

Values and Emotions

Because dignity is a value of the person, it shares the features of other values. Values are what attract us and gain our attention. For example, I may be attracted to the beauty of another person, and turn my attention toward her. However, I don't experience all values as equal, but experience some as more important than others. As a professor, I am deeply attracted to the value of knowledge, and experience it as more significant than the value of drinking a beer. Most of us respond to the things we value in an ordered way. We consider some values as more important than others, and organize our lives around pursuing them. We can classify values into groups, such as those that relate to pleasure, utility, morality, or beauty.[15]

We also experience values both emotionally and cognitively. Our emotional life exhibits a relationship to values that we can discern, discuss, correct, and criticize. For many English speakers, emotions or feelings seem hopelessly subjective and bear no relationship to values. Moreover, in twentieth-century Anglo-American philosophy, feelings were sometimes associated with sensations or irrational aspects of our personality.[16] However, over the past few decades, philosophers have revisited this neglect of the emotions, and thinkers like Martha Nussbaum and Sara Ahmed have emphasized the importance of the emotions for ethics (Nussbaum 2003; Ahmed 2014). They have brought a welcome corrective to earlier generations' neglect of the emotions in ethics.[17]

Following the philosopher Dietrich von Hildebrand I will use the term "affective sphere" to describe a range of feelings and emotions. Today, affect often appears in discussions of "affect theory," a psychological theory focusing on subjective feelings (Tompkins 2008). However, the older philosophical and theological term denotes that someone is aware that she is affected by an object.[18] The affective sphere includes a variety of phenomena. We can distinguish between sensations that are bodily located, and more complex conditions like depression or anxiety that we experience as having less of a connection to specific parts of the body. These differ from affective value responses, which have a more complex structure relating to specific values. These include anger, envy, respect, and veneration.

Phenomenologists considering the affective sphere note that many affective responses *aim* at values in specific ways. They call this object-directed character intentionality.[19] Intentionality includes a cognitive dimension, an awareness of the object toward which I am directed. For example, I may get angry *at* an injustice I observe in a jail, making anger fundamentally different from a sensation of cold in Wisconsin. In this case, the cognitive component of my anger would be injustice, and would accompany whatever physical manifestation my anger takes.[20] Many affective responses resemble anger in containing a cognitive dimension. Using the concept of intentionality, phenomenologists reject understandings of values that see them merely as private emotional states or physiological/neurological reactions. They hold that these accounts of value cannot make sense of the intentional relation between the person and values.[21]

Some people worry, however, that focusing on the affective sphere leads us to accept noxious attitudes and acts. Suppose someone feels disgust at homosexuality, and therefore decides to deny civil rights to gay people. Don't such examples demonstrate the danger of relying on feelings of value? These are legitimate concerns, but we should first note that we could also raise them about reasoning. For example, noted people in the past century used scientific reasoning to support eugenics and forced sterilization. Such errors, however, hardly show that all reasoning is useless and dangerous, but instead call for more careful reasoning.

Similarly, responses to value can go drastically wrong, but this possibility shouldn't mean that we disregard the ethical significance of affections altogether. Instead, we should pay more careful attention to the structure of our affective lives.[22]

In fact, we recognize distortions in our value responses all the time. Suppose I witness a violent crime while walking in the street, but show no emotional reaction to it whatsoever. I am completely indifferent to the victim's screams, and continue along with some mundane task. Or perhaps I burst into laughter as I observe the brutal assault. Most of us would say that I responded *inappropriately* in this situation.[23] We can debate the suitability of my response to the circumstances, and talk about what it reveals about my character. We can also think about how my response to value shapes my action. In these ways, the affective sphere frequently plays a role in our ethical thinking.

By analyzing affectivity, von Hildebrand and Scheler thus free us from the idea that it has no import for ethics. It is arbitrary and careless to banish the affective sphere from our ethical lives. Doing so shuts us off from a whole range of experiences of values. As Scheler puts it, "a philosophy of this sort is like a man who has healthy eyes and closes them and wants to perceive colors only with his ears and nose!" (Scheler 1973c, 122).

Affective Responses and the Transcendence of the Person

When exploring the affective sphere, phenomenologists focus particularly on the person's *self-transcendence* in relation to values. Self-transcendence is the capacity to take "an interest in something having value in itself" (von Hildebrand 2009, 206). The person isn't confined to what gives him pleasure or what benefits him, but can relate to aesthetic and moral values as valuable in themselves. We can transcend ourselves through reason. As Scheler emphasizes, persons not only know that something exists, but also consider its *meaning*. I can take an object out of its physical makeup and local environment, and consider its general nature. For example, if I am in pain I can reflect on the meaning of the pain. What exactly is it? Why does it exist? Why does human life have to include pain at all? With these questions, I take the pain outside its bodily manifestation, and search for its meaning.

The will is also a traditional sign of the person's transcendence in relation to values. I can will to actualize projects that don't yet exist. They may bear little relationship to my immediate needs or my local environment. My will enables me to transcend these parochial factors, and actualize ideas or plans remotely related to me. Philosophers have often noted how the will exhibits the human capacity for self-transcendence.[24]

Phenomenologists add a third dimension to self-transcendence by focusing on our affective relation to values. The person's sensitivity to values through the affections is "precisely the capacity to grasp things important in themselves, to be able to be affected by them, and to be motivated by them in his responses. It is precisely the capacity to transcend the frame of mere immanent trends" (von Hildebrand 1953, 203). For example, we are not only aware of something beautiful, but moved by it in powerful ways (von Hildebrand 1953, 217). When it moves us, we can depart from our narrow concerns, and give ourselves over to the beauty we are experiencing.[25] In our affective response to values like beauty, we respond with our whole person, rather than just with our minds or wills. In other affective value responses like joy, veneration, and anger, we also respond to values and disvalues with our whole selves.

This conception of the person's transcendence enables us to affirm her inherent dignity. We possess dignity not just because of our reason and autonomy, but also because of our transcendence in relation to values. We can know them, be affected by them, and be motivated by them in our affective response (von Hildebrand 1953, 221). These capacities explain why a person differs from impersonal entities. Stones cannot know, be affected by, or respond to values. In contrast, persons *actively* aim at and can reflect values like beauty and truth. We can thus draw a fundamental distinction between persons and things grounded in the person's capacity for self-transcendence.[26]

Dignity and Individuality

Phenomenologists make an additional contribution to contemporary discussions of dignity by grounding it in the person's individuality. As philosopher John F. Crosby puts it, Scheler develops a "neglected source" of dignity (Crosby 2004a, 3–33). Throughout his writings, he worries about the prospect that we could exchange one person for another.[27] If general features of a person are all that ground dignity, why not substitute one person for another? Crosby provides a useful example of this possibility taken from controversial ethicist Peter Singer (Crosby 2004a, 9–10). Singer once proposed that we accord parents the legal right to euthanize their disabled infants.[28] Given the difficulties involved in caring for the disabled, why not enable parents to kill a disabled infant and replace him with a healthy one? Singer's proposal created a storm of controversy among disability rights activists, but Crosby asks why people reacted to it so viscerally. If inherent dignity lies solely in shared human attributes, why not replace a flawed person with a healthy one who properly exercises them?

Scheler helps us understand why this proposal is so appalling. We share dignity because of our common humanity, but also possess it because of our individuality. Each person relates to a common world, but also develops an individual world connected to her acts (Scheler 1973a, 393–394). The general features of humanity never fully capture a person's unique existence and nature.[29] When someone we love dies, for example, we may recall her self-transcendence, but an abstract account of it never sufficiently captures our loss. We have lost not a human specimen, but a unique personality that we will never experience again. Scheler calls this unique feature of the person her "value-essence," the unique and valuable way she exercises her powers within a unique world.[30]

We discover this essence by connecting with the deepest aspect of who we are. A person occupies roles related to work, family, and social activities. Among them, his value essence is often obscured, but as a person explores his roles "the various wrappings which shroud the core of his individual personality fall gradually away" (Scheler 1970, 121). He can initiate this process or others can prompt it, but either way the more a person becomes an individual, *the more he is his inmost personal self* (Scheler 1970, 121, italics original). He discovers not just a common humanity, but also what makes him unique. Often, he cannot express this discovery in words, but with hard work can understand a "pattern of personality" that constitutes his individual value essence (Scheler 1970, 122).

Scheler thus grounds the idea of inherent dignity in both the person's individuality and a shared human nature. Yes, we share general capacities like our capacity for self-transcendence, and they reveal a common human nature. Yet, we cannot reduce any person to a mere instance of general human capacities because she possesses an individual value exhibited by no other. This is one reason we are so horrified at Singer's proposal to replace a disabled infant with a healthy one. Singer ignores the unique value essence of the disabled infant, and falsely concludes that she is interchangeable with a healthier copy.

Grasping the Dignity of the Person

Although inherent dignity is grounded in individuality and self-transcendence, how do we know it exists in other people? The value of the person resembles other values in that we become aware of it both cognitively and affectively. Cognitively, I perceive this value; I am aware of it, even if only vaguely when I encounter it (von Hildebrand 1953, 211–212n39). I don't infer or deduce the person's value. Nor do I discover it by drawing an analogy to my own experience. Instead, I have immediate contact with the value; it stands before me in the encounter with another person. In this encounter, the person's value discloses itself to me, and I develop a direct relationship with it. I gradually learn more about it as I remain in contact with it (von Hildebrand 1953, 231–234; 1991, 171–177).[31]

However, my awareness of human value doesn't often end at perceiving it, but frequently generates responses from me. In crowds or other impersonal situations, I may not notice individual persons. However, in a personal encounter I am often affected by the person, moved in some way by her presence. I don't remain immune to it, but experience something directed at me from the person. Finally, a full recognition of the dignity of others often elicits reactions from me. They include responses like admiration, veneration, benevolence, or love, which can depend on particular circumstances and vary in intensity.

Let me illustrate the affective response to the person by returning to the example I offered earlier of undocumented immigrants in Los Angeles. Cognitively, we become aware of their dignity despite the degrading circumstances of an immigration detention jail. We grasp that those incarcerated are persons, not things. This knowledge moves us, and perhaps we feel a sudden change of mood. We might then respond with anger at the injustice we've witnessed. This example illustrates that knowing the dignity of the person is no vague intuition or sensation.

Nor is it only abstract theoretical knowledge. Instead, it is a complex response to value with cognitive and affective components.[32]

In general, then, we can defend the idea of the inherent dignity of the person by first describing the self-transcendence and the individuality of the human person. We then hold that we apprehend dignity in the face-to-face encounter with another. It is *revealed* in this encounter. On this way of proceeding, we cannot force someone to recognize inherent dignity in persons. However, we can use reason to undermine false understandings of the person or mistaken understandings of the nature of values that prevent him from apprehending it. We can then invite him to rethink his ideas and open himself up to a different kind of encounter with others. Von Hildebrand puts it well when he states that "every value has to be grasped; if a person is blind to a value, all we can do to help him grasp it is to pave the way by removing the obstacles of his will and by trying to draw him under its spell" (von Hildebrand 1953, 79). Because of value perception's cognitive dimension, reasoning about dignity's foundation in the person's nature can influence it. Reasoning also plays a vital role in dismantling poor arguments about the human being that prevent people from experiencing dignity. However, apprehending dignity isn't entirely cognitive, and therefore we cannot expect reason alone to force people to see dignity in others.

Responding to the Dignity Deniers

Bad arguments about values appeared frequently in the era when Scheler, von Hildebrand, and Husserl wrote, and they devoted considerable attention to undermining them. The classic in this genre was Husserl's *Logical Investigations*, which undercuts attempts to reduce logic to psychology. Other phenomenologists developed complex phenomenological arguments against value relativism, nominalism, and psychologism (the attempt to explain logic and values entirely in terms of psychology). Many of these critiques apply to today's efforts to deny that dignity is inherent in the person. Rather than rehearsing all of them, let me make a few general comments. Often, those who reject dignity as an inherent quality of the person have an impoverished account of the affective sphere. They hold that our recognition of the dignity of others is nothing but a subjective feeling. Yet, this overlooks the intentionality of our affective responses, and fails to explain the ontological status of the objects to which they aim. Those who do recognize intentionality often misunderstand its nature and complexity. They ignore the careful distinctions that appear in the phenomenological tradition.

Another common response to our recognition of inherent dignity is to claim that dignity is "socially constructed," a concept that emerged in the 1980s and 1990s in the humanities. It often appears in gender studies and other fields as a way to rebel against biological models of human nature. However, as philosopher Ian Hacking noted in his brilliant and convincing annihilation of the term (*The Social Construction of What?*), it has become "obscure and overused" (Hacking 2000, vii). What does it mean to say that any value, never mind the value of the person, is socially constructed? A value is clearly not a material entity like a brick that we use to construct a house. It seems like something immaterial, but if so, how can we construct things from it? The image of social construction does nothing to answer such questions, and in fact evades them altogether.[33]

A related attempt to deny that persons possess inherent dignity appeals to social agreements. Allegedly, we agree to confer dignity on some people, and all dignity becomes imputed dignity. The consequence of this view, of course, is that we can also choose to overturn the agreements we make. We may, for example, agree at one point to accord inherent dignity to sex offenders, only to withdraw it later and decide to torture them to death. The brutal history of punishment in the United States shows how easily public moods and practices can change. More importantly, however, the social agreement thesis remains as vague as the social construction idea. It entirely ignores the experiences we have of the value of another when we encounter her, claiming falsely that we will it into existence. Moreover, it rarely answers key questions about the ontological character of values. About what is it that we agree? Do we agree on words, feelings, or brain events? All of these candidates for social agreement raise familiar questions about universals (general terms applied to many individuals) that have always interested philosophers. Vague appeals to social agreement cannot substitute for good ontological investigation.

A final and more contemporary way some scholars deconstruct our experience of inherent dignity appeals to neuroscience. We explain values (including the value of person) and our response to them entirely in neuroscientific terms. Values are nothing more than events in our brains. Or they somehow emerge from these events and we collectively respond to them. Given the explosion of research in neuroscience in the past two decades, many philosophers find some version of this understanding of values attractive.[34] Although phenomenologists like Husserl didn't confront neuroscience in its current form, they present strong arguments against attempts to reduce values and our mental life to physical events. They also mount detailed attacks on the idea that science should be the sole source of our knowledge.[35] In contemporary analytic philosophy, such attempts are called naturalism (taking diverse forms), and philosophers have recently begun rebelling against it.[36] It was once a dominant position in analytic philosophy, but some philosophers now find it troubling. For those of us drawing on the phenomenological tradition, this is a welcome development.

Returning to Rosen

This short response to attempts to deny dignity suggests the philosophical difficulties they confront. We can further see the limited character of denials of dignity by returning to Rosen. Recall that for him dignity denotes nothing more than a social agreement to behave in a specific way. He likens it to rules in chess that designate roles for different pieces. In this argument, Rosen ignores the significance of our encounter with another person. We don't decide when to experience another's value. We may turn away from or ignore it, or be blinded to it in some way (a matter I will take up in the next chapter). However, if we honestly consider our reaction to another person, we realize that we are in touch with a being whose attributes and value we don't create. Societies try to deny or suppress the experience of the value of others, but often fail to do so completely. For example, David Brion Davis, a distinguished historian of slavery, has written extensively about how slavery often attempted to "animalize" people. Slave systems used multiple social mechanisms to convince people that slaves were no different from nonhuman animals. However, throughout history people still dimly recognized the slave's humanity, producing strange and contradictory behavior. Davis observes that "I have long interpreted the problem of slavery as centering on the impossibility of converting humans into the totally compliant, submissive, accepting chattels symbolized by Aristotle's ideal of the 'natural slave'" (Davis 2014, xiii). Those who claim that we accord dignity are often captive to an abstract theory, and ignore their own experience of other persons.

Rosen also fails to recognize the nature of the person that grounds her inherent dignity. He rejects the idea of an "inner transcendental core," but offers little argument to support this dismissal. Instead, he focuses excessively on the obscurities of Kant's account of the person. However, many thinkers defend the idea of a moral core of the person without using Kant.[37] For example, the transcendence of the person in relation to values constitutes a non-Kantian ground for affirming human dignity. We have no need to recur to some Kantian transcendental property to understand it.

Rosen also seems entirely unaware of the idea of individuality as a source of dignity. Knowledge of someone's individuality often emerges gradually, unfolding as we understand ourselves or another better. It is *disclosed* in the succession of a person's acts and behavior across time. We lack complete knowledge of it, and shouldn't make quick judgments about others and ourselves.[38] Sometimes, one act may suddenly reveal an important aspect of a person's individual essence (for example, a dramatic criminal or loving act), but these cases are rare.

With a philosophically sophisticated account of inherent dignity, we can also respond to Rosen's other misgivings about it. He expresses a common objection among dignity deniers when he says that dignity is a "Trojan horse for religiously-inspired attacks on equality" (Rosen 2014, 147). Yet, it's hard to know how to understand this concern. Yes, some who discuss dignity defend religious ideas, but we can't say this of many people working in human rights law and prison reform who have no religious affiliations. Many of dignity's defenders (both secular and religious) also affirm basic human equality. It would take a great deal of argument to demonstrate that they really want to undermine it, and Rosen never provides it. Finally, why does Rosen want to arbitrarily cut off discussion of dignity and religion? Perhaps by defending dignity, we will end up adopting certain religious ideas. Or, perhaps we can argue for dignity without using religious concepts. We should take these possibilities as an invitation for discussion rather than fearing dignity as some dangerous "Trojan horse."

Rosen also claims that the idea of inherent dignity undermines autonomy. Recall his example of a French "dwarf" who autonomously agreed to be tossed, but was barred from doing so by judges appealing to dignity. Obviously, Rosen's objection rests on what we mean by autonomy, a topic that would take me too far afield to consider.[39] Nevertheless, Rosen is correct if autonomy means simply choosing without coercion guided by personal ideas about moral issues. If we adopt the idea of inherent dignity, we will say that people should avoid taking certain actions even if they are uncoerced. For example, a legal system that uses dignity as a reason for banning slavery will stop people from choosing to become slaves. Legal systems will often make difficult decisions about when dignity should restrict autonomy.

We can respond in a similar way to Rosen's worry that dignity overrides democratic decisions in a pluralistic society. Yes, ideologues use moral concepts to undermine democracy, and governments or powerful special interests often pervert ethical ideas. Additionally, moral ideas limit democratic choices, and are grounded in controversial assumptions about the human person. For example, philosophers have often debated the basis for ascribing human rights to people. People in democratic societies hold fundamentally different reasons for affirming human rights. This disagreement doesn't mean that we should reject human rights altogether. Legal philosopher Ronald Dworkin once wrote that rights serve as "trumps" that prevent majorities from committing injustice (Dworkin 1978). Inherent dignity functions in the same way; it provides a norm for evaluating the decisions of democratic majorities. Majorities often democratically choose to construct horrific penal systems. A renewed respect for inherent dignity should impede this decision, and we would all be better off if it did.

In sum, Rosen provides only weak objections to the idea of inherent dignity. They lack philosophical depth and contain unexamined assumptions about religion, autonomy, and democracy. He does little to show how inherent dignity is a "deceptive façade" and gives us no reason to doubt that all persons possess it.

Relating Kinds of Dignity

Despite his flawed reasoning, Rosen raises valid concerns about relating kinds of dignity and making sense of the idea of damaging inherent dignity. Like most defenders of dignity, I hold that we should evaluate imputed dignity using inherent dignity. Local ascriptions of dignity that undermine inherent dignity are unjust. Meilaender identifies a real tension existing between dignity as status and inherent dignity (Meilaender 2009). Dignity as a status points to attributes that people actualize in better or worse ways. For example, some people respond to suffering nobly while others respond basely and selfishly. Facing danger, some people act heroically, while others behave in a cowardly manner. In both cases, dignity as status allows for comparisons and success or failure. On the other hand, inherent dignity admits of no talk of success or failure; a being either does or doesn't possess it, and nothing she or others do can change this ontological reality. Inherent dignity and dignity as a status thus coexist in an uneasy tension.

We can mitigate this tension by recognizing both individuality and a nature capable of self-transcendence common to all persons. For example, people often say that child molesters forfeit their dignity, and deserve to be treated like subhumans. At several levels, such statements are false. Because a person possesses inherent dignity, he cannot forfeit it by his actions no matter how heinous they are. Additionally, although he may appear to have ruined his life, we cannot know with any certainty how he will develop his individuality. In the future, he may respond to values in a unique and positive way, and this capacity is one source of his dignity. In sum, no one can forfeit his inherent dignity.

Nevertheless, those who think that child molesters lose dignity have a point. Such criminals debase themselves through selfish and harmful acts. They never lose the capacity to develop their individual value essence, and this remains a source of their dignity. However, we can cautiously say that at this moment, some of them are using their individual capacities badly. A person may even come to this conclusion himself. For example, I have met men who have been in prison for years because they committed horrible crimes. Some have realized that they have failed to actualize what is valuable in them. This realization leads them to make remarkable changes in their lives. They recognize a distinction between who they are and who they can become. They seek to narrow the gap between their terrible past and an ideal of a good person.

If we understand the sources of dignity, we can also respond to the common question about how policies can harm inherent dignity. Rosen wonders how we can damage inherent dignity if it is grounded in a shared humanity that no one can lose. He acknowledges that it makes sense to say that acts symbolically undermine inherent dignity. However, he notes (correctly in my view) that most terrible acts do real rather than symbolic damage. What sense, then, can we make of the idea that acts undermine inherent dignity?[40]

Many years ago, philosopher Herbert Spiegelberg responded to this question by distinguishing between the possession and the expression of dignity. Torture cannot eliminate our possession of dignity, but can prevent us from expressing it. When we practice or witness immoral practices, we confront something incompatible with human dignity (Spiegelberg 1986). Torture's damage is not merely symbolic; it stifles the person's capacity to express her dignity. Torture's victims confront difficulties expressing their self-transcendence because torturers seek to reduce them to suffering creatures. They also have difficulty expressing their individuality; torture often seeks to eliminate what is distinctive in a person, reducing him to a means to an end.[41] In sum, once we distinguish between possessing and expressing dignity, we should no longer be puzzled by the idea that we can damage inherent dignity.

Some philosophers try to eliminate tensions in how we think about dignity altogether, but I think we shouldn't follow them in this step. For example, Waldron maintains that we should see modern conceptions of inherent dignity as the extension of aristocratic dignity to all persons (Waldron 2012). This thesis ignores how inherent dignity appeared in diverse traditions long before modernity (Christianity, Stoicism). Moreover, it too easily subsumes one kind of dignity into another, ignoring dignity's complexities. We can defend inherent dignity while also recognizing other kinds of dignity.

Ways of Attacking Dignity

When moving from a general account of dignity toward specific policies, we cannot operate in an algorithmic fashion. In public policy, we find conflicting values and complex circumstances that require careful consideration. However, we can identify general ways we denigrate dignity. A practice denigrates it when it treats a person merely as a thing, failing to recognize the shared and individual sources of dignity. This was Kant's central insight, and it remains important even if we disagree with him on philosophical issues. Slavery and rape are paradigms of using others merely as objects for labor or for sexual domination. They are not problematic just because they use people for personal benefit; such exchanges occur often in everyday life. Instead, they treat the person *merely* as a thing without recognizing his personhood. For example, when I go to the supermarket, the checkout clerk and I use each other. He provides me with a product, and my payment provides him with a job. However, we are all familiar with people who treat workers merely as things; they yell at them, treat them with disdain, and revel in their power over them.

In some cases, however, people recognize an aspect of another's personhood while also treating him like a thing. For example, a torturer can coexperience someone's feelings, thus recognizing him as a person.[42] However, he then uses what he learns of the other person to torture him. We saw such cases during the administration of U.S. President George W. Bush. Psychologists gained the trust of detainees suspected of terrorism, learned about their phobias, and then reported them so torturers could use them.[43] In this case, torturers initially acknowledged a distinction between persons and things, but then used the person merely as a means for information. Many unethical acts fall under this category, a mixture of recognizing the person while treating him as a thing. Some social practices employ people in activities that only persons can perform, but then treat them as commodities with a price. For example, when Thomas Jefferson had sex with his slave, Sally Hemings, he acknowledged the existence of a person. He thought he was having sex not with a horse or cow but with a human being. However, Jefferson still owned Hemings, and treated her merely as a means for his pleasure, domination, and profit.[44]

In other cases, we recognize that we are dealing with a person, but stifle one of her ways of expressing self-transcendence. We might create or tolerate living conditions that force people to think of little but their survival. People sometimes talk about treating people like animals, but most people wouldn't tolerate allowing their pets to starve to death. Yet, governments starve people through deliberate policy or easily correctable economic imbalances. In such cases, the person finds it difficult to express her transcendent capacities because of a desperate fight for survival.

We also denigrate dignity by enacting practices that refuse to recognize individuality. Totalitarian political movements often repudiate individuality, insisting that a person is merely a member of an economic class or political community. Italian fascists in the 1920s vociferously attacked individuality as a remnant of a decadent political liberalism.[45] Similarly, we disregard dignity when we enact educational policies that ignore each student's unique individuality. I have met prison and jail inmates who cannot recall any teacher who bothered to recognize them as individuals. Instead, they were treated as a mass to be controlled, or seen as numbers in the calculus of a school district's educational failure.

To summarize, treating another merely as a means constitutes only one way of denigrating inherent dignity. Most attacks on it involve complex acts that simultaneously recognize and reject aspects of the person. They include treating people as commodities, reducing them to their bodily functions, and denying their individuality.

Returning to the Jail: Incarceration and the Denigration of Dignity

Sadly, in the U.S. jail system we find many of these ways of denigrating inherent dignity. Once someone enters the jail, her fate depends on where she lives and the conditions of her local jail. She can no longer influence whether she becomes the object of the arbitrary will of others. Many of the acts and conditions I discussed in the last chapter attack inherent dignity. For example, staff and inmate sexual assault in jails represents an obvious assault on inherent dignity. In our culture, jail and prison rape is often the subject of jokes. However, sexual assault in jails scars tens of thousands of people annually. Many of those in jail are legally innocent, but receive a penalty of brutal sexual assault. Rape is such a horrible act that even those convicted of a crime should never be subjected to it. However, jails often serve as enablers of sexual assault through neglect and staff complicity or participation in rape. In 2003, the U.S. Congress took the unprecedented and extraordinary step of passing the Prison Rape Elimination Act (PREA). Congress recognized the horror of jail and prison rape, and enacted monitoring and reporting requirements for penal institutions. We have made progress in dealing with jail and prison rape, but some U.S. states have refused to comply with the PREA regulations. Others have failed to do so properly. Hopefully, this situation will change, but in the meantime, rape remains an enormous problem in U.S. jails.[46]

Staff violence against jail inmates also expresses contempt for inherent dignity. When officials use Tasers to torture inmates, beat them savagely, or subject them to dog attacks, they devalue the person. She is no longer a center of knowing and affectivity, but an object to be controlled. Some staff attacks result from sheer sadism, but many others are a consequence of policies that are open secrets, tolerated as a means to control a difficult population. When violence is revealed, officials may fail to stop it out of inertia or deliberate indifference. Often, the public also disregards it. Some people go as far as to commend officials for giving jail inmates what they deserve. I often read online comments about jail brutality and talk to others about it. I am appalled to hear people fully approve of violently controlling inmates.

Other people find convenient excuses or rationalizations to ignore violations of inherent dignity. They claim to know little about the jails in their community. Or they assume that all inmates are liars who fabricate stories about jail violence. Finally, they may harbor strong views about American exceptionalism that blind them to the brutality of our jails. For many Americans, terrible violence in jails simply doesn't happen in their country; it occurs only in unjust regimes in other countries. Such thinking enables them to turn away from obvious assaults on dignity in their local jails.

Horrible sanitary conditions in jails assault inherent dignity by stifling the person's capacity to express self-transcendence. Recall that knowing and affectivity reveal our capacity to transcend local circumstances and environment. We can know entities far away, and gain access to a universe of objects and values. However, when inmates are forced to live in filth, they think of nothing but their disgusting condition. When undocumented immigrants live in cells stuffed with people, they can often think of little else but their bodies. Whether because of a lack of resources or deliberate policy, unsanitary conditions exhibit a shocking disregard for inherent dignity.

We can say the same of the health disasters that plague U.S. jails. When a jail fails to do an adequate intake examination, it shows contempt for the individual person with special needs. When it refuses to provide medical or dental care to inmates, it disregards a person's bodily integrity. The failure to help those with mental illness displays a particularly appalling disregard for the individual. To respect individual dignity, our society has enacted legislative measures to protect the rights of those with disabilities. We take pride in the passage of the 1990 Americans with Disabilities Act. It seeks to prevent discrimination and helps people (particularly young people in educational institutions) to develop their personalities. In many jails, these concerns disappear, as inmates receive inadequate medication and no therapy. Despite our official concern for disabled people, we allow hundreds of thousands of inmates to suffer with little or no assistance.

Why Dignity Matters

Activists often highlight abuses in jails by using the language of human rights, and they may think that the idea of dignity doesn't contribute anything important to discussions. However, I believe that dignity adds a distinctive dimension to how we think about jail inmates. I have spoken to many inmates who express deep despair at their treatment, and human rights language cannot capture this condition. They talk about the estrangement from family and friends, their job loss, the endless monotony of jail life, the way they are treated as mere numbers, and the sense that society sees them as "garbage." They note the decaying or antiseptic buildings they inhabit, and the lack of beauty in their lives. These inmates experience a deep sense of devaluation. For example, someone might say that inmates have a right to beauty, but rights concepts don't capture the damage a person experiences with little beauty in his life. I once visited a jail that never allowed inmates outside for recreation. Their only recreation occurred in a tiny room with a basketball hoop where inmates walked around in small circles for exercise. Those who remained in the jail for months waiting for trial (and legally innocent) were never exposed to sunlight, lost any connection to beauty, and felt profound hopelessness.

The idea of an individual value essence enables us to acknowledge this suffering. Inmates sometimes feel that they contribute nothing of value to the world. Jails devalue people in subtle and not so subtle ways, making them feel like failures and losers. When compared to staff beatings, sexual assault, and inoperative plumbing, lack of beauty and despair may seem like trivial concerns. However, isolation, loneliness, devaluation, and despair all deeply damage human beings. Sometimes, these powerful feelings lead people to take their own lives while incarcerated. We ought to be attentive to the inner lives of those we confine, and consider how our practices devalue their individual dignity.

Concluding Thoughts on Dignity

In international law, state constitutions, and bioethics, dignity appears as an important ethical concept. However, over the past decade some scholars have rejected it, and their attack has created wide-ranging discussions of dignity's historical and conceptual origins. I agree with Rosen that a twentieth-century consensus about dignity's importance has now weakened. He and others have leveled criticisms of it ranging from calling it "stupid" and "useless" to claims that it denotes nothing but social agreement.

By presenting a phenomenological account of the person, I have shown that contemporary criticisms of dignity are philosophically shallow. They frequently conflate kinds of dignity, failing to distinguish between inherent dignity, dignity as a status, and imputed dignity. Too often, they focus exclusively on Kant or on what contemporary scholars think Kant wrote about dignity. Too often, they disregard how our affective life provides us with knowledge of the person's dignity. Too often, they dismiss the concept of inherent properties of the person like self-transcendence without examining serious arguments for their existence. Finally, those who reject dignity say nothing about individuality as one of its sources. Few contemporary thinkers are even aware of this important idea, long a matter of considerable philosophical discussion.

In addition to their philosophical superficiality, contemporary despisers of dignity ignore how our experience of persons relates to injustice. When we hear about immigrants living in filth, we feel that this condition is unworthy of a human being. This feeling is no irrational sensation, but one that reveals our awareness of human dignity. Far from being useless or stupid, the concept of inherent dignity illumines important dimensions of our penal system. Yes, we violate the human rights of jail inmates and adopt wasteful and senseless policies. However, legal and human rights idioms cannot do justice to the horrible experiences of hundreds of thousands of jail inmates. Once we understand individual dignity, we see this injustice in a deeper manner.

In this chapter, I have also addressed the problem of providing a unified account of dignity. Dignity's critics aim their objections to it without clarifying what they mean by dignity. However, dignity's defenders also don't take the time to clarify how they understand dignity. Too often, as Meilaender points out, they acknowledge inherent dignity and dignity as a status without relating them coherently. I have suggested that we unify concepts of dignity by first emphasizing the nature we share with others. We become aware of it in our personal interactions. Inherent dignity thus provides the basis for general norms about how we should treat others. We should refrain from treating them merely as things or commodities with a price. We should avoid acts that mix an awareness of the person with cruelty and devaluation. Many degrading practices and acts are so troubling because people grasp human dignity while also devaluing it.

Individuality also provides a reason to affirm inherent dignity and explains ideas about status. As persons, we each have a unique existence that gives us value. We discover it in others only imperfectly through our affective responses. Although it grounds inherent dignity, our individuality also allows us to speak of degrees of accomplishment. I can fail to live up to my potential or fall short of an ideal connected to my individuality. This sense of degrees, I think, accounts for some ideas about dignity as a status. A person has value because of her individuality, but can develop it in diverse ways.

If we apprehend the inherent dignity of others, however, why do we disregard it so often? To many people, a phenomenological understanding of dignity seems naïve and foolish in the face of evil and cruelty. In this and the previous chapter, I have uncovered the widespread abuse and violence that plague our jail system, while simultaneously maintaining we apprehend human dignity when encountering people. Although not directly contradictory, this juxtaposition appears puzzling. Why do those operating penal institutions fail to grasp the dignity of inmates? If the distinction between persons and things is so obvious, why do many people discount it? A phenomenological understanding of value perception and dignity may be attractive, but can it really account for the horrors we encounter in penal institutions? To respond to this challenge, we need a better understanding of why we fail to apprehend the dignity of others.[47]

4

Why Do We Stigmatize Inmates?

Disgust, Contempt, and Fear in American Jails

Governing through crime is making America less democratic and more racially polarized; it is exhausting our social
capital and repressing our capacity for innovation. For all
that, governing through crime does not, and I believe, cannot make us more secure; indeed it fuels a culture of fear and
control that inevitably lowers the threshold of fear even as it
places greater and greater burdens on ordinary Americans.
—Jonathan Simon, *Governing through Crime*[1]

Tens of thousands of people exit U.S. jails every day only to find their
lives in tatters. Many lose their jobs and homes while incarcerated.
During their time in jail, they may have amassed considerable debt,
including per diem fees for their incarceration, court costs, and child
support payments. Unable to pay bills that go into collection, they find
themselves hounded by creditors. Unpaid bills can also hamper their
employment opportunities for years. Those who need mental health
care often cannot find it. Just as significantly, many inmates experience
a sense of demoralization. Family members ignore or denounce them.
Many suffered from terrible brutality while incarcerated, and cannot
get over this experience. Whether or not they committed a crime, they
will often be forced to acknowledge their incarceration record to future
employers. For many people, the stigma of incarceration thus can exact
a huge personal and financial toll for years.

Why do we stigmatize current and former jail inmates? If we are
aware of a person's dignity, how can we ignore it in inmates? In this
chapter, I explore how affective responses like disgust, contempt, and
fear blind people to the dignity of current and former jail inmates. First,
I adopt Erving Goffman's famous definition of stigma as a "spoiled iden-

tity." Second, I make general comments about value blindness and approaching affective responses phenomenologically. Third, focusing on disgust, I define it as a reaction to something we think is contaminated and inappropriately located. I discuss how it impedes our experience of the value of others. I also maintain that because disgust often presupposes a subordinate relationship between people, it can lead to contempt. Fourth, I describe several kinds of contempt, and note how they obstruct our experience of oneness with others. Within jails, I show how disgust and contempt lead some staff members to abuse inmates. Fifth, turning to fear, I demonstrate its self-regarding character. Paying little attention to the value of a feared object, we move immediately to protect ourselves. Fear often prevents us from apprehending people's dignity, and produces violent responses to them. Sixth, to illustrate fear's dangers I discuss recent work on actuarial approaches to justice. Grounded in fear and the desire to control risk at all cost, they treat people as an aggregate and disregard their individual dignity. I conclude this chapter by looking at how fear affects the money bail system that dominates our jails. Based on narrow forms of risk assessment, it balloons jail populations and creates a deeply unfair form of social control based on income.

Stigma as a "Spoiled Identity"

As I discussed in chapter 3, imputed dignity involves traits or behaviors that groups, societies, or states attribute to people. Sometimes they include positive ones that accord the person value. For example, we might see a man wearing a top hat as a dignified gentleman. Yet, imputed dignity also takes negative forms that can be transitory. After refusing to wear a top hat and receiving stares, I get the message, don one, and become socially acceptable. However, some negative forms of imputed dignity seem to attach to the person, and we use the term "stigma" to describe them.

Goffman writes eloquently and insightfully about stigma. He notes how categories shape our interactions with others, but we are often unaware of them. We rely on them to reduce complexity, and to navigate our way around the social world. Stigma arises when we have a concept about someone and his attributes that makes us anticipate a negative interaction with him. He is "thus reduced in our minds from a whole and usual person to a tainted discounted one," and as a result he possesses a "spoiled identity" (Goffman 1986, 3). People can be stigmatized for multiple reasons: physical or mental disabilities, sexual orientation, unemployment, family background, racial and ethnic origin, and religious and political affiliations. The individual or group stigmatizing distinguishes between those who are "normal" and those possessing the stigma (Goffman 1986, 5). Those stigmatized are imperfect, and must be avoided, ostracized, corrected, or eliminated.

Stigma may be visible or potentially disclosed. In the former case, the person's identity is already "discredited," while in the latter it is "discreditable" (Goffman 1986, 41–42). People are aware of a discredited identity, and find it unappealing. In contrast, a discreditable identify is one that has the potential to be revealed, but a person keeps it hidden from others. For example, someone may suffer from a stigmatized mental illness about which others are unaware. They would become aware of it only if they gained access to his medical records or learned of the condition from his loved ones.

Goffman brilliantly analyzes how people live with stigma. For example, if someone is born with a disfigured face, she will gradually learn how to respond to the stares and negative responses of others. She may react self-destructively or draw on family or support groups to resist the stigma attached to her. Those with a discreditable identity confront difficulties of information control (Goffman 1986, 41–105). They must ensure that others don't discover information about their stigmatizing feature. For example, I knew two gay men who lived together in New York City for over fifty years. In the early years of their relationship, particularly when they traveled outside of New York, they carefully managed what others knew about them. They didn't want people to know that they were in a relationship. In the 1950s outside of major cities, gay people were heavily stigmatized, and public exposure could prove costly for employment and other opportunities. Gay men and women often had to control information to prevent themselves from going from a discreditable to a discredited identity.

The stigma of incarceration presents complex identity challenges for those experiencing it. Before the advent of Internet technology, an ex-offender had some choice in whether he revealed his criminal record. His stigma was discreditable because someone might know about and reveal it, but it was not easily discreditable. Today, being an ex-offender often quickly becomes a discredited identity. Once a person leaves jail or prison, he may have little choice but to reveal his criminal record to others. Recent years have seen extraordinary growth in private background check services. Many provide accurate information, but some give out flawed material to employers and others using them. Many states also make criminal records readily available to anyone with access to the Internet. An ex-offender is either discredited or easily discredited in the eyes of employers, girlfriends, boyfriends, or anyone using the abundant information available in our society.[2]

Accounting for Stigma

Stigma involves a failure to recognize a person's individual dignity. She is automatically categorized as impure or problematic, part of a group we see negatively. Often, people uncritically employ stigmatizing concepts they inherit from others through language and cultural traditions. However, given the account of dignity I offered in the last chapter, why wouldn't they grasp the individual's value? The reasons why people stigmatize individuals or groups are multiple, and depend heavily on historical and cultural circumstances. When considering stigma, we can distinguish philosophical and theological explanations of its origins from sociological and historical ones. Philosophical/theological accounts focus on ideas like sin, power, self-interest, the emotions, concupiscence, and pride. Sociological/historical understandings explore ethnicity and race, group dynamics, and economic and political forces.

In general, recent economic and sociological developments in the United States have contributed to punitive attitudes toward jail and prison inmates. With the explosion in prison population, an older rhetorical commitment to rehabilitation collapsed and public attitudes turned against attempts to assist inmates in turning their lives around. The disproportionate presence of African Americans in jails and prisons often elicited little concern from white majorities. Finally, the jail and prison system has created strong economic incentives for public and private actors to maintain jails and prisons. It gives them little reason to see the humanity of inmates. These and other factors (chronicled by criminologists, sociologists, and historians) distance people from those who are incarcerated. Today, many people conclude that inmates are flawed human beings who deserve to be stigmatized.

These factors contribute to what von Hildebrand calls "value blindness," an incapacity to recognize the centrality of a value (von Hildebrand 1957). In the case of dignity, value blindness can have many causes.[3] Sometimes, people attach themselves to values like the state or cultural traditions that cloud their perception of the person's value. In other cases, individual or group pride prevents them from apprehending another's dignity. In still other situations, an unwillingness to change or an attachment to pleasure leads people to rationalize devaluating dignity. Finally, education and socialization alter someone's response to human dignity. For example, as I will soon discuss, new corrections officers often adopt negative stances toward inmates that gradually erode their apprehension of human dignity.

Value blindness also takes various degrees. As I noted in chapter 3, people or societies rarely succeed in fully extinguishing all awareness of human dignity. However, our response to it varies in its strength. A person devoted to a political cause may be unable to recognize the dignity of those opposing her. For example, conservatives and progressives in the United States often demonize each other and sometimes move from debating political ideas to devaluing persons. Those embracing social norms above all often cannot see how they devalue certain groups of people. Many people experience only partial value blindness. They may feel a conflict between the dignity they recognize in another and the obligation to adhere to social norms. Or they may make uneasy compromises that recognize the dignity of some persons while denying it to others. Finally, they may have a self-image that blocks their capacity to value others. For example, someone might pride himself on being a modern or scientific person, and be blind to the ways in which modernity devalues dignity. In sum, value blindness exists in diverse forms and degrees depending on the person and his circumstances.

Distinguishing between Affective Responses

To explore in detail how value blindness leads us to devalue inmates, I want to consider how it can originate in negative affective responses like disgust, contempt, and fear. These responses figure prominently in debates about crime and inmates. Frequently, they lead us to embrace policies that degrade and damage people. For these reasons, they are well worth careful examination.

Psychologists devote considerable effort to exploring disgust, contempt, and fear. Some contemporary philosophers draw heavily on this empirical work when discussing the emotions.[4] However, in keeping with the phenomenological focus of this book, I will consider disgust, contempt, and fear philosophically, drawing particularly on the work of Aurel Kolnai. Kolnai was an Austrian philosopher who adopted a phenomenological approach to the emotions. Like other phenomenologists, he held that we could distinguish between kinds of cognitive and affective acts and responses by noting how they aim at objects. Recall phenomenologists call the object-directed character of affective acts intentionality. It enables us to identify a cognitive component of affective responses that is absent from simple sensations. If I step outside during a hot summer day, I experience a heat sensation, but it doesn't necessarily focus on an object. Perhaps I feel a hot blast on my face or have a general bodily sensation of heat. However, this differs from anger, remorse, and resentment, which aim at objects and possess a much more complex structure.

By exploring the intentionality of affective responses, we can distinguish between those that resemble each other or appear together.[5] For example, as we will soon see disgust and fear are both protective affective responses leading us to move away from objects. They often appear together, but differ in how they aim at an object. Similarly, contempt often presupposes disgust, but aims at objects in a different way than disgust does. Thus, by carefully attending to objects and how we relate to them, we can draw fine distinctions between affective responses.

The Nature of Disgust

Turning to disgust, it is a protective affective response that seeks to keep us from being contaminated by an object (Kolnai 2004a, 39–43). Many disgusting objects hold an ambivalence for us; we may find some aspect of them interesting or attractive. My father once saw a large cockroach slowly fall into a big container of soup. A hotel chef had spent several days preparing the soup for famous guests. The sight was disgusting, and the idea of a cockroach in soup revolting, yet the event was strangely interesting to watch. Nevertheless, the aspect that catches our attention usually provokes us, and we want to remove it from our presence. The object seems forced on us in an unrestrained way, and it disturbs our existence.[6]

Disgust powerfully affects our senses, but scholars disagree about whether it appears most prominently in touch, sight, or smell. These three senses bring objects into proximity, and elicit different disgust responses. Few students of disgust argue that hearing by itself provokes it, but they usually say that hearing can evoke what is disgusting. People sometimes associate a sound with a disgusting idea or revolting moral properties. Objects producing disgust are often culturally specific, and include things like putrefied objects, insects, bodily secretions, excrement, dirty bodies, kinds of food, and forms of sexual activity.[7] Disgust also appears in the moral realm; we find vices and crimes disgusting. For example, many people find child molesters and their crimes disgusting. Historically, people have also found certain groups disgusting, and which ones elicit disgust is relative to historical place and time. This deeply problematic kind disgust often persists despite arguments demonstrating its irrationality. For example, disgust at Jews in some societies has often endured despite its unethical and irrational character.[8]

Anthropologists and psychologists sometimes seek to identify objects that elicit disgust in all cultures. Whether they exist is an empirical question that I cannot answer, but if they do, they interact with historically and culturally conditioned circumstances. For example, feces may invoke disgust in all cultures, but how people respond to them takes diverse cultural and historical forms. In sum, the "realm of the disgusting is a remarkably inclusive one. It contemplates disgust at all kinds of offensiveness, whether these have their origins primarily in touch, smell, or taste; or whether they be understood as more complexly moral and aesthetic" (Miller 1998, 109).

Can we identify a general feature of disgust that explains its origins? Scholars propose different answers to this question. For example, philosopher Martha Nussbaum maintains that disgust reminds us of our animal nature and its vulnerabilities, and we recoil from the idea that we are merely animals (Nussbaum 2003, 87–99). She goes further, holding that disgust reflects our shame of this vulnerable nature. For example, excrement disgusts us because it reveals that despite all our lofty cultural achievements, we are no different from dogs or cats in our bodily functions. Nussbaum explains certain kinds of disgust well, but I reject her general account of it. Her fear of our vulnerable animality thesis cannot adequately account for certain kinds of moral disgust. For example, people feeling disgust at child molestation may experience little apprehension of being exposed as vulnerable animals. Instead, they experience disgust because child molesters cross a boundary they shouldn't cross.[9]

Nussbaum also draws problematic normative conclusions from her claim that disgust reflects fear of our vulnerable animal nature. She wants not just to note disgust's origins, but also to demote the human, and get us to accept this demotion. Even if we were to accept Nussbaum's animality thesis, however, we need not (and should not) accept her conclusion. In many cases, disgust reminds us of our vulnerability as animals, but in others it prompts us to recall that we are bodily beings capable of self-transcendence. For example, when we recoil in disgust at learning of undocumented immigrants crowded in a jail cell without functioning toilets, disgust reminds us that such conditions are unfit for human beings. In discussing such cases, philosopher Jay M. Bernstein comes closer to the truth when he says that "disgust at the sight of the degraded human body is a wholly moral response: a visceral repugnance at the sight of *what ought not to be*" (Bernstein 2015, 281, italics original). We shouldn't accept our vulnerable animal status. Instead, we should recall that we are beings with dignity who shouldn't be forced to live in horrible conditions.[10]

Kolnai suggests a better way to understand disgust, maintaining that it responds to something that "adheres in an improper place" (Kolnai 2004a, 55). It reacts to inappropriateness, the breaking of boundaries and the intrusion of entities that don't belong. For example, mucus streaming from someone's nose disgusts us because it's out of place. Excrement belongs in the body or in some proper disposal facility, and shouldn't be all over our hands. People also find putrefying bodies disgusting. As Kolnai notes, dead flesh by itself may not disgust, but the in-between process of moving from living to dead material does (Kolnai 2004a, 52–54). The odor, the maggots, and other signs of decay seem inappropriate to living beings. In all these cases, disgust responds to something improperly located. As Sara Ahmed notes, we often perceive disgusting objects as "sticky," possessing a quality of blurring and undoing of boundaries (Ahmed 2014, 89–92).[11]

In many instances, disgust reacts to something inappropriately related to life. However, in the moral realm it departs from its usual association with life. For example, satiety or excess pleasure often arouses moral disgust (Kolnai 2004a, 63–64; Miller 1998, 112). If I get drunk and suffer from a hangover the next day, I may feel disgusted with myself. We also experience disgust at practices like parent/child incest. Undoubtedly, a child cannot give consent to such an act, and the adult is guilty of a crime. However, in such cases a child also becomes the instrument of an adult's sexual pleasure and domination, both of which don't belong in the child's life. Finally, people often respond to sexual acts with disgust. Debates about the morality of homosexuality, for example, often involve disgust responses. Despite our changing norms and attitudes (a positive development in my view) about homosexuality, some young men still respond with disgust at the idea of men having sex with each other. They react viscerally to the idea of sexual organs in places where they (supposedly) shouldn't be. In sum, disgust arises when we encounter an object that intrudes where we think (correctly or incorrectly) it doesn't belong.

Disgust and Individual Dignity

Scholars evaluate the ethical significance of disgust in different ways. Leon R. Kass once wrote a provocative essay called "The Wisdom of Repugnance." Opposing human cloning, he maintained that repugnance carries with it a wisdom that we should trust even when we lack good arguments for opposing a policy (Kass 1997). Nussbaum strongly opposes this view, arguing that disgust is a dangerous emotion that often leads to unjust actions (Nussbaum 2006, 72–163). Other authors express similar concerns about uncritically relying on our disgust response when making ethical decisions. I share their misgivings, but also think that disgust can connect us with important values in certain situations. Its dangers and unreliability need not mean that we should jettison its ethical significance altogether. Instead, we should allow human dignity to serve as the norm for thinking about disgust.

Disgust poses dangers to human dignity because it impedes our perception of the person's value. Recall that one mark of our dignity is transcendence in relation to values. We are not confined to our individual circumstances, but can move beyond them to relate to aesthetic, moral, and intellectual values. Disgust undermines our capacity to recognize transcendence in others. It draws our attention narrowly to unpleasant features of a person. Even if we find them fascinating in some way, we disvalue rather than value them.

Disgust can also undermine the perception of the value of a group. When my disgust toward others becomes habitual, I no longer perceive value in all humanity. Affectively, I carve out an exception for members of a group (for example, jail inmates). Because they are disgusting, they no longer inhabit my circle of positive valuation. They are outliers, exceptions to a circle of care that can otherwise be quite broad. For example, I sometimes meet people who consider themselves good liberals or progressives who respect human rights in many contexts. Yet when I mention inmates I have taught who have committed violent sexual assaults, our conversation comes to a halt. They are visibly revolted, and evince no benevolence at all toward sex offenders of any kind. They see them as contaminated beings whom we need to quarantine and incapacitate.

Disgust and Contempt

Disgust often leads to contempt because when we feel it we experience a superiority over the disgusting object. Disgust assumes "a certain low evaluation of its object, a feeling of superiority" (Kolnai 2004a, 42). Often, I pay no attention to this superiority, simply noting it in my experience. My father may have had a low evaluation of the cockroach in the soup pot, but didn't think much of the matter. However, in some cases disgust goes in a different direction, becoming "formalized, cool, and regulated" (Kolnai 2004a, 82). We perceive the object in terms of "the mean, the unrefined, the unreliable, the inadequate" (Kolnai 2004a, 82). In such situations, disgust becomes contempt.

Contempt can take passive and active forms. William Ian Miller identifies a "contempt of indifference," an aristocratic coolness where social superiors find inferiors unworthy and lowly. They withdraw from them in haughty ways. Lower persons "simply do not merit strong affect; they are noticed only sufficiently so as to know that they are not notice worthy. One can condescend to treat them decently, one may, in rare circumstances, even pity them, but they are mostly invisible or utterly and safely disattendable" (Miller 1998, 215). A different attitude arises when people respond to disgusting objects with loathsome contempt. Like contempt of indifference, it asserts a superiority over people and relates to social hierarchies. However, rather than indifference it leads to hostility. We let "others know that they have failed, that they are not measuring up, that they are claiming more for themselves than they can worthily discharge" (Miller 1998, 216). This form of contempt displays itself in asserting rank over others, and demanding that they recognize their inferior status.

The value blindness that contempt engenders differs from that of disgust. Contempt contains moments of cold indifference or hostility toward the person that aren't necessarily part of disgust. I not only fail to apprehend valuable qualities in someone, but often develop lasting negative feelings toward him or her. Disgust may lead me to turn quickly away from someone or attempt to remove him from my presence. Contempt, on the other hand, leads me to do so with cool disinterest (contempt of indifference) or with an active attempt to denigrate the person (loathsome contempt). In either case, I experience both a cognitive and an affective failure to respond properly to the person's value.

Disgust and Contempt in the Jail

Contempt and disgust appear often in institutions that deal with vulnerable populations. Those who work in hospitals, mental institutions, jails, and prisons often struggle with the disgust they feel toward others. They encounter people in weakened conditions, particularly bodily ones that people prefer to keep hidden from others. Those with physical disabilities may be unable to control their bodily functions. Those with mental illness may fail to perform daily hygienic tasks. These conditions create powerful emotions in people who work with them.

In jails, the causality of the disgust response is complex and difficult to understand in many cases. In the United States, those arrested are subjected to treatment that often makes them objects of disgust. The police publicly humiliate them, arresting them in violent or nonviolent ways that make clear their subordinate position. Our legal system holds that a person is innocent until proven guilty, but many people automatically assume that an arrest entails guilt. For example, many people don't know the difference between jails and prisons. When they learn of terrible conditions in jails, they proclaim that jail inmates deserve their fate because they committed a crime. As Nussbaum notes, disgust plays such a powerful role in keeping public order and decency because with "its core idea of contamination, it basically wants to get the person out of sight" (Nussbaum 2003, 107). Those entering a jail are thus in a socially subordinate position ripe for eliciting disgust.

The state of inmates entering a jail may stimulate further disgust. Heroin addicts and alcoholics undergo withdrawal symptoms and vomit. Homeless people may stink, and those suffering from mental illness may have defecated or urinated on themselves. Some entering jail are accused of committing acts people find morally disgusting. Child molestation and domestic violence often evoke deep moral disgust. In general, then, those entering the jail are often the target of disgust from the public and from those holding them in jail.

Degrading conditions within jails invoke only further disgust. When jails allow people to live in cells with barely functioning toilets, they create revolting conditions. When authorities refuse to offer medical intake examinations, inmates may import diseases with outward symptoms that elicit disgust. When officials fail to provide psychotropic medication to those who need it, inmates may decompress, and fail to clean themselves. When cells swarm with insects and rodents that find their way into food, staff members can hardly contain their disgust.

Let me offer a concrete example to illustrate disgust in a jail. Many jails isolate those with severe mental illness in solitary confinement. Frequently, solitary only exacerbates their illness, and inmates deteriorate mentally and physically.[12] In other cases, jails put those with mental illness in single cells where staff can observe them. One time when I visited a jail, I turned a corner and smelled the overwhelming odor of feces. I noticed a figure moving behind a cell window covered with feces, but found it difficult to think about him when confronting such a powerful smell. The psychiatrist accompanying me seemed habituated to such a situation. However, the overpowering odor made it difficult for me to think about the inmate at all. I could barely look at him, with his hair and body smeared with feces. In a flow of emotions, I felt ashamed that

I saw him in his vulnerability, appalled at his condition and revolted at his filth. I quickly turned away from him and moved out of his area. I wondered how those working with him could overcome their natural aversion to his disgusting condition.

From Disgust to Contempt

Because of public contempt for jail inmates, jail staff may find themselves moving quickly from disgust to contempt. Those entering jails are the object of public contempt. For many people, someone who is publicly disgusting, mentally ill, or otherwise compromised has brought it on himself. His disgusting condition is a sign of a moral failure worthy of contempt. Often, we impute "moral failing to him as a consequence of his having been rendered ugly, deformed, undignified, and disgusting by victimhood. The victim is held to some moral account for being so degraded unless the victim has the peculiar status we accord to infants and children for whom the demands of dignity are largely suspended" (Miller 1998, 196). He should therefore be removed from public view, and deserves whatever fate awaits him in the jail. Public contempt for jail inmates gives some staff members license to move from disgust to contempt.

The arrest and booking process in the United States expresses this contempt for people, sending a clear signal that they occupy a subordinate position in society. When police officers arrest people, they often make a public spectacle. For example, police often parade suspects before the public in a "perp walk," a practice outlawed in many European countries. Officers may meet any sign of insubordination or disagreement with harsh language or violence. Authorities make it clear to the person, her family, and anyone else present that her status has been officially lowered.

We see the degrading character of the arrest process in the case of Chicago policing, which has often exhibited racism and violence toward those arrested. The Chicago Police Department is an enormous institution with many fine employees who treat people well. However, for decades it also employed officers who tortured, brutalized, and abused suspected criminals. For example, in the 1980s Jon Burge and officers under his command tortured dozens of African American men in police precincts on Chicago's South Side. They suffocated them with plastic bags, threated them with guns, and shocked them with electrical devices. After years of litigation and investigation, Chicago finally acknowledged this torture, and compensated some of the victims.[13]

Sadly, although Burge's torture was extraordinary in its scale, the Chicago Police Department's relationship with African Americans and poor people in Chicago has remained deeply problematic. In 2015, the Chicago police were involved in several high-profile deadly shootings of young black men. A Task Force convened to examine police conduct, and concluded that police officers often treated African American and Latino citizens with contempt. It interviewed numerous people who reported that they were "stopped without justification, verbally and physically abused, and in some instances arrested, and then detained without counsel" (Police Accountability Task Force 2016, 5). The Task Force detailed pervasive physical and verbal abuse by police, deprivation of human and constitutional rights, death and injury at the hands of the police, and a lack of accountability for abuses.[14]

The attitudes toward African Americans and Latinos noted by the Task Force are particularly important for understanding the contempt for inmates in the Cook County Jail. The Task Force "heard over and over again from a range of voices, particularly from African-Americans, that some CPD [Chicago Police Department] officers are racist, have no respect for the lives and experiences of people of color and approach every encounter with people of color as if the person, regardless of age, gender or circumstance, is a criminal" (Police Accountability Task Force 2016, 7). Statistics about traffic stops, Taser use, and arrest and street stops all showed significant racial disparities. In these encounters, African American and Latino citizens reported a general attitude of contempt toward them.

We can also display contempt for people by refusing to acknowledge that they have been harmed. We declare that their complaints of abuse or mistreatment are unworthy of a response; they are liars or complainers or people who are of lesser value in society.[15] The Chicago Task Force reported that in Chicago "the public has lost faith in the oversight system. Every stage of investigations and discipline is plagued by serious structural and procedural flaws that make real accountability nearly impossible. The collective bargaining agreements provide an unfair advantage to officers, and the investigating agencies—IPRA and CPD's Bureau of Internal Affairs—are under-resourced, lack true independence and are not held accountable for their work. Even where misconduct is found to have occurred, officers are frequently able to avoid meaningful consequences due to an opaque, drawn out and unscrutinized disciplinary process" (Police Accountability Task Force 2016, 11). Police brutality, verbal abuse, and unjust police shootings all seemed to go unpunished. This process sent a clear signal that the lives and concerns of African Americans and Latinos in Chicago were undervalued.

In January 2017, the DOJ issued a scathing report about the Chicago Police Department that supported many of the findings of the Police Accountability Task Force (U.S. Attorney's Office, Northern District of Illinois 2017). After an extensive, yearlong investigation, the DOJ emphasized the importance of improving trust between the Chicago Police Department and Chicago citizens. However, it also concluded that the police engaged in a pattern of unnecessary use of force that resulted in avoidable shootings. In grim detail, the DOJ report highlighted numerous cases of excessive force against children and people suffering from mental illness.

Equally disturbing, the DOJ found little accountability for excessive use of force by Chicago police officers. Citizens who made complaints received little response, officers filed inadequate reports of incidents, and investigations rarely proceeded in a thorough manner. For those making complaints, procedures seemed opaque and completely lacking in transparency. Finally, the DOJ report also supported the Police Accountability Board's findings that police displayed widespread bias against African Americans and Latinos.

The DOJ report and the Police Accountability Task Force findings illustrate the myriad ways in which those arrested in Chicago can become objects of contempt. By the time they arrive at the Cook County Jail, many people have already been degraded and devalued. Those receiving them may feel that they have license to continue to treat them contemptuously. Or their disgust at certain people may develop into contempt because they deal with a police department that often shows contempt for those it arrests.

The degrading character of the jailing process also encourages contempt. Strip searches, the removal of private property, and many of the things that happen in jail all signal subordination and degradation. In the 1960s, Goffman wrote insightfully about degradation in the context of mental hospitals. He famously used the term "total institution" to describe an institution in which a person spends twenty-fours a day. Such institutions demand (with varying degrees of success) a separation from the outside world. To accomplish this aim, they must degrade and reshape someone's identify. Goffman describes this process as "mortifying" it, changing an identity from one kind to another (Goffman 2007, 14). A jail demands deference to staff, creates rituals that signal obedience, provides uniforms, and in many other ways seeks to alter someone's relationship to her previous identity. It aims to force her to conform to a new institutional one.

Goffman was keenly aware that total institutions often fail to mortify old identities entirely. In fact, he wrote extensively about how patients in large mental institutions acted subversively to create their own worlds (Goffman 2007, 171–320). Today's jails house inmates for only brief periods of time, and because of gang and other affiliations inside them, inmates retain important aspects of their outside identities. Total institutions have diverse aspirations, and rarely succeed in shaping identities in the way they think they can. Nevertheless, Goffman shows how rituals of mortification indicate hierarchy and degradation. I believe these rituals make it easier for staff members to move from disgust to contempt. They know that society often sees those who are arrested as disgusting and loathsome. They encounter people who have already been degraded and demoted in status by police authorities. They deal with a population that at times presents itself in disgusting ways. They exercise power over people who often lack legal power to resist. Finally, they are empowered to mortify the identities of inmates and make them docile occupants of a total institution. All these factors create a toxic brew that encourages both disgust and contempt.

The Deadly Consequences of Contempt

In many cases in U.S. jails, contempt yields deadly consequences. Let me offer three examples, two from Rikers Island and one from a smaller jail. In 2013 Bradley Ballard arrived at Rikers Island. He suffered from diabetes and schizophrenia, and apparently made a lewd gesture at a

.staff member. He was put in a cell and ignored. Ballard received no insulin or medication of any kind, and he covered himself with feces. Days passed, and dozens of staff members went by his cell without entering it. A nurse came in only once to give Ballard medicine. Occasionally, people peered into his cell through a window, and corrections officers passed food through a slot in the door. No one entered it. Finally, after seven days someone noticed that Ballard was on the floor and unresponsive, and opened his cell door. Balland had tied a rubber band around his penis, and it had become infected. He died shortly after being taken out of his cell. In this case, we see an appalling contempt where staff members paid no attention to a sick person who desperately needed help. Disgust at his behavior and condition produced a cold contempt, a sense that he was a creature unworthy of minimal attention.[16]

In a second case at Rikers in 2014, Jerome Murdough, a Marine Corps veteran suffering from schizophrenia, was arrested for trespassing after he sought shelter in a stairwell during the winter. While at Rikers, he was placed in an observation cell. However, corrections officers left him in it overnight without checking on him. The temperature of the cell rose to over 101 degrees Fahrenheit. Authorities discovered Murdough's dead body the next morning, and his body temperature had reached 103 degrees Fahrenheit. He had baked to death in his cell while corrections officers ignored him completely. Those working the night shift revealed their contempt by abandoning a person with a history of mental health problems. The Department of Corrections expressed further contempt by failing to promptly notify Murdough's family of his death. Family members learned of it from an Associated Press reporter. A corrections officer was later arrested, and charged with falsifying documents about the episode. The family sued the City of New York, and settled the case before it went to trial.[17]

In a final example of contempt for inmates, in 2015 Jesse Jacobs entered the Galveston County Jail to serve a thirty-day sentence for DUI (driving under the influence). He carried a letter from his doctor indicating that he took antianxiety medication, and shouldn't go off it because he might suffer from seizures. However, apparently, the Galveston County Sheriff encouraged jail staff to detox inmates, and they refused to provide Jacobs with his medication. Consequently, after four days he had a seizure, but staff members didn't take him to the hospital. After a second seizure, he was placed under suicide watch in another cell, but he still didn't see a doctor. It was only after his third seizure that a doctor arrived, but rather than providing him with proper medication, she prescribed a new drug. Finally, Jacobs suffered a fourth seizure, and staff members discovered him dead in his cell the following morning. In this case, authorities showed utter contempt for Jacobs, and instead of serving his thirty-day term he received a death sentence.[18]

Without interviewing staff members in these cases, we can't ascertain what kind of contempt they displayed toward inmates. Perhaps they loathed them for their compromised conditions and incapacity to control their behavior. Or perhaps they simply reached a point after dealing with so many inmates that they developed complete indifference toward their suffering. Either way, we see how value blindness can produce terrible consequences.

The Nature of Fear

Like disgust, fear is a defensive and protective affective response, but differs from it in how the subject relates to the object. When someone fears an object, he flees it and feels that it "threatens his survival, safety, welfare, or any of his vital interests—the integrity of his possessions, body, or status in any sense (including chances or prospects)" (Kolnai 2004b, 97). At its most basic level, flight means putting oneself at a distance from an object, moving beyond its reach. It need not be a physical object; a person can set himself at a distance from imaginary objects without ever moving. For example, I can flee a terrible thought without ever running from it. Fear's initial movement, then, involves a flight from an object.

However, unlike disgust, fear also has another motion, a turning toward the self or its interests. When I am afraid, I take little interest in aspects of the object, focusing only on those creating fear in me. Fear takes no "intrinsic interest in the object" (Kolnai 2004b, 98). Once I realize its threatening aspect, I quickly turn toward myself or what relates to me. Fear then is an impoverished response because it leads me to consider only narrow aspects of objects. I turn away from the rich experiences of them.

Fear and Dignity

Fear's double movement makes it deeply problematic for human dignity. When we fear an object, we focus on its disvalue for us. Fear blocks appreciation of aspects of a person that reveal her individual dignity. Our interest lies solely in the real or perceived part of her that threatens our existence or interests. Nothing else matters. Fear can also overwhelm us, undermining our capacity to experience unity with others. It damages our capacity for self-transcendence, and can lead us to react to threats with little awareness of the personhood of others. They become things we flee simply because they threaten us.

Fear's motion from the object to the self also narrows our concern by diminishing our openness to aesthetic and moral values. The transcendent character of our response to values disappears, replaced by a constricted focus on the self. In political or social relations, fear can be a unifying force that moves people to collective action. This action might produce beneficial results and enhance the common good. However, in other cases collective fear pits one group against another or one group against an individual. In these cases, it leads to a unity that produces value blindness.

Fear and Actuarial Justice

This value blindness appears frequently in matters of crime and punishment, and I devote the rest of this chapter to showing how it influences jail policies. In an important article written more than twenty years ago ("The New Penology: Notes on the Emerging Strategy of Corrections and Its Implications"), Malcolm Feeley and Jonathan Simon discussed an emerging pattern in American criminal justice. Rather than focusing on language of therapy, it emphasized risk and probability. Rather than seeking rehabilitation, the new approach accentuated crime control. Instead of considering individual characteristics of offenders, the new penology adopted techniques that "target offenders as an aggregate in place of traditional techniques for individualizing" (Feeley and Simon 1992, 450). Feeley and Simon predicted that the new penology would gain popularity, and warned of its dangers to American institutions.

Their warning turned out to be prescient, and the new penology became an important way of approaching crime. Since the Feeley/Simon article, many scholars have buttressed their thesis. Some have focused particularly on the techniques of treating people as aggregates, sometimes calling them "actuarial justice." Scholars have considered two forms of it. The first concentrates on masses of people without considering them as individuals at all. For example, racial profiling pays little attention to individuals, approaching them instead as a group that may be statistically likely to commit crimes. It has played a prominent role in policing and antiterrorism strategies. A different actuarial approach uses aggregate data to control individuals more tightly. Through it, we "place people in categories and assess risk factors in order to know the individual better" (Harcourt 2007, 193). In this case, we have recourse to general categories as a means of regulating individual behavior more precisely.

These approaches present different dangers to individual dignity. The first simply ignores it. The stigma of incarceration effaces what makes me unique and special. I have the spoiled identity of "inmate," and it remains with me throughout my incarceration. It also stays with me once I leave the jail. The second actuarial approach bears a more complex relationship to dignity. On one hand, the aggregating techniques enable authorities to pay more attention to me. However, they aim to control me, shaping me in their image. Policy makers, politicians, and police authorities promise to mitigate fear by controlling and predicting behavior. They approach me not with an openness to my individual dignity, but with information they think controls me maximally.

Fear and Minimizing Risk

Actuarial justice requires new tools of risk assessment that authorities can use to incapacitate actual and potential criminals. Simon has drawn attention to how ideas about risk assessment and crime have changed over the past few decades. Risk assessment played a role in the U.S. penal system for much of the twentieth century. Until the 1970s, authorities often used it to make judgments about an individual's prospects for rehabilitation (Simon 2005, 399). However, Simon describes a paradigm shift in risk assessment in criminal justice since the 1980s. It

is now "deployed as a mechanism for extending confinement or surveillance over persons either not yet convicted of crime or who have already
served their penal sentence. Increasingly, risk assessment is being
brought into the criminal justice process to select people for extended
incapacitation through a variety of means ranging from registration and
notification requirements attached to many sex offenders to civil commitment, to the death penalty" (Simon 2005, 399–400). For multiple
reasons, policy makers, politicians, and penal authorities came to believe
that risk assessment could do little to predict future positive behavior.
Instead, they employed it simply to reduce risk. They held that if an
inmate posed even the slightest risk of reoffending, we should incarcerate or control him for as long as possible.

Fear dominates this form of risk assessment, blinding us to the value
of the person. We fear the slightest risk of violent crime. We have media
that sensationalize horrible instances of violence, opportunistic politicians who pass draconian legislation, and victims' rights groups that
demand legal protection. These familiar dynamics have played themselves out in U.S. politics over the past three decades.[19] Through them,
fear leads people to think about certain people only as risks, and focus
narrowly on real or imagined dangers to themselves. We also see false
promises to control all risk. As Bernard Harcourt notes, actuarial approaches seem to reduce fear by conquering it. Today's advocates of risk
assessment claim that if we only employ new, sophisticated statistical
tools, we can "shape chance," reducing the risk of crime to a manageable
minimum (Harcourt 2003). Many people are only so happy to accept a
promise of psychic and physical security, even if it carries the enormous
moral and financial price tag that comes with mass incarceration.

This form of risk assessment also serves the larger goal of what Simon
calls "total incapacitation" (Simon 2014). Total incapacitation is a cluster
of ideas accentuating punitive measures against offenders. It sees custody as the only meaningful way to incapacitate people. It emphasizes
preventative control within jails and prisons while disregarding education and treatment. Total incapacitation also acts indiscriminately, using
categories to incapacitate people regardless of the risk they pose to a
community. Finally, total incapacitation recognizes little capacity for
change in criminals and inmates, and seeks to lock them up for as long
as possible (Simon 2014, 41–42).

Total incapacitation accentuates fear and promises minimal risk. Those endorsing it often use scare tactics and images of inmates going free and hurting people. For example, Simon notes that for years the image of the serial killer and the violent revolutionary buttressed California's extraordinary growth in prisons and prisoners (Simon 2014, 28–36). By emphasizing fear, total incapacitation enjoys a considerable advantage in the political arena. A person who proposes a different approach to criminals "would appear to choose hope about the future behavior of criminal offenders over fears for the harms that their victims have suffered or might suffer" (Simon 2014, 43). In such cases, fear of violence usually prevails, and the public is only too willing to embrace extreme measures to minimize perceived or real risks. The result is a profoundly punitive approach to crime that incarcerates people in extreme ways.

Bail, Fear, and the Attempt to Eliminate Risk

To illustrate how the total incapacitation/fear dynamic affects jails, let me return to the topic of money bail. Ostensibly, jails exist to hold people who are dangerous, who won't show up for trial, or who are serving short sentences. However, as I have argued, they also control those with mental illness and poor people who cannot afford bail. As I noted in chapter 2, in the past twenty years the United States has seen an extraordinary increase in the use of and the amount of money bail. In 1990, "most felony defendants who were freed from jail pending the resolution of their cases were released on non-financial conditions."[20] However, in 2009 "those released on their own recognizance (also referred to as ROR) made up only 23 percent of all felony defendants released pretrial." Of the remaining 77 percent, 61 percent were required to post financial bail of some kind, either the entire amount or a percentage of the bail. Many had to work through a bail bondsman to come up with the bail. Moreover, the "average bail amount in felony cases increased 43 percent (in constant dollar values) between 1992 and 2009, from $38,800 to $55,400." These developments reflect a growing fear of crime, a determination to control risk, and a drive to incapacitate those accused of crime.

The increased use of money bail and its higher amounts have played a significant role in the growth of jail populations. In fact, "current policies and practices around money bail are among the primary drivers around growth in jail populations" (Justice Policy Institute 2012, 3).[21] Municipalities and counties throughout the United States use imperfect risk-assessment tools to decide whether and how to grant money bail. The use of bail is "so problematic because there is no definitive association between a particular accusation and the amount of money that would guarantee appearance at court (or deter future criminal activity) for the offense" (Justice Policy Institute 2012, 23). Like conditions in many jails, bail policies depend entirely on where a person is arrested. For example, in Cook County, Illinois, someone must pay 10 percent of her bail, and can use the services of a bail bondsman. However, where I live, Brown County in Wisconsin, she must pay 100 percent of her bail, and bail bondsmen are illegal. In some counties, pretrial services play a role in arranging the bail amount, while in others prosecutors and judges do this work. In many counties, a judge consults a "bail schedule" that indicates appropriate bail for offenses. Because of the decentralized character of the U.S. jail system, bail decisions thus depend on local factors that often have little correlation with flight risk or a danger to the community.

The Damaging Effects of Money Bail

Sadly, scholars have known about the damaging effects of our current bail system for decades, but this knowledge hasn't halted its growing influence and power. Studies and public committees back in the 1960s drew attention to the irrationality and unfairness of our bail system. Since then, further studies have shown "over the years that people in jail pretrial end up with worse trial outcomes than people who are free while awaiting trial" (Justice Policy Institute 2012, 13).[22] Financial pressure often makes it difficult for jail inmates to pursue their cases. While incarcerated, they often lose their jobs and sources of income. They may be evicted from their apartments or houses because they can't pay rent or make mortgage payments. Gradually, as the days, weeks, or months drag on before trial, their financial situation deteriorates.

Incarceration also makes it hard for someone to prepare for trial. She cannot easily meet with legal counsel, particularly if she relies on an overworked public defender. Phone conversations of any kind are expensive. Many jails sign contracts with phone companies that make phone calls costly. Only in recent years have counties made modest attempts to control these outrageous costs.[23] If an inmate has witnesses she wants to assemble for trial, she may encounter difficulties contacting them. If she wants to locate legal materials, she may be unable to find them in grossly inadequate jail libraries. All these factors make it difficult to mount a legal case while inside a jail.

Perhaps of equal concern, the conditions of jails put inmates at a disadvantage in relation to prosecutors. Those who live in constant fear of violence from other inmates or staff cannot easily concentrate on their cases. Those who live in filthy conditions seek to escape them rather than languish for months in jail waiting for a trial. The sheer boredom, inactivity, and lack of access to fresh air and sunlight drive many people to settle their cases at all costs. They may take a plea bargain rather than go to trial. In many cases, plea bargains turn out to be unfavorable to the accused, but they take them anyway because they simply want their jail ordeal to end.

Jail incarceration may also increase the likelihood of more severe punishment. For example, a 2013 study found that "defendants who are detained for the entire pretrial period are much more likely to be sentenced to jail and prison" (Arnold Foundation 2013, 4). It also found that those who remained in jail for their trial received longer sentences. This was particularly true for lower-level offenders, for whom jail time correlated with longer sentences. The study's authors don't speculate about why this is the case, but perhaps lack of access to good counsel played some role in this outcome. Other reasons may include how inmates present themselves at trial. Those who are free on their own recognizance can appear in civilian clothes and may appear less demoralized. Those in jail sometimes come to court beaten down and disheveled. Perhaps such factors affect how judges and juries respond to them.

There are many reasons for the extraordinary growth in the use and amount of money bail in the past few decades. In some municipalities, lobbyists for the bail bondsman industry work hard to retain a profitable industry. Prosecutors may find money bail useful because it pressures defendants into making plea bargains rather than going to trial. For example, in 2010, Human Rights Watch issued a report on money bail in New York City that concluded that "judges, prosecutors, and defense counsel all know that defendants at arraignments who face the prospect of pretrial detention because they cannot post bail are likely to agree to plea bargains. This is not to say that judges or prosecutors always deliberately seek bail as a means to a plea bargain, but the money bail system often gives prosecutors a decided advantage when it comes to encouraging a plea bargain" (Human Rights Watch 2010, 31–32). In this case, the money bail system seemed to serve the interests of prosecutors and judges.

Additionally, the money bail system enables municipalities to control large numbers of people without convicting them. Recall that in Cook County, thousands of people are arrested, given a bail they can't afford, and then sent to the Cook County Jail. Days or weeks pass, the charges against them are dropped, and they are released. They are thus punished without ever having been convicted of a crime. Years ago, Malcolm Feeley titled one of his books *The Process Is the Punishment*, and some scholars and activists have applied his title to the money bail system (Human Rights Watch 2010, 27).[24] Judges and prosecutors may or may not intend this outcome, but the money bail system effectively penalizes those without financial resources.[25]

Money Bail and the Fear of Violent Offenders

We thus have a money bail system for many reasons, but one certainly is fear of violent crime. Money bail puts judges (who are in many cases elected officials) in a difficult position because they often lack information about defendants and can't risk releasing them on their own recognizance. In counties where pretrial services exist, they are often poorly managed. Officials have little time to verify information they receive about defendants, are often overworked, and provide imperfect information to prosecutors and judges. For all these reasons, judges can have little confidence that they are receiving reliable information about defendants. If they do have the discretion or time to make a risk assessment, it is likely to be a conservative one that errs on the side of caution.

We see this problem in the history of Cook County's Pretrial Services. Recall that in Cook County's Bond Court, proceedings for each defendant take only a few minutes. Cook County's Bond Court was not supposed to be so dysfunctional. In 1990, Cook County created its Pretrial Services to provide judges with better information about arrestees. However, as a 2014 report of the Illinois Supreme Court exhaustively detailed, Pretrial Services often failed in this function. It suffered from management problems, interviewed inmates in difficult physical conditions, and often failed to verify information provided by those arrested. Bond Court judges often had little or no knowledge of Pretrial Services, and distrusted the information they received from it (Illinois Supreme Court, Administrative Office of the Illinois Courts 2014).

Problems with Pretrial Services only contribute to an environment where court authorities fear the risk of violent crime. Judges worry about releasing someone who might commit a terrible and newsworthy crime. In 2013, Cook County Chief Judge Timothy Evans (to whom I will return in the Conclusion) put it well when he said, "There's the issue of being afraid of being the Willie Horton judge. I'm sure at some point a judge is going to consider all these factors from the statute, and the risk assessment, and end up releasing someone who either doesn't come to court or does something dastardly when they're out. And I hope people will stand with that judge if he's considered all these factors and followed the law. If the judge does everything he could do, it still could happen" (Dumke 2013).[26] Judge Evans expresses the fear of taking the blame for releasing dangerous criminals. Given a broken system and a public demanding freedom from risk, judges may choose incarceration as the least risky course of action.

Unnecessary and damaging pretrial confinement illustrates how fear plays a role in our penal system. The total incapacitation approach to risk and crime populates our jails with people who cannot afford bail. It produces overcrowding, and creates deep management challenges for jail administrators. Most importantly, it inflicts terrible damage on inmates. It forces them to live in intolerable and dangerous institutions. It drives many people into financial ruin, saddling them with debt that stays with them long after their incarceration. In this case, we again see how value blindness spawned by a negative affective response harms hundreds of thousands of people.

Conclusion

Throughout this book, I have maintained that when we encounter other people, we recognize their value. If I walk into a room with a wet coat and hang it on a chair, few people will find this behavior problematic.

However, if I take the coat and hang it on someone's neck, most people will be horrified. They recognize that treating a person like a coat stand is inappropriate to her value, even if they cannot articulate why they think this is true. In this case, they display an appropriate emotional response to value, and recognize an action showing contempt for it.

However, if we recognize the person's value when encountering him, how can we account for human cruelty, brutality, and neglect? To respond to this question, I think it's helpful to consider specific instances where knowledge of the person's value becomes distorted. I have presented a phenomenological account of value blindness originating in disgust, contempt, and fear. These affective responses often appear together, but we distinguish them by analyzing how they relate to objects. Disgust, contempt, and fear are all aversive responses, leading us to react negatively to what we encounter. Disgust responds to something out of place, often (but not always) something biological, and it includes a sense of contamination. Contempt presupposes a moment of disgust, but has a cooler, more calculating character. It can take the form of indifference, where I pay minimal attention to the object of my contempt. Or, it can take a loathing form, where I want to damage or eliminate the object. Finally, fear differs from contempt or disgust because it involves a double motion of the person. I focus narrowly on an aspect of the object that threatens me and flee from it. I then turn back to myself in a protective manner.

I have maintained that fear, contempt, and disgust distort our awareness of the human dignity in different ways. Disgust exerts a powerful influence on me through sight or smell. It leads me to concentrate not on what makes a person unique or on our common humanity, but on what elicits my disgust. Sometimes, the disgust response so overwhelms me that I can think of little else. Contempt revels in subordination; I stand in a positon of superiority over someone and enjoy it. This subordination relation often dominates any sense of equality I share with others. Finally, fear is particularly threatening to human dignity. When I fear you, I rarely consider anything else, but what I think threatens me. Fear is a self-regarding affective response that draws me back toward myself, my property, or my loved ones, and away from what might be valuable in you.

Fear, disgust, and contempt play a powerful role in supporting the degrading and violent conditions in contemporary jails. Cities and counties often use jails to remove from public view those they consider disgusting. Homeless people, those suffering from mental illness, and those who engage in disruptive behavior often find themselves in jails. Because cities seek to attract to their downtown areas tourists and young people with money, they cannot tolerate too much disgusting behavior in public. Jails become the means to control it. Disgust also operates within jails. Jail staff must deal with people in states that usually elicit disgust, and the revolting conditions in many jails bring about only further disgust. Disgust doesn't necessarily have to lead to contempt, but our society's harsh attitude toward inmates provides warrant for it to harden into contempt. We encourage this dynamic through an arrest and booking process that degrades and subordinates people. All these factors combine to produce a dangerous contempt and disgust in jails.

Finally, I have discussed one example in our penal system where fear devalues individual dignity. As Simon notes, we have increasingly embraced an incapacitation approach to risk and crime. We aim to minimize risk, reduce fear, and completely incapacitate inmates. Often, judges, politicians, and prosecutors refuse to take even the slightest risk that someone accused of a crime will reoffend. Consequently, over the past twenty years we have dramatically increased the use and the amount of money bail. The result has been disastrous for both our jail system and the inmates.

As I have argued throughout this book, affective responses to values are not irrational sensations, but instead aim at objects and contain a cognitive component. We can ask critical questions about these objects, and consider if our responses aim at them appropriately. Nevertheless, changing affective responses is never easy. For example, we can't simply point out (as many do) that our money bail system is irrational, costly, and unfair. Nor can we merely tell people to reconsider their fear of the violent behavior of inmates because crime rates have fallen. These arguments often fail to move people trapped by negative responses to others. If we want to alter responses that distort how we value people, we need to link policy changes with personal transformation. To this issue I now turn.

5

What Can We Do?

Responding to a Crisis

All jailed persons look alike to the ordinary virtuous citizens, all look equally dangerous. It is curious how the mere fact of a man's being admitted to bail operates as a suspension, of even a reversal of this harsh judgment. In that case, the legal presumption that a man is innocent until proven guilty is also the proper presumption and this is notwithstanding the fact that in nearly all the cases (all in fact but cases of murder which are few in number), the only difference between the bailed and the jailed offender is that one had money enough to procure a bail-bond which the other lacked. Doubtless the character of the jail and the nature of the treatment to which the inmates are subjected have a good deal to do with this irrational attitude on the part of the public.
—Chicago Community Trust, *The Cook County Jail Survey*, 1922[1]

In 1794, philosopher Jeremy Bentham published a plan for new kind of institution called the Panopticon (made famous in a book by Michel Foucault). This institution would contain its inhabitants with minimal physical force. The Panopticon would be a circular structure that confined people in cells in solitary confinement. At its center, an Inspection House would stand where inspectors could continuously see the occupants of the cells. Cell occupants would never know if or when they were being watched. Merely conceiving that they might be watched would influence their behavior. They would adjust their behavior accordingly, obeying rules even without violent coercion. Bentham called this idea the "Inspection Principle," and held that it could serve as a source of power in prisons, hospitals, schools, and juvenile facilities.[2]

Bentham never succeeded in building the Panopticon, and his proposal reflects a frightening vision of totalitarian social control. Some architects have constructed prisons based on his ideas, but the Inspection Principle has rarely proven an effective means of controlling inmates. However, despite the horrors of Bentham's ideas, his critics often overlook an intriguing moment in his Panopticon letters. Bentham was convinced that those who watched inmates in the Inspection House should also be watched. Under no instance, Bentham wrote, could the inspector's "subordinates either perform or depart from their duty, but he must know the time and degree of their doing so" (Bentham 2011, 46). Like the inmates, the guards and inspectors would never know when and if they were being observed. Like many in the eighteenth and nineteenth centuries, Bentham proposed that penal institutions open their doors to the public so people could observe what occurred inside them. This proposal presents the horrifying prospect of treating inmates like zoo animals, but it also reflects Bentham's concern about abuses of power. We cannot simply trust those watching inmates to do the right thing, but must watch them as well.

Unlike Bentham's ideal prison, today's jails lack transparency. Federal and state laws govern them, but jail authorities exert decentralized and local power. Information about what happens inside jails is scant, and access to inmates is highly restricted. The public often shows little interest in holding jail officials accountable for how they treat inmates. In their mind, jails are for troublemakers and undesirables who deserve whatever bad treatment they receive. They uncritically trust those exercising power, and leave them to their own devices. In general, Americans ignore Bentham's conviction that even the inspectors need to be inspected.

In this chapter, I maintain that to protect human dignity in jails, we need monitoring and transparency to counter abuses of power. I also focus on how institutional change and free choices can respond to the moral blindness engendered by disgust, contempt, and fear. To explore these topics, I first comment on the tension between short-term and long-term change, emphasizing the urgent need to respond to injustice. Second, I describe the problem of decentralization in the U.S. jail system. The United States has an extraordinary number of jails that punish in hidden ways and with little oversight. Those proposing that we improve jail conditions must recognize how decentralization impedes their aspirations. Third, I recommend greater jail monitoring through state and citizen monitoring organizations and more investigative journalism. Fourth, I support additional federal and state oversight and greater litigation on behalf of inmates. Fifth, moving inside the jail, I return to mental health issues and inmate abuse. I focus particularly on proper medical intake procedures and medication. I also support specific use-of-force policies and timely reporting of inmate abuse. Sixth, calling for the gradual end of the money bail system, I explore the trend toward adopting new forms of pretrial risk assessment. I argue that they hold promise for reducing jail populations, but pose dangers for human dignity. Seventh, I consider the complex interaction between institutional structures and our affective response to human dignity. Policies, institutions, and leadership deeply affect how we respond to values. I conclude this chapter by reflecting on changing disgust, contempt, and fear. We cannot will to directly change these affective responses, but can indirectly influence them in ways that respect human dignity.

Reformism and Abolitionism: Facing the Tension

Those writing about injustice in jails and prisons often note a tension between calls for reform and more radical approaches to change. In fact, some scholars argue that when we seek to improve jail conditions, we merely perpetuate an unjust system, making it appear to be "slightly more comfortable or humane" (Schept 2015, 236). They criticize such efforts for putting a better face on injustice. For example, counties sometimes expand their jail capacity in response to overcrowding. Overcrowding in penal facilities almost always brings problems, and relieving the suffering of those stuffed into a jail seems imperative. However, counties often fail to consider the human and financial costs of jail expansion. They adopt expensive bonding schemes to expand the jail, putting local government in debt for years. They may then be tempted to fill empty jail spaces with state prisoners or undocumented immigrants. Before long, we have a bigger jail with all the problems of overcrowding we faced before the expansion.[3]

The tension between reform and the goal of dismantling an unjust system is very real, and I will discuss it in more detail in the conclusion. However, I think it's important to consider the immediate ethical demands of responding to assaults on human dignity. To do otherwise is to ignore the suffering of inmates. I resist the urge to label all attempts to alter penal institutions as useless "reformist" policies. Instead, I think we can address immediate problems in jails while also pursuing the long-term goal of dismantling jails. We should, however, think carefully about how responses to injustice do or don't strengthen our penal system.[4]

Decentralization: A Key Challenge

Turning to the need for immediate action, the local character of the U.S. jail system poses significant challenges to any attempt to change degrading and abusive punishment. Federal laws govern county jails, but local officials administer them, and we often have little information about what goes on behind jail walls. For example, my state of Wisconsin has seventy-two counties and seventy-nine adult jail facilities (National Institute of Corrections 2013). Its landscape is dotted with a variety of work camps and juvenile holding facilities, about which it is difficult to obtain accurate information. A sheriff administers each of Wisconsin's jails, and he or she is elected and answerable to local constituents. In my years in Wisconsin, I have learned how the culture of each jail differs according to community mores and the management style of its administrator. Wisconsin is a small state, and larger states contain multiple jails in diverse communities. Those administering them are often unwilling to share information with researchers or citizens. In fifty states, sixteen territories, and hundreds of Native American lands, U.S. jail punishment remains local and largely hidden from public view.[5]

We often learn about jails only when something terrible happens, and then get a sense of the bureaucratic difficulties inmates and their families experience. For example, in 2015 Jamycheal Mitchell, a twenty-four-year-old African American man, allegedly stole five dollars' worth of soda and snacks from a Virginia store. He was arrested, and transported to the Hampton Roads Regional Jail. He suffered from mental illnesses, and a judge determined that he wasn't responsible for his crime and should be sent to a psychiatric hospital. However, because of bed shortages at the local psychiatric hospital and paperwork errors, Mitchell remained in the jail for four months. During this time, family members contacted the jail repeatedly, and while in court noticed that Mitchell's physical condition had deteriorated. But authorities assured them that he was fine. However, after four months his mother received a phone call informing her that her son had died of "natural causes."

Struggling to understand why their son died, Mitchell's family received few answers. Apparently, he hadn't taken his medication, hadn't eaten, lost forty pounds, lived in a cell by himself, and died. Despite this horror, a jail investigation found that officials acted appropriately. The State Inspector General's Office claimed that it lacked authority to investigate the case, and the Department of Behavioral Health and Developmental Services found no fault with the jail. Because the Hampton Roads Regional Jail serves five cities, Mitchell's mother couldn't go to one county or city official and hold him responsible for her son's death. As of the writing of this book, the exact circumstances of Mitchell's death remain unclear. No one has been held legally responsible for it.[6]

Although not so tragic, tens of thousands of Americans confront similar bureaucratic nightmares in U.S. jails. Anyone who has ever visited an inmate in jail knows the obstacles visitors face. Often, families lose contact with loved ones who cannot make phone calls. If family members try calling a jail, they go through a seemingly endless series of connections before they receive information. At the jail, they meet indifferent or hostile authorities who make it clear that visitors are wasting their time. Family members are often made to feel ashamed for having someone in jail. They receive little or no information, and must find things out themselves. In sum, to visitors, jail authorities often seem to know little and take no responsibility for their actions.

Therefore, proposals to improve jails must consider the local character of jail administration in the United States. Too often, public discussions of punishment assume that the federal government possesses more power than it does. Alternatively, they overlook the real configuration of power in communities throughout the United States. Recall that almost twelve million people pass through our jails annually, and many come under the control of local officials wielding considerable power over their lives. Realistic policies to make jails better must recognize this power.

Jail Monitoring

One way to improve jail conditions and enhance transparency is to develop jail monitoring mechanisms. These can take the form of state-sponsored organizations, accrediting agencies, or citizen organizations. Commenting about prison monitoring, Michelle Deitch and Michael B. Mushlin note,

> Designed correctly, an oversight body can provide an early warning system about patterns of complaints against certain prison employees, assess the appropriateness of discipline meted out to staff members, address concerns about inadequate health care or protocols for dealing with mentally ill inmates, highlight programs that are ineffective, point to areas for improved staff training, and identify policies that need to be adjusted. A monitor could also identify practices worth replicating at other prisons. (Mushlin and Deitch 2016)[7]

To act effectively, monitoring organizations must have several characteristics (Deitch 2010, 1757–1759). They should enjoy free access to the jail, making both scheduled and unscheduled visits. Monitoring organizations must be able to speak freely with inmates. Additionally, they need to operate independently from departments of corrections. Too often, bureaucracies use words like "due process" and "monitoring" to describe processes that lack independence or fairness. Independence ensures a minimal level of impartiality. Finally, monitoring organizations must exercise oversight functions. They should issue official reports to government bodies or make public their findings about what occurs in a jail.

Jail monitoring serves several important functions. It makes it difficult for penal authorities to hide abuse. Monitors can warn lawyers who can take legal action against abusers. They can help families struggling to find out what has happened to their loved ones. Finally, monitors can break down barriers between inmates and the public. Citizens' groups that monitor jails can contact inmates and share their experiences with others. This contact reduces the dehumanization and disinformation that often exists when people think of jail inmates.

Unfortunately, the United States currently possesses poor jail monitoring arrangements. Our jail system provides little access to monitoring groups. In a major 2010 study of U.S. jail and prison monitoring, Michelle Deitch concluded that "it should be clear upon closer examination that formal and comprehensive external oversight—in the form of inspections and routine monitoring of conditions that affect the rights of prisoners—is truly rare in this country" (Deitch 2010, 1762). Some states like New York and Illinois have old monitoring organizations, while others like Wisconsin have few at all. Such a paucity stems not from ignorance or lack of funding, but from an absence of will and concern. Governors, legislators, sheriffs, and citizens don't think it's important to shed light on what happens behind jail walls. Until they change this outlook, our jail system will continue to lack transparency and be ripe for abuse.

Investigative journalism offers one other means of enhancing jail transparency. Journalists of all kinds can investigate and expose abusive jail practices. However, print journalists enjoy some advantages. They often have the resources to devote to sustained examination of records needed to investigate penal institutions (Freedom of Information Act requests, open record searches, etc.). Journalists who work for a prestigious newspaper may be able to gain access to a jail. Or they can speak to former inmates or relatives of inmates. Additionally, they have editors and legal counsel who can help them navigate the dangerous territory of publishing stories of abuse. Jails, particularly large urban ones, can often retaliate against investigative journalists, and they must operate carefully when writing stories. Journalists also need to learn to interview people properly so to avoid being taken in by fabricated stories. For all these reasons, print journalists are in a good position to perform investigations into jail abuses.

With the advent of new media and corporate control over old media, investigative journalism has seen a decline in recent years. However, important newspapers have devoted considerable resources to jails and prisons. I have already noted how the *New York Times* has printed stories about the horrors of Rikers Island. It also devoted considerable attention to alleged abuses after inmates escaped from the Clinton Correctional Facility, a maximum-security prison in New York State. The *Milwaukee Journal Sentinel* has done excellent work exposing alleged abuses at the Lincoln Hills School for Boys in Wisconsin. In 2015, the FBI raided this prison, investigating allegations of sexual assault and abuse and neglect of inmates, and repeated local coverage has kept this scandal in the public eye.[8] These examples illustrate that investigative reporting remains an important tool for informing people of what occurs in our penal system. It counters institutional abuses of power, and gives voice to people in jails and prisons who often have no way to tell their stories.

Legal Challenges: A Necessity

Investigative journalists can reveal abuses of power, but lacks the legal power to make change. In the U.S. political system, legal mechanisms play a vital role in forcing institutional change. For example, although the federal government doesn't directly administer county jails, it exercises some power over them. Throughout this book, I have drawn extensively on DOJ investigations of jail conditions. The DOJ plays a limited but important role in monitoring jails. It takes cases under the Special Litigation Section of the Civil Rights Division. The section employs a small staff that can respond to only major cases of abuse and degradation. Nevertheless, it exerts significant power when it takes them on. As I have already detailed, it launches investigations, brings lawsuits, and develops Consent Agreements. This form of monitoring gets the attention of county and state officials in a dramatic fashion.

I have a friend who works in a jail that negotiated a DOJ Consent Decree. Monitors conduct regular inspections, and the jail has seen some important improvements. Jail conditions remain imperfect, and problems at the facility persist. However, my friend welcomes the DOJ's presence, likening it to parents keeping an eye on their children. He believes that such a watchful eye is a positive development, and hopes that the DOJ will bring enduring changes. The DOJ operates from at a distance from local conditions, and often can't fully understands what's occurring in a jail. Nevertheless, it can exert important influence, and those concerned with injustice in our jails should urge that we devote greater resources to its efforts. The Special Litigation Section is small and underfunded, and could expand its operations considerably. Whether it gains this power depends on the goals and character of the DOJ and how it operates under different presidents, a topic I will return to in the conclusion.

In addition to DOJ investigations, nonprofit organizations can litigate on behalf of inmates. I have drawn attention to the ACLU's work, and it supports the National Prison Project.[9] It has operated since 1972, and works at a national level. It takes cases from jails and prisons throughout the United States, and initiates lawsuits against municipalities. It then goes through a trial or settles with the municipality. The National Prison Project has enjoyed important successes in altering jail conditions. It has triggered state and federal investigations leading to wide-ranging changes in jail leadership and structure. For example, the ACLU issued a report on the Los Angeles County Jail that focused on officer abuse of inmates. It drew attention to an issue that eventually led to FBI and DOJ investigations of the jail.[10]

The problems in jails often seem overwhelming in their complexity, and people learning about them wonder if individuals can make a difference. Nonprofit organizations like the ACLU (and many lesser-known groups) do improve the lives of inmates. Despite popular misconceptions, inmates cannot easily sue jails. Organizations like the ACLU bring experienced litigators to cases, and draw attention to abuse and degradation. With our renewed concern with mass incarceration, we can encourage people to enter public interest law on behalf of inmates. However, like the DOJ, organizations like the ACLU have limited resources to devote to jail litigation, and those concerned about the issue can help them by providing financial support.

Stopping the Abuse: The Need for Good Policies

Litigation, however, is an imperfect tool that usually enters the picture only once conditions have reached a crisis point. In the 1960s and 1970s, judicial authorities intervened actively to stop abuses in penal institutions, sometimes supervising reforms of entire correctional systems. However, since the 1980s and 1990s scholars have debated the wisdom and efficacy of judicial intervention in penal systems. Many judges also backed away from it, maintaining that prison and jail officials knew best how to manage their institutions. Recently, however, with the unprecedented growth of prison populations, particularly in places like California, we have seen judicial authorities who are more willing to respond to abuses. For example, a federal judge recently took over operations of the New Orleans Parish Prison after years of dysfunction. These are positive developments, but often come only once an institution or system faces serious legal challenges or can no longer function.[11]

Ultimately, penal authorities must exercise leadership to develop and enforce policies that minimally respect human dignity. Let me begin with staff violence toward inmates. DOJ Consent Decrees provide guidelines for how jails can prevent it. They call for prohibiting the use of force as a means of retaliation, control of movement, or punishment. They define acceptable uses of force, limit the kinds of technologies of force officials can use, and discuss what constitutes excessive force. They also recommend that authorities install surveillance cameras to record use-of-force incidents and examine them.

Perhaps more importantly, DOJ documents recommend that authorities quickly review use-of-force incidents.[12] Jails differ from prisons because the inmate population is transient. People who leave a jail may be disinclined to revisit their experience by pursuing legal cases against officers. Additionally, lawyers seeking to build cases against a jail may encounter difficulties locating inmates who have been released. These factors present unique challenges to those investigating use-of-force problems in a jail.

Because of these unique circumstances in jails, DOJ agreements often urge swift and proper reporting of use-of-force incidents. They specify that inmates must be able to lodge complaints without retaliation, insist that officers involved write detailed reports, and require supervisors to review incidents. Use-of-force recommendations also include provisions for medical examinations for inmates after they have been subjected to violence. Finally, DOJ agreements call for discipline of officers who repeatedly use excessive force.

Helping Those with Mental Illness

Good leadership can also produce changes in how we treat inmates with mental illness. From numerous DOJ and ACLU documents, we gain some idea about how to improve care for these inmates.[13] To begin with, competent authorities, not corrections officers, should provide intake examination for all incoming inmates. We could prevent many tragedies in jails with these examinations. Proper expertise plays a particularly important role in dispensing medication and keeping good records. Unlike prison authorities, those working in jails confront acute difficulties with medical records. Often, inmates don't have them, may not have seen a doctor in a long time, or may provide information that requires time to verify. These complex realities make it essential that medical authorities interview patients to find out their medication needs. A nurse or doctor examining inmates sometimes must decide which medications to prescribe. Unfortunately, jails often restrict medications for cost considerations, and inmates cannot continue taking their current medication. However, at least proper medical authorities will make medication decisions, and keep accurate medical records. Investigative documents repeatedly show an appalling failure to record medical conditions and medications.

Finally, licensed medical authorities must work with inmates while they live in jails. As I mentioned in chapter 2, jails experience many failures in chronic and acute care. Staff often lack adequate suicide-prevention training, particularly as it relates to those suffering from mental illness. Inmates cannot easily access sick call, and languish while waiting for mental health care. Jails cannot transfer acute-care patients to hospitals because of the lack of available beds. Proper acute and chronic care mitigates many problems and reduces the disruption that occurs in jails caused by those experiencing confusion and decompression. Finally, proper care helps corrections officers struggling to respond to those with mental illness.

In fact, some jails have linked corrections officers and mental health staff in what is known as Crisis Intervention Training (CIT). This training (also employed by police departments) teaches officers how to recognize signs of mental illness. It trains them to deescalate violent situations so that they don't result in severe injury or death. Not all officers in a jail participate in CIT training, and it is no panacea for all problems. Nevertheless, it shows how mental health and custodial staff can work together to ameliorate the conditions of those with mental illness. CIT training has the added benefit of reducing tensions between these two groups in a jail.[14]

In sum, jails can take minimal steps to help those with mental illness. We have no excuse for the disgraceful failure to care for those we arrest and jail. Jails have a moral and legal obligation to help those suffering from mental illness, and cannot evade it by blaming others in society.

The Failure to Confront the Real Problem

Nevertheless, we won't adequately address the crisis of mental illness in jails unless we radically reconsider mental health care in society. As I noted in chapter 2, jails contain an extraordinary number of people suffering from mental illness. Estimates based on 2014 data run to at least 149,000 jail inmates who suffer from serious psychiatric illness (Torrey et al. 2014, 101).[15] Some of them end up in prison, where perhaps over 350,000 suffer from serious psychiatric illness (Torrey et al. 2014, 101). Jails will always be ill-equipped to treat people because they aren't hospitals. Moreover, they put people in cages and in conditions that often exacerbate their illness. At best, jails can serve a Band-Aid function until inmates receive serious mental health care outside the penal setting.

In this book, my goal has been to draw attention to the mental health crisis in our jails rather than to provide comprehensive ways to overhaul our mental health care system. Nevertheless, let me briefly indicate some of the dimensions of this extraordinarily complex problem. People often call for greater funding for mental health care. Incarcerating people with mental illness is expensive, and we could reallocate resources so that they don't end up jailed. We also could spend more money helping those suffering from mental illness. We could provide health insurance for them, and operate smaller community clinics where they could receive medication. By allocating greater funding for mental illness, we would help people before they reach the point where they end up in jail.

However, jails often deal with the most difficult cases in society. Community treatment can't help those who fail to show up for appointments or refuse to take medication. Penal and medical authorities often confront significant problems with compliance and medication. These problems don't disappear once someone is released from a controlled environment. Moreover, many communities won't allow mental health clinics for low-income people to operate in them. They will need to be more welcoming of clinics and community housing for ex-offenders suffering from mental illness. Proposals for treatment in lieu of punishment often ignore the hard cases, and if enacted would help only some of those suffering in our jails.[16]

Some thinkers reject the call for more funding for community-based treatment altogether, and lobby instead for reopening large state mental health hospitals. They want the state to have more power to forcibly commit people who refuse to take medication and who pose a public nuisance. For them, the great evil was "deinstitutionalization," the closing of large state institutions and changes in civil rights laws making it difficult to civilly commit those with mental illness. We often hear a familiar refrain that blames our current mental health care crisis on liberal ideas about excessive individual freedom and rights gone wild.[17] However, this narrative suffers from historical amnesia and revisionism. It ignores the horrors of life in many twentieth-century mental health institutions. Until the 1960s in the United States, those with mental illness often lived in overcrowded horror houses like Willowbrook, Pennhurst, and Camarillo.[18] Many received no treatment at all, and languished for years in filthy and overcrowded conditions. People who lived in mental institutions were often brutally abused by incompetent and underpaid staff. With little due process, they could be committed and incarcerated for years or their entire lives. Thousands received "treatments" like lobotomies and insulin shock therapy. Tens of thousands were coercively sterilized by asylum superintendents or eugenics boards who arbitrarily decided that they were unfit to procreate (Hansen and King 2013).[19] Anyone familiar with this history should hesitate before recommending that we return to some golden age before the evils of deinstitutionalization.[20]

A final point I want to make regarding mental health care concerns mass incarceration and mental hospitals. Contemporary criminologists and historians debate why the U.S. penal population has ballooned so incredibly in the past few decades. They offer competing explanations (the New Jim Crow, the power of prosecutors, the war on drugs, the rise of victims' advocacy groups, economic interests), all of which illuminate this shocking phenomenon. However, only a few scholars (like Bernard Harcourt and Liat Ben-Moshe) have examined mass incarceration in light of the long U.S. tendency to incarcerate marginalized people. As I noted in chapter 2, Harcourt describes the extraordinary figure of 559,000 people in state mental hospitals in 1955. If we add to this figure other coercive institutions (juvenile facilities, forestry camps, etc.), we have an extraordinary level of coercion in the United States even before the advent of mass incarceration. As Harcourt notes, "simply put, when the data on mental hospitalization rates are combined with the data on prison rates for the years 1928 through 2000, the incarceration revolution of the late twentieth century barely reaches the level of aggregated institutionalization that the United States experienced at midcentury" (Harcourt 2006, 1754).[21] When thinking about jails and mental illness, we should locate this phenomenon in the United States' long and ugly history of incarcerating marginalized people. Only if we honestly confront this history will we be able to avoid simplistic responses to our current crisis in mental health care.

Reducing the Size of Jail Populations: The Pretrial Process

Jails will also continue to confront difficulties if they remain overcrowded. Overcrowding only magnifies problems with mental health, inmate and staff violence, and sanitation. As I already mentioned, many municipalities respond to overcrowding by expanding their jails (my home county, Brown County, is currently considering expanding its jail). However, expansion often just creates additional problems. We would be better off reducing the jail population rather than building new jails. One way to reduce jail populations would be to gradually replace the money bail system with a fairer and more rational pretrial process. A pretrial process aims at ensuring that people arrested return for trial or present no further threat to communities. The current money bail system fails miserably in achieving these goals. It often releases those who can afford bail, yet may still be a threat, while jailing tens of thousands of people who present no threat to the community.

Many U.S. counties lack pretrial services that might provide alternatives to incarceration in jail. In a 2011 study of pretrial risk assessment, Cynthia A. Mamalian estimated that "about 200 to 300 pretrial programs provide services to defendants across fewer than 1,000 of the 3,000 U.S. counties. Though there may be some core pretrial services beyond these programs, there is no information at the national level about the availability or lack of core pretrial services (i.e., interviewing and investigating defendants, assessing risks of pretrial misconduct, providing supervision of pretrial release conditions set by the court) in more than 2,000 counties in this country" (Mamalian 2011, 12). For a long time, counties have shown little interest in developing pretrial services or more sophisticated bail systems.

The District of Columbia and Money Bail

Recently, however, several large municipalities have seen the fiscal and moral folly of retaining expensive jails that house low-level offenders in abysmal conditions. Seeking change, they have looked to the example of the District of Columbia, which for many years had an overcrowded jail. Using diverse tools, D.C. officials reduced their jail population by keeping out low-level offenders. The city prohibits money bail, thus banishing the pernicious role of money from the pretrial process. A sophisticated Pretrial Services office guarantees legal counsel at pretrial hearings, prepares detailed risk assessments, and helps judges release offenders guilty of misdemeanors. It also uses drug and mental health courts as alternatives to jail, and exercises a range of supervision over pretrial defendants in lieu of incarceration. Some violent crimes automatically lead the accused to be detained in jail (Keenan 2015). Because of these policies, the District of Columbia releases 85 percent of its pretrial defendants. Of them, 88 percent return for trial and 89 percent avoid arrest again before their trial date (Keenan 2015).

The District of Columbia exercises strong social control over those it arrests, and its methods are not without ethical and political problems. It also enjoys the advantage of having federal dollars supporting its programs. It operates a jail system that is far smaller than those that exist in New York City, Chicago, and Los Angeles. I see its efforts as a short-term, imperfect response to problems in jail, but as preferable to jailing thousands of people.

Reforming the Bail System: Is Better Risk Assessment the Answer?

We see a similar kind of response in the contemporary trend toward improving pretrial risk assessment. Confronting the irrationality of the bail system, scholars, policy makers, judges, and politicians have begun embracing new pretrial risk-assessment tools. Social scientists developing them recognize that municipalities fear the prospect of releasing violent offenders. Consequently, before implementing risk-assessment tools, they conduct large studies to demonstrate their effectiveness. They then recommend that a municipality adapt instruments to local circumstances. They usually implement pilot programs before putting the risk-assessment tool into practice in a larger setting.

In this way, organizations like the Arnold Foundation, the Vera Institute, and the Pretrial Justice Institute work with municipalities to implement risk-assessment tools. They vary in their specific nature, but generally seek to replace money bail with an evidence-based risk-assessment mechanism. It focuses on aspects of a person's past that can predict if he will show up for trial or commit a violent crime. These include things like the nature of the charge, whether a defendant has warrants, his prior criminal record, his history of appearing before the court, whether he lives in a stable residence, and his family relations. Drawing on this information, researchers locate people into risk categories (low, moderate, high). Judges can then use these categories to release those who pose little flight risk or threat to the community, and jail those who are dangerous.[22]

One pretrial risk assessment called the Public Safety Assessment (PSA) has recently gained popularity. The Arnold Foundation promotes it, and numerous counties and several states have adopted it. The PSA considers nine factors about a defendant before she appears in bond court.[23] They include her current offense, pending charge, prior misdemeanor offenses, prior felony convictions, prior violent convictions, prior failure to appear pretrial in the past two years, prior failure to appear pretrial more than two years previous, prior sentences to incarceration, and age at current arrest (Arnold Foundation 2013). Using these criteria, pretrial authorities develop a composite score for the accused. They then forward it to judges, who use it and other factors to decide whether to release the person before trial.

Those promoting the PSA insist that it holds several advantages over other approaches to pretrial decision making. First, it is rigorous and evidence-based, grounded in extensive studies of thousands of defendants in several municipalities. Second, it can strongly predict whether someone poses a risk of flight or violence. Its predictive power far exceeds that of money bail, bail schedules based on offense type, or subjective judgments of prosecutors or judges. Third, the PSA doesn't consider criteria like family ties, income, race, or gender. Bail decisions have long been plagued by subjective judgments that are often racist or sexist (Harcourt 2007, 7–77). The PSA, its advocates say, avoids these controversial judgments. Finally, the PSA may significantly reduce jail populations. It doesn't necessarily require a personal interview with those arrested (although some states still require one). Pretrial authorities can easily verify information they gather about people. The PSA can also ease the fear judges have of releasing dangerous offenders into the community (Lowenkamp and VanNostrand 2013). For all these reasons, numerous municipalities and several states have adopted the PSA as their primary pretrial risk-assessment tool.

Dignity and Risk Assessment: Some Misgivings

The current emphasis on better pretrial risk assessment holds promise for reducing jail populations and for moving away from our current unjust and irrational money bail system. Pragmatically, it appeals to municipalities struggling with budget problems and looking for ways to reduce jail expenditures. It also appears hardheaded, promising to reduce both cost and risk. For these reasons, it seems like an attractive way out of our current money bail disaster.

Nevertheless, philosophically I have serious misgivings about the current focus on pretrial risk assessment. First, when I read documents from the Vera Institute, the Arnold Foundation, and the Pretrial Justice Institute, I find a remarkable confidence in "evidence-based" policy and "data." Degradation and torture have existed in U.S. jails since their inception. Punishment has unleashed passions and horrific violence. However, today's researchers confidently believe that if we only confront irrational people with evidence, we can change their evil ways. I discern little sense of unintended consequences, difficult choices, or human folly in the work of those who promote pretrial assessment.

Sadly, we have been here before, and those familiar with the history of American punishment should approach today's research cautiously. As David Rothman, Bernard Harcourt, Gerald Grob, and others have detailed, those with good intentions and statistics have often aspired to reorder our penal and mental health systems (Rothman 2002; Grob 1991; Harcourt 2007). Confronting its brutality and irrationality, they longed for and institutionalized "evidence-based" approaches to criminals and those with mental illness. However, in many cases they displayed scant self-criticism and showed little awareness of unintended consequences. Consequently, their projects frequently ended in failure, disaster, and hypocrisy. Nearly four decades ago, David J. Rothman wrote a reflective essay contrasting the Progressives and social policy in the 1960s (Rothman 1978). The Progressives, he wrote,

> did not pause to ask if the dependent had to be protected against their own well-meaning interventions. It was as if the benevolence of their motives together with their clear recognition of the wretchedness of lower-class social conditions guaranteed that ameliorative efforts would unambiguously benefit the poor. The problem, it now appears, is not only that Progressives could not accomplish their grand designs but that policies whose legitimacy rested on their promise to do good may actually have produced substantial harm. (Rothman 1978, 72)

Today's researchers possess better analytic tools, but display the same attitudes that created problems for their ancestors. Those of us who are aware of this history shouldn't condemn the recourse to evidence or data altogether. However, we can't share the unbridled confidence of researchers who uncritically promote "evidence-based" public policy.

In addition to excessive confidence in evidence, pretrial risk assessment researchers demonstrate scant interest in the life experiences of inmates. We hear little about how particular policies affect people's lives and instead learn about risks and cost. For example, pretrial authorities meet a person when she's in a difficult state of mind. She has been arrested and degraded, and may be utterly confused about what's happening to her. Pretrial authorities aren't lawyers, and yet they demand a great deal of information from people who often lack legal representation. The person, we hear, will be assured that authorities won't use this information against her at trial. Why, however, should anyone give detailed information without legal representation? How will authorities use this information, and how might it negatively affect someone's life? Most of us without knowledge of the court system would hesitate to answer questions from authorities. If we have financial means, we would make sure we had a lawyer present before providing any information to them. Why should things be any different for those who are poor? These questions about due process rarely appear in documents promoting "evidence-based" risk assessment.

Moreover, those promoting the PSA claim that it's neutral about race and class, but they are often uncritical about its criteria.[24] For example, the PSA assigns a score for past failures to appear at trial, but doesn't explore why people miss their trial dates. Some low-level offenders don't appear in court because they forget their dates. Others suffer from mental illness, and can't remember them at all. Still others are overwhelmed with family troubles or live hand to mouth. The PSA takes none of these matters into consideration, instead abstractly assigning a score for failure to appear for trial. This is particularly unfortunate because we can help people show up for their trial dates. Pretrial Services in the District of Columbia discovered that many people appear in court if they receive a phone call reminding them of their court date. D.C. authorities now send out reminders via text message, and have found success with this communication method.[25] Rather than resting content with the current system, they changed it with positive results.

Similarly, the PSA provides a score for misdemeanors, but asks no questions about why people are arrested. As I argued in chapter 2, many municipalities trap people in cycles of arrests and rearrests because they cannot afford to pay court fees or traffic tickets. Municipalities like Ferguson, Missouri, and New Orleans, Louisiana, have funded local government by repeatedly arresting African Americans for minor offenses, and then making them pay court fees. Many large cities employ some form of aggressive policing that nets many misdemeanor offenders. The PSA perpetuates this kind of system by assigning weight to misdemeanor arrests without exploring their context. It accepts the status quo rather than asking critical questions about it. It purports to address complex issues in our criminal justice system with purely technical solutions based on "evidence" and "data." Yet, such solutions always presuppose controversial background assumptions that aren't ethically neutral, and we should carefully examine them.[26]

A final reservation I have about pretrial risk assessment regards individual dignity. The PSA demonstrates a statistical correlation between past and future behavior. It may be useful for judges and prosecutors, but doesn't mean that I will behave in a specific way in the future. My individual circumstances, personality, and value should all come into play in a decision about my freedom. In a bond court, authorities consider whether to send me to an institution where I may be assaulted, raped, and forced to live in filth. While in jail, I may lose my job and home and face financial ruin. Why should society make an important decision about my life based on statistical correlations that may not apply to me individually? Those defending the PSA insist that it serves as only one tool that judges will use in deciding someone's fate. However, this is remarkably naïve; it is exactly the PSA's "evidence-based" character that makes it so attractive to overworked judges and prosecutors. In fact, those proposing the PSA accentuate its "objective" character when they promote it to municipalities. Numbers and evidence hold a peculiar fascination for many people today. Once a municipality adopts a pretrial assessment tool, busy judges and prosecutors will rely heavily on it if they think it is scientific and objective.

In sum, the current emphasis on greater precision in pretrial risk assessment may reduce jail populations. Even with its flaws, it is an improvement over putting someone through a brutal jail system. However, too often those proposing it display excessive confidence in technical rationality and ignore how risk assessment threatens individual dignity. As theologian Reinhold Niebuhr wrote in the 1930s, they make the error of believing that "with a little more time, a little more adequate moral and social pedagogy and a generally higher development of human intelligence, our problems will approach solution" (Niebuhr 1960, xiii). Sadly, our penal history gives us little reason to affirm such an idea.

Bail and the Right to Counsel

Realistically, despite its ethical flaws, jurisdictions will likely use risk assessment because it seems like a scientific way to control fear and risk. However, rather than focusing excessively on it, perhaps we should work harder to ensure that all defendants have legal representation at a bond hearing. In many municipalities, those without resources face the judge and prosecutor alone. They confront an asymmetry of knowledge and power in situations that can decide their future decisively. One side knows all the legal terms and the consequences of different courses of actions. The other may understand little about the proceedings, may misunderstand the consequences of future decisions, and may be confused and frightened.

This knowledge and power disparity has dire consequences for many people. Generally, "defendants appearing alone before a judicial officer lack the knowledge and skill to identify the statutory factors that would be persuasive in arguing for pretrial release on personal recognizance or an affordable money bail" (Constitution Project 2015, 27). Those without representation and knowledge cannot challenge controversial judgments about risk assessment. They may be unaware that the state is using past information it shouldn't use. Finally, without a lawyer people often don't know that in lieu of incarceration, they could be on electronic monitoring or other supervision.[27] Consequently, they end up languishing in jail while awaiting trial.

For most of the past century, those entering bond hearings faced a murky legal situation if they demanded a right to counsel. Legal scholars debate whether late twentieth-century Supreme Court cases established this right. However, this seemed to change in 2007 in a case involving a Texas man named Walter Rothgery.[28] He was arrested on a felony charge of firearms possession. The police arrested him based on erroneous information about his actions in another state, but he was brought before a judge. Rothgery asked for a lawyer but wasn't afforded one, was assigned a bond he couldn't pay, and was jailed for six months. Once he received court-appointed counsel, his attorney prepared his case and renegotiated bail, and Rothgery was released. The lawyer discovered the erroneous information in his case, and all charges against Rothgery were dropped. He then sued the state of Texas for civil rights violations.

Rothgery's case made its way to the Supreme Court. The Court ruled that Rothgery had a right to counsel at his bond hearing. Its majority maintained that a "criminal defendant's initial appearance before a magistrate judge, where he learns the charge against him and his liberty is subject to restriction, marks the initiation of adversary judicial proceedings that trigger attachment of the Sixth Amendment right to counsel."[29] This ruling seems to recognize that someone's legal right to counsel begins at a bond hearing when his liberty is at stake.

The *Rothgery* case prompted some states and municipalities to alter their approach to pretrial hearings. However, generally people arrested in the United States still lack adequate legal representation at bail hearings. In a 2015 report, the nonprofit Constitution Project noted,

> While *Rothgery* persuaded considerably more states and localities to guarantee legal representation, today's public defenders and assigned lawyers still remain missing from first bail hearings in numerous state courts. Lawyers are never present at the first bail hearing in eight states, while defenders appear infrequently or in token jurisdictions in 17 states. In 11 other states, a poor person stands a 50% or better chance of obtaining an assigned lawyer's representation, depending upon where the arrest occurred. In these hybrid states, however, unrepresented defendants still appear alone at "freedom hearings" conducted in many counties where counsel is not present. (Constitution Project 2015, 24)

In our "constitutional system of checks and balances, the criminal defense lawyer assumes the essential role of curbing judicial officers' and prosecutors' improper use of bail to keep an accused person in jail until trial or final disposition" (Constitution Project 2015, 30). However, too often those without resources are defenseless against the state's power, and end up incarcerated because of their poverty.

When prosecutors and judges face opposition to their action, we have some check on their power. Good legal advocates force authorities to justify their decisions to incarcerate people because of bail amounts they cannot afford. Good lawyers can demand that judges and prosecutors keep people out of violent and abusive jails. They can try to block municipalities from using poor people as sources of revenue. Good lawyers may also contest the many court fees and fines that authorities levy on unsuspecting defendants. Most importantly, good legal representation can draw attention to the dignity of the individual by focusing on the details of a case. This can go a long way toward preventing people from being treated like an anonymous mass that must be managed. For all these reasons, I think those seeking to reduce jail populations should advocate for better access to good legal counsel.

Structures and Inner Change

I have identified specific ways jails can prevent abuse against inmates and made suggestions for reducing jail populations. I have not offered an exhaustive set of proposals; others would include reducing the power of prosecutors and changing police practices that result in too many arrests of low-level offenders.[30] In general, however, what we need are structures that provide defendants and their advocates with the power to counter abuses. The structural changes I recommend minimally protect the dignity of inmates. In the next chapter, I will relate them to debates about the long-term future of the jail. However, by itself, policy change often cannot alter the disgust, contempt, and fear people experience in relation to inmates. Legal and penal authorities can go along with policies without changing their affective responses toward inmates. They may still view them as animals or scum and respond to them with disgust and contempt. Notoriously, corrections officers often resist policy changes or sullenly go along with them out of self-interest. Even when policies change, people continue to make bad choices and retain negative affective responses.

A more serious problem confronts us if we think about whether we can control our affective responses. Can we really change our disgust, contempt, and fear? In most of us, the origins of disgust are mysterious, linked to biological and cultural realities about which we remain largely ignorant. If swarms of insects disgust us, we can't will to alter our response. Disgust has a powerful immediacy that we often can't control. We can say the same of contempt. Gradually, it seems to develop through choices and interactions with others. We may inherit attitudes of contempt toward kinds of people, or develop new ones as we join a group. For example, I have known young corrections officers who developed contempt for inmates. They adopted it from more experienced officers, and I noticed how it gradually deepened as they remained on the job. To me, it didn't seem like they woke up one day, and decided to have contempt for inmates. Finally, fear seems the least amenable to our voluntary control. It often takes control of us suddenly. It would be absurd for me to command myself to "experience fear now." If I am healthy, I can raise my hand at will, but I can't command myself to feel fear.

In sum, we generally lack direct voluntary control over affective responses. We cannot will that disgust, contempt, and fear appear directly. We also can't will some causal sequence that will guarantee that they immediately come into existence (von Hildebrand 1953, 215, 314). Through my will alone, I can't light a fire, but can light a match to wood so it will appear. This doesn't seem to be true of many of our affective responses. The causal sequences I initiate have a more tenuous relationship to my disgust, contempt, and fear. If this is true, we seem incapable of changing our perception of the value of others. If homeless people wandering our streets disgust us, we seem doomed to devalue them. This incapacity to exert direct control over affective responses accounts in part for why some scholars dismiss their ethical significance. Ethics seems to concern what we can directly will and what we can control.

The Importance of Indirect Freedom

Dismissing affective responses from ethical evaluation entirely, however, comports ill with our common attitudes toward them. Suppose I know someone is wrongly convicted, but nevertheless take joy in his suffering. People would naturally criticize me for this response. Similarly, if someone says interracial marriages disgust him, we would fault him for this response. Finally, someone who repeatedly exhibits contempt for those with disabilities would be worthy of moral condemnation. In all these cases, we attach ethical significance to affective responses. We also presuppose that people retain some degree of freedom over them.

We are justified in this presupposition because we *do* possess some freedom in relation to affective responses. We can respond freely but *indirectly* to them in many ways. We can "turn away from them, we can struggle against them with our will, we can try not to think of the object which has motivated them, and so on" (von Hildebrand 1953, 336). These acts vary in how they influence affective responses. Perhaps they will continue to arise but we will become habituated to them less, or perhaps they will arise less often. Free choices interact with affective responses in complex psychological ways that vary from person to person. For example, medical professionals often freely choose to relate differently to objects of disgust or fear. I teach nurses who initially feared dead bodies, but chose diverse techniques to relate to them differently. Some also found human feces revolting, but learned to deal with their discomfort with patients who need help using the bathroom. Some of these nurses continued to experience disgust or fear, but learned to control their responses. Others gradually altered these negative responses so that the issue arose less frequently. These examples illustrate how free choices can indirectly influence affective responses.

Indirectly, we can make other free choices to counter the moral blindness engendered by disgust, contempt, and fear. Suppose we experience disgust, contempt, or fear when meeting an inmate. We feel guilty about these responses, but they continue to arise, shaping our interaction with people. In these cases, we can exercise what von Hildebrand calls "cooperative freedom" toward our affective responses. We can "take a position toward them which greatly modifies the character of the experience and which can also be of great moral significance in itself" (von Hildebrand 1953, 316). When we encounter an inmate, we may have some vague sense of his value despite our difficulties in perceiving it because of disgust, fear, or contempt. We can then choose to take different stances toward this value. We can "abandon ourselves to this experience, we can open our soul in its very depth, we can expose our soul to the action of the value" (von Hildebrand 1953, 317). These stances will have different consequences depending on the circumstances and the people involved in the encounter.

A final and more profound stance I can freely adopt toward negative affective responses involves sanction or disavowal. The objects that elicit disgust or fear in me are deeply contingent; I don't choose them, and may not understand their complex biological and psychological causality. However, no matter their causal origins, I can embrace or refuse to identify with aspects of my character or affective makeup. For example, I might find myself unable to control my fear of formerly incarcerated people, and worry that it will influence how I hire people. I know that a blanket policy of fearing and discriminating against them is wrong, but cannot seem to eliminate my fear. Nevertheless, I can disavow it, denying that it constitutes a valid affective response (von Hildebrand 1953, 322). When I disavow fear, I resist it even if it remains somehow a part of me. In contrast, when we sanction an affective response, we go along with its presence. As von Hildebrand puts it, "not to actualize our freedom by disavowing a morally negative response suffices to make us to a certain extant responsible for its moral ugliness. In other words, the undisputed solidarity with this response suffices to stain us morally" (von Hildebrand 1953, 333). The capacity to sanction or disavow affective responses constitutes one of the deepest elements of our freedom. Difficult to understand and exercise, it nevertheless remains of central importance for those struggling to value the human person properly.

Concluding Thoughts: Changing Structures and Value Perception

In my years teaching in prisons and jails, I have a spent a lot of time talking to corrections officers. Sometimes I meet veteran officers who work hard to respect the dignity of inmates. They avoid the hotheaded behavior of some of their younger colleagues, and know how to deescalate dicey situations before they turn violent. They give orders and expect inmates to follow them, yet speak respectfully to them. They also strive to treat inmates fairly. Finally, they show a deep understanding of the troubles inmates encounter, and recognize the broken and unjust character of our penal system.

These officers model positive behaviors for new officers coming into the jail and prison system. In talking to them, I notice how they are often self-conscious about how their job affects them. They work in an environment of constant distrust, and know that this toxic atmosphere impacts them personally. They acknowledge that negative emotions can blind them to the dignity of the inmates. Some officers reach a point where their work has taken too great a moral and personal toll, and they leave corrections altogether.

The time I have interacted with these officers has convinced me of the importance of both structural change and individual free choices. Structural changes mitigate the violence, abuse, and degradation that jails engender. They force penal authorities, politicians, and society to minimally respect human dignity when they are inclined to disrespect it. Structural changes also support those who want to do a difficult job in a professional way that respects human dignity.

My encounters with conscientious corrections officers have convinced me of the significance of free choices in jails and prisons. Officers are not determined to act in specific ways by institutional structures.

Daily, they make decisions to relate to inmates positively. These choices depend only partially on the character and culture of the institution. Group pressures, horrible conditions, job insecurity, and other factors constrain choices in penal settings. However, ordinary people also make free choices about human dignity in difficult circumstances. Some refuse to sanction the disgust, contempt, and fear that pervade our jails. These important choices are of deep ethical significance, and make a difference in the lives on inmates. Whether they can bring about long-term change is an entirely different question.

Conclusion

Can We Reform the Jail?

Of course, prisons and penal servitude do not reform the criminal; they only punish him and protect society from further attacks on its security. In the criminal, prison and the severest hard labor only develop hatred, lust for forbidden pleasures and a fearful levity.
—Fyodor Dostoyevsky, *House of the Dead*[1]

Mass incarceration has become a popular topic among contemporary scholars and pundits. We are becoming aware of the terrible consequences of our decision to incarcerate millions of people over the past few decades. We are also beginning to back away from some of the disastrous policies we have adopted in our penal and legal system. We are also learning more about the racial discrimination that pervades our criminal justice system. This growing awareness of mass incarceration's deleterious consequences marks a welcome departure from decades of draconian punishment.

Unfortunately, the discussion of imprisonment sometimes takes simplistic turns, ignoring the true challenges of reversing the damage of irrational and violent policies. Pundits blame one political party or the other for the rise of our massive prison complex. Or activists harken back to a golden age of rehabilitation in punishment, ignoring the long history of racism and torture in American penal and mental institutions. Some scholars write insightfully about race and the New Jim Crow, but show little understanding of how the United States has long incarcerated marginalized people in mental hospitals and other coercive institutions. We also have younger scholars who thoughtfully explore how modern liberalism helped produce mass incarceration. However, they often self-righteously condemn the difficult choices of their ancestors. They confidently believe they can reverse our current folly by dismantling penal institutions and constructing new political structures.[2] Finally (as I have already noted in this book), we have an army of social scientists who think the answer to the ills in our jails and prisons is to employ more "evidence-based" public policy. Ignoring the long history of failed attempts at this enterprise, they completely disregard the power of ugly emotions in public life.

In this conclusion, I reflect on the long-term future of the American jail. I first summarize the argument I have made in this book. If we care about human dignity, we cannot see the contemporary jail as a morally legitimate institution. Second, I explore the long-term prospects of reforming the jail. To illustrate one example of reform, I return to the Cook County Jail, noting important changes it has made to address staff violence and mental health issues. Third, however, I express skepticism that reform efforts can create jails that respect human dignity. Reforms are often precarious, and the long history of abuse in U.S. coercive institutions provides little reason to believe that future jails will justly punish. Moreover, caging people often elicits the negative affective responses I have discussed in this book. Fourth, I turn to a more radical approach to the jail that declares it unreformable, and seeks to substantially diminish its power. After discussing contemporary debates about "abolitionism," I hold that we will need coercive institutions to deal with some violent people, but maintain that they are unlikely to do so unjustly. I then describe what it would mean to take a more radical stance toward the jail. It would require different approaches to criminalization and preventative justice, and a greater awareness of the dangers of alternatives to jails. I end by showing how a more radical critique of the jail helps focus on ethical concerns. I maintain that no change in our approach to the jail will succeed without an inward change in our perception of human dignity.

Taking Stock: The Jail and Human Dignity

It is time to take stock of this book's argument, and to consider the contemporary jail's moral legitimacy. I want to emphasize again that in raising this question, I am not indicting all those who work in jails or claiming that all jails are similarly unjust. Instead, I am asking a systemic question about the jail as an institution. Individual jails may perform specific tasks better than others, but they all confront similar problems that raise questions about the jail's moral legitimacy.

Let's begin with inmate-on-inmate and staff violence. As I have noted throughout this book, most inmates in jails are *legally innocent*; they have yet to be convicted of any crime. However, in many jails we expose them to a high risk of violence. Large urban jails in the United States process an extraordinary number of inmates annually. Recall that the "largest jails (those with an average daily population (ADP) of 1,000 or more inmates) held 48% of the inmate population at midyear 2013, but accounted for 6% of all jail jurisdictions nationwide" (Minton and Goloinelli 2014, 2). However, in many of them, inmates face the possibility of assault by inmates or staff members. Jails in cities like Miami, Dallas, Houston, Cincinnati, San Francisco, Philadelphia, St. Louis, and Baltimore would be considered unsafe by any standard.

In fact, politicians, citizens, law enforcement officers, and judges often concede that jails are dangerous places. For example, when she dismissed the MacArthur Center's 2014 motion for a preliminary injunction against the Cook County Jail, Judge Virginia Kendall remarked that penal experts recognize that "even the best run jails have incidents of violence."[3] Legally, U.S. judges like Kendall cannot sanction jails for the mere existence of violence. Instead, they operate within a legal architecture requiring them to determine if penal authorities act with "deliberate indifference." However, ethically, statements like Judge Kendall's should give us all pause. Why should someone who is legally innocent be exposed to *any* risk of violence in a jail? Why should we accept the idea that even the best-run jails will be violent? Our tolerance for such violence is extraordinarily high and often goes unquestioned.

This is particularly problematic when we think about sexual assault. I have detailed an exceptionally high level of sexual assault in our jail system. Jails are not supposed to be places of punishment for those awaiting trial, yet many people find themselves raped by inmates or staff. More importantly, rape is a morally indefensible act, and we shouldn't approve it as a punishment for anyone. Jails often lack the staff necessary to prevent sexual assault, but this neglect can't justify exposing people to the risk of it. It certainly can't excuse allowing tens of thousands of people to suffer its horrors.

In this book, I have also drawn attention to the terrible problem of mental illness in our jails. Jails are ill-equipped to help people suffering from it. Nevertheless, they must deal with tens of thousands of people who need mental health care. Some jails do a minimally competent job, but find themselves confronting problems they cannot address. Many others fail miserably in their responsibilities to help inmates. They provide inadequate medications, keep poor medical records, and offer no access to competent medical staff. Consequently, those with mental illness suffer and their conditions worsen. They face violence from inmates and staff, and commit suicide at an alarming rate. Any society that cares about dignity should find this situation horrifying.

I have also detailed how jails contain hundreds of thousands of low-level offenders who simply cannot afford bail. They present no serious threat to the community, and if they possessed greater financial resources, they wouldn't be jailed. This system has operated for decades, but in past twenty years it has expanded, with bail amounts and bail requirements growing. Additionally, those who are jailed are often trapped by demands that they pay various fees. They can be billed for the time they were incarcerated, forced to pay money to private probation companies, and charged numerous court fees. While incarcerated, many inmates lose their jobs, and have difficulty supporting their families. For those with few financial resources, the jail system is a financial nightmare from which it is difficult to awaken.

Finally, jails degrade their inhabitants in multiple ways. As Irwin showed decades ago, jails do more than simply detain people. They search them intrusively, demand their obedience to authorities, and demean them. The physical environment of many jails sends an unambiguous message to people: they are inferior beings who deserve to be debased. Jail incarceration constitutes an attack on someone's identity, an attempt to render her an obedient occupant of a controlling institution.

An ethic of dignity emphasizes the person's self-transcendence, inner life, and individuality. It draws attention to how institutions treat people merely as things, and neglect their individual value. These dimensions of ethics reveal the grave injustice of the contemporary jail. Officially, it exists to contain dangerous people or those who won't show up for trial, but it performs even this task in ways that denigrate human dignity. More significantly, unofficially, it controls the lives of hundreds of thousands of people who present neither a flight risk nor a danger to others. If we judge an institution by how it enhances human dignity, we can only conclude that the contemporary jail fails miserably.

Prospects for Reform

One natural response to this ethical critique is to seek reforms that will make the jail a more just institution. In this book, I have made specific suggestions for improving jail conditions and respecting the dignity of jail inmates. If enacted, they would reduce jail populations and respond to immediate dangers to inmates. The larger question, however, is the end to which these initiatives aim. For some critics of jails, such policies aim at making the jail more humane while enhancing public safety. For example, many nonprofit organizations support bail reform and changes in juvenile justice. They do important research, focusing particularly on the grossly inefficient and expensive character of jails and prisons. They also enter policy debates at the state and federal levels, seeking to make significant reforms to the jail.[4]

These efforts can produce positive results. For example, I have emphasized the need for bail reform, and several nonprofit organizations have led the way in changing our broken bail system. Throughout the United States, municipalities have adopted new bail reform measures that have positively changed how jails process inmates. For example, in 2017, New Jersey took the extraordinary step of eliminating money bail. In its place, the state adopted the Public Safety Assessment (PSA), passed a speedy-trial provision, and developed ways to monitor those charged with crimes without incarcerating them The New Jersey bail reform will hopefully prevent thousands of people from languishing in jails simply because of their poverty (see "N.J. Will Eliminate Cash Bail" 2016).

Returning to Cook County

We see a similar promise of reform at the Cook County Jail. Since 2010, the state of Illinois has faced deep financial problems. It has made massive cuts to expenditures for public and social services. It has confronted budget crises, only to resolve them at the last moment. Republicans and

Democrats in the State House, and legislators and the governor have repeatedly clashed over fiscal issues. Budget battles have created an unstable environment, rendering it difficult to make positive changes in mental health care and corrections ("Tribune Coverage: Illinois Budget" 2017).

Despite these challenges, Cook County officials have made improvements to the Cook County Jail since the 2010 DOJ Consent Decree. The jail remains a horrible, violent place that treats people in degrading ways and houses thousands of people with mental illness. However, Sheriff Thomas J. Dart and others have worked within the byzantine bureaucracy to bring about structural changes. As I mentioned in chapter 5, in 2014 the Illinois Supreme Court issued a scathing report about the failures of Cook County's Pretrial Services. It exposed dysfunction at multiple levels, and recommended forty major changes. They included technical and administrative changes, including adopting a more accurate risk-assessment tool. Chief Cook County Circuit Judge Timothy J. Evans adopted all these recommendations (Illinois Bar Association 2014). For example, on a pilot basis Cook County adopted the PSA as its new risk-assessment tool. In 2017, Judge Evans also issued an order requiring that Bond Court authorities consider a person's ability to pay a bond (Evans 2017). Given the long history of difficulties in Pretrial Services in Cook County, conditions for those arrested are unlikely to get better overnight. However, with the new structure, I hope Pretrial Services will improve.

More promising, Sheriff Dart has made changes in and outside of the jail. Working with others, he supported the passage of the 2015 Accelerated Resolution Court Act (Illinois General Assembly 2015), which established a pilot program that seeks to reduce the number of minor property offenders residing in the Cook County Jail. Those charged with these crimes who meet certain conditions and cannot afford bail can qualify for this program. If the courts fail to hear their cases within thirty days, they will be released on their own recognizance or with supervision. The Accelerated Resolution Court Act, combined with Judge Evans's bail reforms, will mean that many low-level offenders will be spared the fate of long-term confinement. However, these steps remain flawed ways of addressing the presence of alleged offenders within the Cook County Jail. Like the District of Columbia, Cook County should find ways to keep low-level offenders out of the jail altogether. However, it has long had trouble with its electronic monitoring program, police practices, and social services outside the jail. It also lacks many of the supervisory services for offenders that exist in the District of Columbia. Hopefully, the steps Cook County is taking will habituate political actors and the public to keeping low-level offenders out of jail.

Within the jail, Sheriff Dart has worked to comply with the 2010 DOJ Consent Agreement. Cook County Jail remains a place marked by both staff and inmate violence. However, Sheriff Dart has taken steps to hold corrections officers responsible for abusing inmates. In accordance with the DOJ Consent Agreement, the DOJ and Cook County adopted an official monitor to oversee use-of-force policies. They agreed on measures to reduce staff violence toward inmates (U.S. Department of Justice, Civil Rights Division 2010, A, 31). These include defining excessive force, prohibiting the use of force to retaliate against inmates, and properly reporting use-of-force incidents. Finally, the Consent Decree requires that the Cook County Jail install cameras so that authorities can review use-of-force incidents.

In the 2015 monitor report, the federal monitor found that the Cook County Jail was in "substantial agreement" with the Consent Agreement's use-of-force provisions. This is equivalent to the highest grade a monitor can accord a jail. In the interest of transparency, Sheriff Dart has also made public videos of violent encounters between officers and inmates and transcripts of disciplinary hearings. The Cook County Jail is an enormous institution, and abusive officers can find ways to evade monitoring. However, authorities at Cook County have developed procedures for preventing some of the terrible abuse that has characterized the jail's history.

Sheriff Dart has also tried to address the mental health care crisis at Cook County. In 2015, he appointed a psychologist, Dr. Nneka Jones Tapia, as executive director of the jail. Director Jones Tapia is one of the few psychologists to serve as director of a large urban jail. Her appointment signaled Cook County's commitment to dealing with mental health issues. Sheriff Dart has also ensured that all inmates receive intake mental health screenings from competent authorities. Most of those suffering from mental illness now get treatment in the Residential Treatment Unit (RTU). As I noted in chapter 1, we will need to wait some time before evaluating the RTU's successes in improving mental health care. However, it represents an attempt to address the crisis of mental illness in the jail.

The jail still confronts a shortage of psychiatric and psychological staff. Recall that Cook County operates with a dual chain of command. It has the sheriff's office and Cermak hospital, which provides medical care for inmates. In 2015, the federal monitor indicated concern about the shortage of mental health staff, a problem that has plagued the Cook County Jail (and many other jails) for years. She noted that "mental health staffing continues to fall short of the needs of the jail's inmate population. As noted by the psychiatric monitor, the Cermak mental health staff in place are doing the best they can. However, Cermak's inability to hire and retain mental health staff, in my opinion, negatively impacts the safety of inmates and staff" (U.S. District Court for Illinois 2015, v). The shortage of psychiatrists in corrections continues to create problems for the Cook County Jail.

Two other developments at Cook County are worth noting. Since the passage of the Affordable Care Act (2010), the jail has been able to sign inmates up for Medicaid if they qualify. Cook County ensures that all those who are eligible can enroll in Illinois's CountyCare, which provides health insurance under Medicaid. This can benefit inmates who need medication, particularly those who require it to treat mental illnesses. The jail has enrolled many people in CountyCare who lacked health insurance when they entered the jail.

Sheriff Dart and Director Jones Tapia have also tried to help inmates exiting the jail who need mental health care. Many receive only a limited supply of medication and have nowhere to turn for treatment. Cook County created the Mental Health Transition Center, which helps inmates transition out of the jail. It provides therapy and job counseling, and helps inmates plan what they will do when they are released. Inmates spend time in the center before leaving the jail. As of the writing of the book, a small number of inmates participate in this program, and Cook County has yet to study its effectiveness. Additionally, the closing of public mental health clinics in Chicago has created significant problems for those exiting the Cook County Jail. However, through their efforts, authorities have sought to address the mental health crisis at the Cook County Jail.

In 2017, Judge Kendall determined that the Cook County Jail had met the terms of the 2010 Consent Decree. For the first time in forty years, it would no longer be under federal supervision ("County Jail Exits Federal Oversight of 40 Years" 2017). Judge Kendall held that Cermak Health Services had yet to meet all the Consent Decree's requirements, but praised Sheriff Dart for his work. The Cook County Jail remains a dangerous place that incarcerates thousands of people who need mental health care. Without addressing this need, problems at the jail will persist. However, under DOJ monitoring and with good leadership at the top, it has taken steps to mitigate some of the horrors that have plagued it for decades.

History and the Precarious Nature of Reform

The recent changes at Cook County are positive, but whether they endure depends on local circumstances, good leadership, and other factors. The gains at the jail can easily disappear. Circumstances such as the high murder rate in Chicago, public responses to crime, and leadership changes in corrections can bring the Cook County Jail back to previous practices. Additionally, the United States has recently undergone a change in presidential leadership that may herald big shifts in federal policies. For example, the Medicaid program may undergo significant changes, which could affect how Cook County can help inmates who need mental health care.[5] People could lose access to mental health care, leading to more jail admissions for those with mental illness. Additionally, the Civil Rights Division in the Justice Department may lose some of its power to investigate jails and prisons. Members of the Trump administration have expressed skepticism about the value of civil rights investigations of police departments and penal institutions (see Bazelon 2017). Without the watchful eye of the Justice Department, conditions in jails that have recently completed Consent Decrees could deteriorate. Finally, significant federal budget cuts could put additional strains on state budgets, stifling attempts to positively change jails. Such contingent factors can easily undermine reforms at a place like the Cook County Jail.

Sadly, the history of the jail in the United States provides reasons for deep skepticism about the durability of reform in U.S. jails. John Irwin was a sociologist rather than a historian, but in his famous study of the jail he briefly described its history (Irwin 1985/2013, 1–18). He held that from its inception, the jail served the function of controlling marginalized people. Although historical scholarship on jails remains thin compared to that of the prison, what we have tends to support Irwin's musings. In many cases, we find a depressing tale of brutality and inhumanity. Attempts at reform come and go, but often jails fail to achieve their humane aspirations.

Let's consider an earlier period at the Cook County Jail as an example of an attempt to reform the jail. In 1922, the Chicago Community Trust, a philanthropic organization, issued a report on the jail. At that time, the county was considering expanding it. It asked a group of experts connected with the Chicago Community Trust to inspect the jail and issue a report (a summary of the report is available today). The authors condemned the Cook County Jail as a place of punishment rather than detention before trial. It held three to five people in cells built for one, and mixed juveniles and adults, hardened and first-time offenders. Incoming inmates received only "perfunctory" medical examinations, and the jail housed inmates with contagious and other dangerous diseases (Chicago Community Trust 1922, 10). Inmates received little or no medical care, and the institution was filthy and teeming with rodents and insects.

In eloquent language, the report also condemned the absurd bail system that imprisoned low-level offenders. The money bail system, it held, "works to the advantage of professional crooks and against the poor" (Chicago Community Trust 1922, 27). It incarcerated large numbers of people who couldn't afford bail, and who shouldn't have been jailed in the first place. According to the report, 75 percent of the inmates in the jail were eventually released without being convicted. It concluded that they were likely detained without sufficient evidence, but because of their indigence, they endured the hell of the Cook County Jail.

Although the Chicago Community Trust report painted a grim picture of the Cook County Jail, it also confidently predicted that jail conditions could change. The distinguished criminologists and social scientists who authored the report believed they lived in a new era of science and progress. The jail's problems existed because of ignorant public officials, brutal penal authorities, and an apathetic public. However, the authors noted that "at last the scientific method which has revolutionized our hospitals and asylums is making inroads and Chicago will doubtless join the procession" (Chicago Community Trust 1922, 19). With proper expert guidance, Chicago could overcome the evils that plagued its penal system.

Sadly, the report's vision of a better jail never materialized. Six years after the report came out (1928), Cook County expanded its jail. It soon filled up, and became a house of horrors for decades. Reading the 1922 report, several points stand out to me. At one level, it is remarkable that similar problems have plagued the jail for decades. At another level, it is deeply depressing that people of good will recognized them, yet the problems failed to disappear. I also note the extraordinary confidence in science and progress that we find among some of today's prison and jail reformers. We have the same appeal to "evidence" and "statistics," although today they take more sophisticated forms. I hasten to add that I don't condemn the recourse to social science at all, but am instead wary of the excessive confidence that by itself science can overcome deep social problems. Like the men and women in the 1920s, today's critics of jails and prisons often believe they are on the right side of history. For them, rather than moral problems involving human dignity, the emotions, and the will, prison reform is a technical matter we can address with better data.

The Chicago Community Trust document also illustrates Irwin's thesis about the jail. The Cook County Jail in the early part of the twentieth century held dangerous people who threatened the community and presented a flight risk. However, it also controlled large numbers of young men and a small number of women arrested by the police for minor charges. Police authorities would arrest hundreds of people for minor theft, disturbing the peace, drunkenness, or prostitution. They would be held in the Cook County Jail, only to be released after charges were dropped. On this score, Chicago in the early part of the twentieth century seems no different than New York City today, which jails thousands of people on misdemeanor charges. Contemporary cities use policing techniques and statistics to track and mark people for effective social control. Today, the very tools the Chicago Community Trust reformers linked to positive change have instead been adopted to dominate people more effectively.

If we look at other points in U.S. history, we find similar instances when communities used jails to contain those they considered marginalized or undesirable. Historians have explored the famous Tombs jails in New York City, and found a history of neglect, abuse, and degradation. They have also examined jails in small towns in the nineteenth-century American West, detailing how they contained inmates in horrific conditions.[6] Recently, scholars have begun doing work on the history of jails in bigger cities in the West. For example, Kelly Lytle Hernàndez has written about how the Los Angeles Jail responded to an influx of white male "hobos" in the late nineteenth century and the early part of the twentieth. Gripped by a fear of hobos, the city saw a huge surge in its jail population. Police aggressively arrested and jailed vagrants and others whom people perceived as threats to the social order. Hernàndez notes that in 1904, over 60 percent of jail commitments nationwide were for "arrests on public order charges, led by public drunkenness, disorderly conduct, and vagrancy" (Hernàndez 2014, 423).[7] Los Angeles built new jails, which were continually overcrowded. If convicted of a misdemeanor, inmates would remain in the jail and be forced to labor on chain gangs in a brutal regime supported by physical punishment. Hernàndez details how these chain gangs worked on projects throughout the city of Los Angeles.

In sum, historians who have begun excavating the jail's history in the United States have found that jails rarely held only dangerous people or those unlikely to show up for trial. Instead, scholars have identified loci of punishment, where counties and municipalities contained and controlled those they considered offensive or disturbing.

The Case for Abolition

Generally, if an institution has a long history of failure in its stated purpose, we seek to develop alternatives to it. A minority of thinkers take this position about the jail and prison, calling for its gradual elimination. They often adopt the term "abolitionism" to describe their position. Before the advent of modern mass incarceration, movements for abolitionism lived and died in the late 1960s and early 1970s. With the failure of our current system, they have reemerged. Today's abolitionists insist that any attempt to ameliorate conditions for inmates is a morally bankrupt enterprise. Some speak vaguely of a "revolution" that will dismantle our current penal system (Alexander 2016). Others propose replacing jails with practices like restorative justice that bring together offender and victim to repair the harm of a crime (Schept 2015).[8] Still other abolitionists present critiques of the jail and prison that call for their gradual abolition. They differ on tactics and ultimate goals, often disagreeing about the nature and scope of change needed in political and social institutions. They also endorse diverse philosophical positions. Some argue that we can't justify punishment at all while others reject this idea.[9] In whatever form it takes, jail abolitionism sees the jail as an entirely illegitimate institution that should have no place in a just society.

To many Americans, the idea of abolishing the jail seems self-evidently absurd. This institution plays such a vital role in our society that we can't imagine doing away with it. However, the jail isn't an immutable feature of the social order, and hasn't in fact existed in many societies. It also doesn't exist in many parts of the world today. Past societies punished people through mediation, nonviolent conflict resolution, reparations, banishment, flogging, mutilation, crucifixion, and a variety of other means. Historically, punishment has often been local. Parents, employers, and military officers were empowered to administer punishments to both children and adults. In the United States before the advent of jails in western states, communities used lynching to punish those they considered lawbreakers or undesirables. A cursory look at the history of punishment reveals that the jail has been only one among many means of dealing with those who contravene social or legal norms. We can certainly consider whether it's worth retaining.[10]

The idea of abolishing jails cannot mean that we immediately eliminate them without finding alternative modes of dealing with crimes. Nor can it mean that we ignore the real need to deal with violent people whom society needs to contain. Instead, in its most sophisticated forms, abolitionism applied to the jail would begin with the conviction that in the United States, we are unlikely to bridge the gap between the jail's official and unofficial purposes. If this is true, then the jail will remain a fundamentally unjust institution no matter how many reforms we institute. Given the historical failures of the jail to perform its official purpose, we have little reason to believe that our generation will succeed in reform when others failed.

Jail reformers often respond to such arguments by pointing to other countries (particularly Scandinavian countries) to draw inspiration for their reform efforts. In these countries, they hold, penal institutions succeed in confining human beings while respecting their dignity. If we just copy them and work harder, the reformers maintain, we can make our jails and prisons into just institutions. We are more progressive than our ancestors were, and possess technical skills they lacked, and all we need is greater expertise, education, knowledge, and will.[11]

However, such an ahistorical approach ignores our violent history toward those who are marginalized.[12] We can certainly learn from other penal systems to make positive changes in how we treat inmates.[13] However, we bear a burden of history and memory that differs from that of the Netherlands, Denmark, or Norway. Our history of slavery, Jim Crow, abusive mental institutions, and violent prisons differs from those of many European countries. Historians of the jail and prison have long discussed the context and impetus for the development of penal and mental institutions in the United States. They have debated whether religious, economic, humanitarian, or other motivations moved people in the eighteenth and nineteenth centuries to construct coercive institutions.[14]

However, whatever the motivations of their architects, the structures they built were inhumane. Early jails were often dumping grounds where people waited to enter terrible prisons. Guards at the famous Auburn and Sing Sing prisons in nineteenth-century New York flogged and tortured inmates into submission. At Auburn, authorities enforced a regime of inmate silence with the lash and water torture. The Auburn model for discipline became a popular one in the United States, and remained powerful for decades. Scandals often led to reforms, but jails and prisons would then return to abusive conditions. This pattern of scandal and reform often repeated itself throughout the past two centuries. Anyone looking for a narrative of progress in our penal history will be sorely disappointed.

The negative affective responses of disgust, contempt, and fear provide some explanation for our long history of brutality. Scholars exploring prison violence often cite psychological work like the 1970s Stanford prison experiment to explain the destructive dynamics of captor and captive.[15] In this book, I have offered a different understanding of this phenomenon, grounded in our negative affective responses toward the person. We use the jail to contain those we find disgusting or threatening, but jailing people creates a dynamic that only enhances our disgust and contempt for them. Arresting and caging human beings often elicits a profound devaluation of those behind bars. I have also noted how fear often dominates our debates about pretrial defendants. Yet, confining people in institutions often does little to quell this fear, and in fact often creates more demand to expand overcrowded jails. Negative affective responses often produce a value blindness to human dignity that can lead to violence and degradation. The short-term policy recommendations I have endorsed can mitigate these responses. Individuals working in jails can respond to the negative affective responses they experience. However, systemically, these efforts are unlikely to counter the powerful negative forces operating within and outside of U.S. jails. Instead, they act as dikes, holding them back temporarily. The problem remains the institution, which segregates people in cages, demeaning both them and those who endorse their captivity.

What Would It Mean to Reject the Jail?

Concretely, what difference would it make if we adopted a more radical approach and declared that the jail is unreformable? I don't have a complete blueprint for what should replace jails. I think we need ideas from people from diverse academic disciplines and from policy makers with expertise. However, I want to end this book by reflecting on how a refusal to affirm the jail's moral legitimacy changes our approach to some public policies. The major challenge for rejecting the jail's moral legitimacy will always be confronting those violent people who must be contained. We should be clear that this population represents a minority of jail inhabitants. The best estimates we have suggest that 25 to 30 percent of people in jail have been accused of a violent crime (Prison Policy Initiative 2017). How many people in this group constitute a danger to others depends on what we mean by "violent," a notoriously difficult concept to define. Sometimes abolitionists call this population the "violent few."[16] They correctly point out that focusing on violent people draws attention away from how jails incarcerate large numbers of nonviolent offenders. I have made this case in this book, showing how the contemporary jail targets the homeless, those suffering from mental illness, and those too poor to pay for bail. Abolitionists also do good work in questioning the concept of "dangerousness," showing how we often quickly classify people as dangerous when they pose little danger. As I have maintained in this book, fear often drives us to seek to minimize risk, and this means we expand the class of dangerous people very easily. When receiving statistics about violent offenders, we should carefully scrutinize the methodologies for arriving at them.

Nevertheless, I think abolitionists dismiss the problem of the "violent few" far too quickly. Let's consider domestic violence. Over the past few decades, we have fundamentally altered our approach to it. We no longer see domestic violence as a private or family matter, but hold that it is a criminal affair that should concern us all. Many police departments make domestic violence calls a priority, and arrest alleged offenders even if victims refuse to press charges. Police officers devote substantial resources to dealing with domestic violence, and intervene in disputes often at considerable personal risk. For most of us, these changes are positive, an improvement over a time when authorities left men and women to their own devices or to the aid of family members.

The jail serves as a tool for fighting domestic violence. Those accused of it are often jailed until they can demonstrate that they no longer present a threat to spouses, partners, or children. At the Cook County Jail in 2012, more than nine thousand inmates were admitted for domestic battery (Olson 2012, 5). In the same year in my home county, Brown County, Wisconsin, police made over six hundred arrests for domestic violence (Wisconsin Department of Justice 2014, 9). Most county jails hold people accused of domestic battery. In recent decades, jails have thus become one of the means police (imperfectly) use to protect people from domestic violence.

Some scholars recognize a need to delink movements opposing violence against women from the police and incarceration. For example, philosopher Sarah Tyson notes "a recalcitrant and troubling problem in much feminist antiviolence work that presents a formidable obstacle to reaching its ultimate goal: many feminists working to eradicate violence have come to rely on prisons and the apparatus of the carceral state more broadly" (Tyson 2015, 210). She insightfully explores how feminist organizations can think differently about offenders and their crimes. However, she provides little in the way of concrete proposals to protect people from immediate harm in domestic violence situations. Given the extreme danger domestic violence poses, we will likely need some kind of coercive institution to control violent offenders.

Contemporary jails also hold those accused of child molestation, rape, assault, and murder. We tend to forget that those jailed for these crimes are innocent until proven guilty. Those accused of sexual offenses often have their lives ruined by accusation and arrests. Nevertheless, authorities confront the immediate task of containing people they believe to be a threat to a community. For example, someone charged with serial rape cannot be allowed to roam free in a community. I have met people who have been convicted of raping multiple people within a few weeks, and when they were arrested, authorities needed to prevent them from committing additional rapes.

Because I acknowledge the need to incapacitate violent offenders, I think we will continue to need some coercive institutions. However, we should see the violence of these institutions as a last resort, acknowledging "that even if a person is so awful in her violence that the threat she poses must be forcibly contained, this course of action ought to be undertaken with moral conflict, circumspection, and even shame, as a choice of the lesser of two evils, rather than as an achievement of justice" (McLeod 2015, 1171). Considering their history, how they assault dignity and the negative affective responses they evoke, jails are unlikely to be just institutions. We also shouldn't take refuge in a comfortable narrative that celebrates our capacity to rehabilitate people. However, this certainly doesn't mean we should abandon efforts to protect inmates from abuse. Nor does it mean that we should refuse to recognize the personhood of those we control. Whatever coercive institutions we adopt, we will need to fight to protect the dignity of those inhabiting them. Although I hold that we will continue to need coercive institutions, these should be nothing like our current jails. An ethic of dignity demands that we confine only those in jail who present a violent threat or a flight risk and in nothing like the caged conditions of contemporary jails.[17]

As legal scholar Allegra M. McLeod notes, reconceiving alternatives to jails would also require that we develop "positive forms of social integration and collective security that are not organized around criminal law enforcement, confinement, criminal surveillance, punitive policing, or punishment" (McLeod 2015, 1164). We need to move away from the extraordinary level of criminalization in our society, and decriminalize a host of behaviors that fall under the law's domination. For example, I have drawn attention to ordinances that criminalize begging and other behaviors associated with homelessness. Municipalities have often used them to jail people. We should eliminate these kinds of ordinances. Decriminalization without finding alternatives to the jail might increase public disorder. We would need to decide whether to tolerate it or to invest in the alternatives necessary to respond to it. For example, the National Coalition for the Homeless has highlighted communities in the United States that refuse to respond to homeless people in draconian ways. Rather than jailing people, they provide temporary places where the homeless can stay, and respond creatively to those who people see as a public nuisance (National Coalition for the Homeless and National Law Center on Homelessness and Poverty 2006). Such policies aren't easy to implement, but given the nature of our penal institutions, jailing the homeless should no longer be an option.

As McLeod argues, we should also develop preventative justice tools that exist outside of the criminal justice system. For instance, these would require moving away from the kinds of aggressive forms of policing that sometimes go under the rubric of "broken windows" policing.[18] Adopted by many cities since the 1990s, broken windows focuses on stopping and arresting large numbers of people for misdemeanors, vandalism, or suspicious behavior. Such policing responds to genuine concerns people harbor, and constructing alternatives to it is no easy matter. Moreover, whether aggressive policing reduces crime is a complex empirical debate that I can't settle here. However, an ethic of dignity rests not on complex calculations of consequences, but on a recognition of the person's value. Acknowledging the true character of the jail means that incarcerating thousands of people for misdemeanors is morally indefensible. Municipalities and citizens need to find alternatives.

Other measures we could adopt would include ending the pervasive presence of police in our school system. It has produced what some scholars call the "school-to-prison pipeline," where students end up in the criminal justice system.[19] Since the 1990s, we have tolerated a remarkable police presence in our schools. Municipalities spend hundreds of thousands or even millions of dollars annually to have police officers in schools. We have criminalized behavior that used to be a matter of school discipline, with the predictable increase in arrests. Decreasing police presence in schools would require finding creative ways to respond to the fear of violence and disorder in schools. Much of the increase in police presence occurred after prominent school shootings in the 1990s. Many parents and school administrators endorse it, and in this book, I have noted the difficulties in changing our fears. However, ethically, we can't justify responding to school disciplinary problems by putting children in hellish jails where they may be subjected to violence and degrading conditions.

A more radical approach to jails also alerts us to how alternatives to jail incarceration may enhance coercive social control. Many proposals for jail reform emphasize mechanisms like drug and mental health courts. They provide alternatives to the jail, but can also be deeply coercive.[20] In many cases, they create new surveillance methods that extend the power of penal authorities outside the walls of the jail. If we begin with the idea that the jail is unjust, we become attentive to ways other institutions damage human dignity. I have hinted at this kind of analysis when I discussed the ethical problems with the PSA. In a rush to provide alternatives to jailing, we may adopt institutions that only further damage human dignity. A radical approach to the jail would subject all alternatives to the jail to ethical scrutiny.

This concern about coercion is particularly important because of our history of abusing vulnerable people in institutions. Liat Ben-Moshe writes insightfully about the need to "reconceptualize institutionalization and imprisonment as not merely analogous but as in fact interconnected, in their logic, historical enactment, and social effects" (Ben-Moshe 2017, 123). The crisis of mental illness in our jails illustrates the urgency of Ben-Moshe's point. On this issue, a more radical stance toward the jail differs significantly from a reformist one. In documents from organizations like the Vera Institute and the Justice Policy Institute, I rarely read about the dangers or unintended consequences of community mental health care. What forms of coercion might emerge from efforts to help those with mental illness? Will we move to just institutions or simply create more problems in the name of "community" mental health? We may end up reducing jail populations by forcing those with mental illness into therapeutic communities that deny people rights and pacify them with medication. By focusing on human dignity, we are compelled to consider these questions.[21]

The Importance of Ethics

By acknowledging the jail's injustice, we also refuse to allow ethical concerns to recede into the background of policy debates. Even though I don't embrace the abolitionist label, I agree with McLeod, who notes that the abolitionist stance "more accurately identifies the wrong entailed in holding people in cages or policing them with the threat of imprisonment, as well as more fully recognizes the transformative work that would be required to meaningfully alter these dynamics and practices" (McLeod 2015, 1207). Too often, critics of jails and prisons provide simplistic understandings of human motivation. They ascribe all the ills of mass incarceration to economic motives or claim that it benefits an elite class. They insist that people will be motivated only by self-interest, and will be unresponsive to moral arguments. Or, they pretend to be the only hardheaded realists in the discussion, the ones armed with the "data" that move politicians and bureaucrats to act. However helpful these approaches may be, they overlook the ethical scandal of our jail system. The value of the person and the assaults on it in our penal system elicit powerful responses in us. Social and political movements opposing mass incarceration deny an important aspect of our humanity when they ignore our response to value. The assault on dignity in places like the Cook County Jail demands a response from authorities and citizens.

Recently, in a welcome development, some scholars writing about incarceration have recognized the ethical dimension of human motivation. For example, Jonathan Simon has published a book dissecting an important 2011 Supreme Court case called *Brown v. Plata* (Simon 2014). In an important decision, the Supreme Court ordered the state of California to release tens of thousands of prison inmates. California held them in overcrowded conditions, and brutalized them in horrific ways. Simon details how in the *Brown v. Plata* case the Supreme Court justices were moved by arguments about dignity. During hearings before the Court, they saw photographs of inmates with mental illness who were held in tiny outdoor cages in their own urine. The majority decision made extensive use of the concept of dignity in its interpretation of the Eighth Amendment. Far from being a useless or stupid concept, it played an integral role in an important Supreme Court case.

Marie Gottschalk also emphasizes political and ethical arguments when she analyzes penal conditions. In several works, she condemns the tendency to focus excessively on the cost of incarceration. She points out that reducing the size of institutional populations in a just manner may end up being costly in the immediate future. This is probably true with jail populations, particularly if we intend to help those who need mental health care. Gottschalk notes that "many criminologists have sought refuge in producing state-of-the-art, ostensibly apolitical, evidence-based research centered largely on how to reduce crime or on how to help government agencies or other groups reduce crime" (Gottschalk 2012, 233). In contrast, she thinks those seeking to reverse mass incarceration must address political and moral issues of fairness and justice.

However, many who do employ moral concepts fail to examine them critically, and assume that we all agree with their views of human rights, dignity, or justice. We are seeing an increasingly sophisticated scholarship on the history of U.S. incarceration and penal institutions. Often, scholars link their research directly to their political activism and determination to end mass incarceration. Yet, their work and activism contain implicit and explicit appeals to complex philosophical terms whose meaning is not at all self-evident. Mass incarceration is a moral scandal, but responding to it requires more than outrage and assertions about injustice. Instead, we need careful analysis of ideas of justice, dignity, and human rights that have always been a matter of dispute.

In this book, I have added the philosophically sophisticated perspective of phenomenology to contemporary discussions of the jail. It awakens us to the diverse values that attract and move us. Among these values are economic ones, but these are not the only ones motivating us. Phenomenology draws our attention to all values, making them objects of wonder and interest. The experience of incarceration includes not only a loss of liberty, but also a struggle to remain in contact with aesthetic, moral, and other values.

For those of us thinking about our local county jail, this experience of values is particularly significant. Jails sustain their unjust practices partially because people are ignorant of jail conditions. Or they are disinterested in them or approve of brutal punishment. By developing greater transparency, we can shed light on jail practices, and thereby expose the abuses in our jail system. In the short term, jail monitoring, media attention, and lawsuits all provide information to people who may be simply unaware of penal conditions. They can come to understand the assault on dignity that may be taking place within their own community. In the long term, becoming aware of the dignity of those incarcerated can lead them to seek alternatives to the jail.

Information and transparency also provide opportunities for us to examine our affective responses of disgust, contempt, and fear toward the socially marginalized among us. Should we have a low tolerance for public "nuisance" crimes? Should we turn away in disgust from those in public whom we find weak, repellent, or disorderly in some way? Is calling the police the best response to them, or can we react to the disorderly differently? Can we discover what is valuable in people we usually find disgusting and undesirable? Perhaps we can find ways to interact with inmates, former inmates, and others whom we find troubling. Throughout this book, I have emphasized the encounter between persons as one way to understand human dignity. Even when fear or contempt dominates our interaction, we retain indirect freedom to examine our affective responses and actions. Our disgust, contempt, and fear often give authorities the license to abuse those they arrest and incarcerate. We're not condemned to give sanction to these negative and exclusionary responses to others. We are not compelled to turn people over to an abusive jail system. We are certainly not forced to accept the existence of the jail.

Recognizing Human Dignity

More information, policy changes, and education alone won't alter our affective responses. In both short-term and long-term approaches to the jail, we need to consider how we exercise indirect freedom. How do our affective responses lead us to respond to others in ways that value or devalue human dignity? In thinking about these questions, we can be inspired by examples that move us to make the right choice. Max Scheler wrote of the importance of exemplars in our lives, teachers or others who embody certain values and elicit affective responses in us (Scheler 1987, 127–196). In my years of teaching in jails and prisons, I have repeatedly met remarkable inmates and staff members who reminded me of the importance of human dignity. For example, in one of the confusing days

I spent at the Cook County Jail, I had an unusual experience. My guide from Cermak Health Services of Cook County told me that I should meet an expressive therapist named Eric Spruth. Expressive therapists use various art forms to work with patients suffering from mental and physical illnesses. I agreed to spend the morning sitting through sessions conducted by Spruth and his assistant.

Spruth works with some of most severely disturbed inmates at Cook County. When I entered his room, I noticed walls covered with all kinds of art done by inmates. At a table sat a small group of women. When I spoke with them, it was clear that they had been through some terrible trauma in their lives. Spruth begin by asking the women to write letters to loved ones, which he promised to mail when they were completed. He observed how well they could write and communicate. Afterward, he played some music, and encouraged everyone to sing together. Spruth insisted that I participate in the session. He urged everyone to draw or color, and asked us to talk about what we had created. Some people had problems talking at all, while others shared difficult stories that related to their pictures. Spruth then played more music, we talked some more, and the session ended. He and his assistant wrote observations about each person. They would later share them with psychologists and others trying to help the inmates.

What moved me in these sessions was how Spruth connected with a creative part of inmates that seemed to be lost. He treated each person as an individual worthy of respect and attention, and proudly displayed completed artwork in his room. Inmates who spent only a few minutes with psychiatrists or psychologists responded to Spruth because he attended to them as persons. I later got to know Spruth better, and learned that my one morning with him was no aberration. In the brutal and confusing environment of the Cook County Jail, he recognized the individual dignity of both staff members and inmates. In a bureaucracy that did everything to crush all creativity and initiative, he located and cultivated creativity in deeply traumatized people. Most remarkably, Spruth has been an expressive therapist at the Cook County Jail for more than twenty years. Despite the horrors of this institution, he retains a deep commitment to those he encounters.

I have met corrections officers, correctional psychologists, and social workers who are deeply cynical about their work. They view inmates with disdain or have lost an idealism they once had years ago. Some now believe the worst of human beings. Yet I have occasionally met people like Spruth, who exemplify a commitment to human dignity. In dark places, they quietly work to overcome the degradation around them. They show us that despite its awful history and current brutality, we need not accept the jail's assault on human dignity. Even among those accused of the most heinous crimes, the dignity of the person remains. Even among those most damaged by violence or mental illness, the beauty of the human person exists. It remains our task to remember the basic truth of inherent dignity, and to struggle to prevent our jails from obscuring or denying it altogether.

ACKNOWLEDGMENTS

The inspiration for this book came from my experiences teaching religion and philosophy classes at the Green Bay Correctional Institution and at the Brown County Jail in Wisconsin. I have spent many hours talking to inmates about topics like love, anger, evil, and punishment. I have learned a great deal from these conversations, and I am grateful to all the students I have taught for their passion for learning. At the Brown County Jail, I am grateful to Brian Laurent, superintendent of the Brown County Juvenile Detention Center. Brian welcomed me when I expressed a desire to develop a teaching program at the jail, and helped me develop it. He displays a deep concern for the lives of inmates. At the Green Bay Correctional Facility, I am grateful to the men who worship at the Chapel and to Chaplain Mike Donavan and Father Jim Baraniak. I deeply value the time I spend talking and worshiping with the men in the Chapel, and appreciate their willingness to share their life experiences with me. I also thank Virginia Vanden Branden, organizer of the prison's "Challenges and Possibilities" program. This program provided inmates with three months of lectures and a restorative justice seminar, and I will always be grateful to Ginny for inviting me to participate in it. With her quiet presence and deep faith in humanity, she has inspired me to hope for positive change even when it doesn't seem possible.

At the Cook County Jail, I want to thank Sheriff Thomas J. Dart. I had the opportunity to talk with him about his work, and he graciously granted me access to the jail. I also am grateful to Benjamin Breit, director of communications for the Sheriff's office. Ben helped me navigate the Cook County Jail's confusing physical and bureaucratic landscape. I am also thankful to the inmates and staff who took time out to talk to me about their lives and experiences. Finally, I thank Eric Spruth, whose wonderful work with inmates I discuss in this book.

I particularly appreciate my good friend Rhonda Bell in Chicago. In my visits to the Cook County Jail, I shared many of my impressions with her in helpful and spirited discussions. She was always willing to listen to me as I returned from my jail visits.

For beneficial conversations or correspondence, I thank Christine Agaiby, David Coury, John F. Crosby, Amy Fettig, Paul J. Griffiths, Bernard Harcourt, Cliff Keenan, Eric Maciolek, Ellen Mommaerts, Michael Mushlin, Sharon Shalev, David Shapiro, and Marie VanNostrand.

At New York University Press, I thank Jeff Ferrel, editor of the Alternative Criminology series. Jeff read my manuscript submission, and recognized that it would be a good addition to his series. I also thank Ilene R. Kalish, executive editor of NYU Press. Ilene has been very helpful in her editorial comments and suggestions. Finally, I appreciate the comments of the anonymous referees who carefully read the manuscript from different perspectives. Several urged me to clarify my approach to penology. One reader read the manuscript philosophically, and pressed me to develop my arguments about dignity with greater precision. Another strongly urged me to explore prison abolitionism more sympathetically, and challenged me to take a clear stance on the jail's moral legitimacy. All the reviewers enabled me to improve my argument substantially.

My wife Celestine has lived with me as I struggled to understand what is happening in our jails. She listens patiently when I relate the difficult things I see in jails and prisons. Yet, she also knows when to turn conversations away from the degradation and misery of our penal system. She has taught me a spiritual balance that I deeply value.

Finally, I dedicate this book to my beloved twin sons Zachariah and Caleb. They are now entering the world as adults, full of excitement and promise. It is my hope that their generation will begin to turn away from the madness of mass incarceration.

NOTES

INTRODUCTION

1 Dostoyevsky (2004, 258).

2 For information about Ismaaiyl Brinsley's case, I have relied on the following articles: "New York Officers' Killer" (2014) and "Many Identities of New York Officers' Killer" (2015).

3 For a good discussion of this terminology, see McConville (1995).

4 For one example of this genre, see Dubler (2014).

5 For discussions of racism in the U.S. penal system, see Alexander (2012) and Hinton (2016). For the statistics on Wisconsin, see Pawasarat and Quinn (2013).

6 Many nonprofit organizations publish reports detailing the costly and wasteful character of our criminal justice system. For one good example, see the website for the Justice Policy Institute at www.justicepolicy.org. The Vera Institute of Justice takes a similar approach; see its website at www.vera.org. I find the materials from both these organizations informative.

7 I thank an anonymous reader at New York University Press for suggesting I use the term "marginalized" instead of the older sociological term "deviant." Although sociologists in the 1960s often used "deviant" in a nonmoral sense, today it carries a stigmatizing sense, and I think "marginalized" is a preferable term to capture the population of people the jail targets.

8 I take these figures from the Vera Institute of Justice (2015). Another good source for statistics on jail numbers is Prison Policy Initiative (2017).

9 For a good discussion of why U.S. jails are decentralized, see McConville (1995, 320–323).

10 For two exceptions to this general trend, see Tyson and Hall (2014) and Guenther (2013).

11 I am grateful to an anonymous reader at New York University Press who challenged me to engage the abolitionist tradition more carefully. Debates about abolition appeared frequently in the 1960s and early 1970s, but died out with the rise of mass incarceration. For thinkers from this earlier tradition, see Davis (2003), Mathiesen (2006), and Christie (2007). In the United States, Angela Davis is one of the most famous advocates of prison abolitionism. However, I won't discuss her work at length. Philosophically, I reject her Marxist approach to abolition and other issues, but explaining my differences with Davis would take me too far afield from the main themes of this book. Instead, I will engage a younger generation of scholars today who are revisiting abolitionism.

12 I have learned from the work of Nicolas Carrier and Justin Piché. For one of their articles that describes the complexities of the abolitionist movement, see Carrier and Piché (2015b).

CHAPTER 1. DEGRADATION AND DISORIENTATION

1 Wines and Dwight (1867, 317–318).

2 Eugene V. Debs, the famous socialist, provides a vivid account of conditions in the Cook County Jail in 1894; see Debs (2000, 25–29). For a sensationalist account of how officials fought the "barn-boss" system, see English (2007). For a detailed study of Illinois jails in the 1960s, see Mattick and Sweet (1970).

3 *Dan Duran et al. v. Richard Elrod et al.*, no. 83–1574 (7th Cir., July 22, 1983), www.openjurist.org.

4 John P. Walsh provides a good history and analysis of the *Duran* decree and its aftermath; see Walsh (2013).

5 I haven't presented anywhere near a full history of the Cook County Jail in this chapter. Melanie D. Newport (2016) offers a detailed history of the jail in her Temple University dissertation, which I have found very informative. I thank Professor Newport for sharing her dissertation with me.

6 For the lawsuit, see *Gary v. Sheahan*, no. 96-cv-07294 (N.D. Ill., 1996), www.clearinghouse.net. Tori Marlin (1998) provides a good analysis of this case.

7 *Young v. Cook County*, no. 06–552 (N.D. Ill., April 2, 2009), http://il.findacase.com.

8 *United States of America v. Cook County, Illinois, Agreed Order*, no. 10 C 2946 (N.D. Ill., May 13, 2010), www.justice.gov.

9 *Hudson et al. v. Preckwinkle et al.*, no. 13cv8752 (N.D. Ill., February 27, 2014), intro., sec. 1, http://uplcchicago.org.

10 Ibid., intro., 8.

11 Ibid., intro., sec. 1.

12 Ibid., intro., 9.

13 Ibid., sec. 2, 50.

14 Ibid., sec. 2, 51.

15 Ibid., sec. 3.

16 Ibid.

17 Deliberate indifference requires that there exists a serious harm or risk of harm and that authorities knew of this harm. This is a very difficult legal standard to meet.

18 I have learned much about police lockups from an excellent document written by Charles Hounmenau (2010).

19 The statistics in this paragraph come from Olson and Huddle (2013).

20 For information about pretrial services in Cook County, I have relied on the report "Circuit Court of Cook County Pretrial Operational Review" (Illinois Supreme Court, Administrative Office of the Illinois Courts 2014).

21 For information about the organization of the Cook County Jail, see www.cookcountysheriff.org.

22 Information about Cermak comes from http://hmprg.org.

23 For a discussion of the difficulties in attracting qualified mental health professionals to the Cook County Jail, see Trotter (2015).

24 Mike Dumke (2013) offers a good account of the problems with Cook County's
bond hearings.

CHAPTER 2. WHAT IS THE PURPOSE OF A JAIL?

1 Nietzsche (1969, sec. 2, 14).

2 I have discussed philosophical accounts of punishment in Jeffreys (2013, 83–103).
For other useful discussions of theories of punishment, see Murphy (1994) and
Boonin (2008).

3 Nietzsche rejects the idea that we can arrive at a philosophical justification of
punishment. I disagree with him on this point. For my views on punishment, see
Jeffreys (2013, 83–103). Although I don't think it can morally legitimize the American jail and prison system, I think we can defend a version of the "expressive
view" of punishment, arguing that it can express values to the offender, victim,
and society. It has appeared in the work of thinkers like Joel Feinberg, R. A. Duff,
and Jean Hampton.

4 For details about this clash, see "At Rikers Island" (2014).

5 For this discussion of the Los Angeles County Jail, I have relied on the following
sources: American Civil Liberties Union (2011); "18 Current, Former L.A. County
Sheriff's Deputies Face Federal Charges" (2013); *Alex Rosas et al. v. Leroy Baca et
al.*, no. 12–00428 DDP (SHx) (C.D. Calif., February 13, 2013), http://cases.justia.
com. As of the writing of this book, some of the deputies involved in beating
inmates have pleaded guilty, while former Los Angeles County Sheriff Lee Baca
was convicted of obstructing a federal investigation and sentenced to three years
in federal prison.

6 The Department of Justice investigations are available at the website of the U.S.
Department of Justice, Civil Rights Division, Special Litigation Section, Cases and
Matters (www.justice.gov).

7 For the articles from the *Miami Herald*, see "Beyond Punishment" (2015).

8 *Mark Butler et al. v. Suffolk County et al.*, no. 2:11-cv-02602-JS-GRB (E.D. N.Y.,
April 5, 2012), sec. 2, www.nyclu.org.

9 Ibid., sec. 41.

10 For other cases involving terrible sanitary conditions, see U.S. Department of
Justice, Civil Rights Division (2008a, sec. III, E); *Davis et al. v. Canyon County,
Idaho, et al.* (D. Idaho), Class Action Complaint for Declaratory and Injunctive
Relief (November 12, 2009), secs. 21–33, www.aclu.org; U.S. Department of Justice,
Civil Rights Division (2011b, sec. IV, D); *Angel Colon v. Passaic County* (D. N.J.,
September 3, 2008), II, C, www.aclu-nj.org; U.S. Department of Justice, Civil
Rights Division (2009b, sec. II, D); U.S. Department of Justice, Civil Rights Divi-
sion (2008b, sec. II, D); U.S. Department of Justice, Civil Rights Division (2006a,
sec. C); and American Civil Liberties Union (2015, 27–31).

11 For the proposed settlement, see American Civil Liberties Union (2012).

12 Jails sometimes use dogs to search for drugs and to keep order. For a horrifying video showing dogs attacking inmates in the Iberia Parish Jail in Louisiana, see "Shocking Jail Video" (2015).

13 *Shreve v. Franklin County, Ohio*, no. 2: 10-cv-644 (S.D. Ohio, November 3, 2010), 2, www.justice.gov.

14 Ibid., 5.

15 *Shreve et al., Michael Reed, individually v. Franklin County, Ohio, et al.*, no. 13–3119 (6th Cir., February 6, 2014), www.ca6.uscourts.gov. One judge on the Sixth Circuit wrote a stinging dissent, but the majority held that Reed did not suffer a violation of his Eighth Amendment rights. Those suing a penal institution for Eighth Amendment violations must show a pattern of official knowledge and intent, a difficult standard to meet. Tasers are used frequently in jails and prisons. For two good discussions of this trend, see Cusac (2009, 212–220) and Rejali (2009, 225–255).

16 I have taken my account of the York Prison events from Reutter (2015). For other cases involving staff violence, see *Tabitha Gentry et al. v. Floyd County, Indiana, et al.*, no. 4:2014 cv00054 (S.D. Ind., June 12, 2014), secs. 39–107, http://media.ibj.com; U.S. Department of Justice, Civil Rights Division (2011a, sec. IV, 1–4); U.S. Department of Justice, Civil Rights Division (2009d, sec. III, A, 1); U.S. Department of Justice, Civil Rights Division (2017). The Westchester County Jail in Westchester County, New York, came under investigation by the DOJ in 2007 for staff abuse and substandard sanitary conditions. For its findings letter that describes staff abuses, see U.S. Department of Justice, Civil Rights Division (2009a, sec. III, A, 1). For years, the Maricopa County Jail in Phoenix, operated by Sheriff Joe Arpaio, was sued numerous times for abuse of force. It was also the subject of DOJ investigations. For a useful story detailing this history, see Dickerson (2007). The Harris County Jail in Texas has frequently been the subject of lawsuits and media stories about staff violence. The *Houston Chronicle* has done good investigative journalism on this problem; see "Jailhouse Jeopardy" (2015). David Reutter has written on inmate abuse in Pennsylvania jails. For one of his articles, see Reutter (2007, 1–13). I have found *Prison Legal News* to be a useful source for information about conditions in U.S. jails.

17 David Kaiser and Lovisa Stannow have written extensively on rape in jails and prisons, and have detailed how often it occurs in juvenile facilities. For their articles, see Kaiser and Stannow (2011, 2012). For some cases detailing the failure of California to humanely deal with its juvenile population during the 1990s and early 2000s, see *Walter Hixson and Andrea Hixson v. Chris Hope*, no. CV029154 (Calif. Super. Ct.), Complaint for Injunctive and Declaratory Relief (April 25, 2006), www.prisonlaw.com; *Margaret Farrell v. Jerry L. Harper*, no. RG03079344 (Calif. Super. Ct., September 18, 2003), www.clearinghouse.net. The California Youth Authority housed youth in a variety of short-term and long-term facilities. Since this lawsuit, it has reduced its population substantially, and made improve-

ments in what was a hellish system. It has also changed its name. I thank the Prison Law Office for its legal work and for making its documents available. For these documents, see www.prisonlaw.com.

18 U.S. Department of Justice, Civil Rights Division (2011d, 1). The case was settled, and the institution made improvements to its sexual assault prevention procedures; see Mire (2014). Some officers were convicted of sexual assault and others fired from their jobs.

19 In the early 2000s, officers in the adolescent wing of Rikers Island created "The Program," where juvenile trustees kept order by savagely beating other inmates. Young inmates were also encouraged to fight each other with weapons in a kind of "fight club"; see "Rikers Island Fight Club" (2008). A corrections officer was sentenced to six years in prison for orchestrating "The Program"; see "Six Year Sentence for Guard in Rikers Island Beatings" (2010). Penal institutions have a long history of using inmates as "trustees," producing a brutal environment controlled by the most violent inmates. For decades, Texas had one of the strongest "trustee" systems, but it was dismantled under court order in the 1980s. For an excellent history of this system, see Perkinson (2010). For a good account of how inmates and their allies battled the Texas trustee system, see Martin and Ekland-Olson (1987).

20 Other cases dealing with inmate-on-inmate violence include U.S. Department of Justice, Civil Rights Division (2009d, sec. III, A, 2–4); *Angel Colon v. Passaic County* (D. N.J., September 3, 2008), II, B, www.aclu-nj.org; U.S. Department of Justice, Civil Rights Division (2005, sec. II, 1); and *Quentin Hall v. Margaret Mims*, no. CV-F 11–02047-LJO-BAM (E.D. Calif., May 16, 2012), www.leagle.com. In 2015, Baltimore finally closed its city jail after years of neglect during which gangs often used violence against inmates; see "Gov. Hogan Announces 'Immediate' Closure of Baltimore Jail" (2015). The Wayne County Jail system serving Detroit has long had problems with inmate-on-inmate violent. For a recent investigation of the jail and its problems, see "Deplorable Conditions on Display at Wayne County Jails" (2015). In 2015, San Francisco rigorously debated whether to build a new jail, with all sides of the debates agreeing that the old one was dangerous for inmates. For this debate, see "In S.F. Debate" (2015). The city decided not to construct a new jail. Philadelphia operates jails that are often overcrowded, and the city has often responded by putting three inmates in a cell. This creates dangers for both inmates and staff. For one good discussion of this situation, see "As City Jail Death Rates Rise, Will Reforms Help?" (2015).

21 U.S. Department of Justice, Civil Rights Division (2009c, sec. III, a). For similar cases, see U.S. Department of Justice, Civil Rights Division (2008b, sec. B); American Civil Liberties Union (2015, 13–16); and *Gray v. County of Riverside*, no. JC-CA-0105-0003 (C.D. Calif., April 30, 2013), www.clearinghouse.net.

22 For other cases, see U.S. Department of Justice, Civil Rights Division (2008a, sec. B, 7); U.S. Department of Justice, Civil Rights Division (2008b, sec. III, b); and U.S. Department of Justice, Civil Rights Division (2006a, sec. III, a, 4).

23 Human Rights Watch (2015). This report provides numerous examples of staff violence against inmates with mental illness in jails and prisons.

24 I have discussed segregation and mental illness in my book *Spirituality in Dark Places: The Ethics of Solitary Confinement* (Jeffreys 2013).

25 For example, see U.S. Department of Justice, Civil Rights Division (2007, sec. II, A).

26 U.S. Department of Justice, Civil Rights Division (2006a, sec. III, B, 2).

27 U.S. Department of Justice, Civil Rights Division (2011b, sec. IV, 2, D).

28 U.S. Department of Justice, Civil Rights Division (2012a, sec. III, a); and U.S. Department of Justice, Civil Rights Division (2006a, sec. III, a, 7).

29 U.S. Department of Justice, Civil Rights Division (2005, sec. III, B, 3).

30 The cases involving failures in mental health care are numerous. For only a few of them, see U.S. Department of Justice, Civil Rights Division (2006a, sec. III, B); U.S. Department of Justice (2011); U.S. Department of Justice, Civil Rights Division (2009c, sec. III, B); U.S. Department of Justice, Civil Rights Division (2012a); American Civil Liberties Union (2015, 16–19); *Quentin Hall v. Margaret Mims*, no. CV-F 11–02047-LJO-BAM (E.D. Calif., May 16, 2012), sec. 1, www.leagle.com; U.S. Department of Justice, Civil Rights Division (2009d, sec. III, C); and U.S. Department of Justice, Civil Rights Division (2005, sec. II, B, 3).

31 For another case involving inmates and suicide, see U.S. Department of Justice, Civil Rights Division (2015b, sec. V). Broward County in Florida has had a Consent Decree with the federal government since 1994. This is one of the longer lasting Consent Decrees with a jail in the United States. Part of the reason it has continued so long is the jail's persistent problem with mental illness and inmate suicides and deaths. For a good investigative piece on this jail, see Hobbes (2016).

32 I take this figure from American Psychiatric Association (2004, 2). I owe this reference to Harcourt (2006).

33 The literature on the closing of mental institutions is substantial. For some good sources, see Grob (2011), Grob (1991), Scull (2016), Scull (1977), Rothman and Rothman (2005), Isaac and Armat (1991), Torrey (2013), and Johnson (1990).

34 Bernard Harcourt has discussed this phenomenon in detail; see Harcourt (2011). I will discuss Harcourt's work later in this book.

35 See also Steadman et al. (2009). I owe this reference to the Vera Institute report on jails (Vera Institute of Justice 2015).

36 For an account of the history of bail in the United States, see Schnacke, Jones, and Brooker (2010, 13).

37 I take the over 90 percent figure from an excellent article written by a former judge who decries the injustice of our plea-bargaining system; see Radkoff (2014). In the 1990s, Malcolm M. Feeley wrote an influential article and later a book describing how jails punish people without bringing them to trial; see Feeley (1992).

38 For the Arnold Foundation report, see Lowenkamp, VanNostrand, and Holsinger (2013).

39 For the original study, see Baradaran and McIntyre (2011).

40 Baradaran and McIntyre (2011, 511) think that some factors can be predictive of violence, but maintain that judges make little use of them. I will discuss issues of risk assessment in the next chapter. I share Bernard Harcourt's skepticism about it; see Harcourt (2007). For a good source of information about pretrial services and bail, see the Pretrial Justice Institute website, www.pretrial.org.

41 The ACLU report on the OPP and Katrina noted the history of this system; see American Civil Liberties Union (2006, 12).

42 See also U.S. Department of Justice, Civil Rights Division (2012b). In 2016, the Orleans Parish Prison became so troubled that the federal judiciary finally took over operations of it from local authorities, see "Judge: Sheriff Gusman 'Relinquishing Operational Control' over Troubled Orleans Jail" (2016).

43 The organization ArchCity Defenders, based in St. Louis, has initiated a series of lawsuits against Ferguson and other cities surrounding St. Louis. It charges that they use jails to pressure inmates into paying legal fees. The lawsuits also detail terrible sanitary conditions in jails. For these lawsuits, see www.archcitydefenders. org.

44 In chapter 5, I will consider ways to change this system. For good discussions of the problem, see Stillman (2014) and Rosenberg (2015). Alice Goffman wrote a controversial ethnographic study of people who live in constant fear of being jailed; see Goffman (2014).

45 Vivien M. L. Miller has produced a fine study of the brutal Florida prison system in the first half of the twentieth century; see Miller (2012). Ethan Blue describes the difficult lives of inmates in prisons in Texas and California during the Depression; see Blue (2012). The convict-lease system, which dominated many southern states for decades after the Civil War, showed no interest in rehabilitating inmates. Inmates, particularly African American inmates, were rented out to companies where they worked in terrible conditions and were often abused and tortured. For two excellent books on this topic, see Blackmon (2008) and Oshinsky (1997). Daniel E. Macallair has written a fascinating history of the California Youth Authority that chronicles its cycles of abuse and reform. He reveals the gap between rhetoric and reality in one of America's most famous juvenile systems that often touted its commitment to rehabilitation; see Macallair (2015).

46 Eric Cummins details the rise and fall of rehabilitation in California in an excellent study; see Cummins (1994). For a well-known attack on prisons and rehabilitation in the 1970s, see Mitford (1973). George Jackson wrote a famous prison memoir in which he rejects rehabilitation; see Jackson (1994). Jackson was killed under suspicious circumstances when he attempted to escape from San Quentin Prison in California. He brutally murdered several corrections officers during the escape attempt. In 1974, Robert Martinson wrote a controversial article in which he questioned the efficacy of rehabilitation programs. Although he later disavowed it, the article exerted a significant influence in debates about rehabilitation. For this article, see Martinson (1974). For a well-known conservative attack on rehabilitation, see Wilson (1975). For good philosophical works on punishment

that include extensive discussions of philosophical problems with rehabilitation, see Duff (1986) and Boonin (2008).

47 For an older but still interesting reflection on justice and public disorder, see Mitchell (2003). I thank my colleague Marcelo Cruz for recommending Mitchell's book.

CHAPTER 3. A MATTER OF DIGNITY

1 Irwin (1985/2013, 67).

2 For good discussions of the growth of immigration incarceration, see Markowitz (2015); Carson and Diaz (2015); and Gottschalk (2016, 215–241). For access to ten reports about conditions in immigration jails during the Obama years, see Ray (2012).

3 For Cicero's account of dignity, see Cicero (2000, 6–8, 93–100). For discussions of Cicero, see Rosen (2012, 11–14) and Ober (2014, 53–64). For Pico della Mirandola, see Pico della Mirandola (1998). Some scholars see Pico as initiating a new, secular understanding of dignity. I disagree with this interpretation, instead reading Pico in light of his religious convictions. Piet Steenbakkers reads Pico this way; see Steenbakkers (2014). The literature on Kant and dignity is substantial. For some discussions, see Hill (2014), Kerstein (2014), Rosen (2012, 19–31), and Waldron (2012, 23–27). For one scholar who uses the image of God to defend human dignity, see Gushee (2014).

4 For a fascinating argument about the origins of inherent dignity in the Irish Constitution, see Moyn (2014).

5 For Waldron's discussion, see Waldron (2012, 13–14). For an account of the importance of human dignity in the South African Constitution, see Cameron (2014). For discussions of European constitutions and dignity, see Dupré (2014), Costa (2014), Dreir (2014), and Grim (2014). Jay M. Bernstein defends dignity by grounding it in ideas about trust; see Bernstein (2015).

6 I have discussed kinds of dignity in Jeffreys (2013, 113–124).

7 W. Norris Clarke, S.J. (1996) offers an excellent discussion of Thomas Aquinas and dignity. Although some contemporary thinkers argue that premodern thinkers like Aquinas and Pico reject inherent dignity, I think they support it on multiple theological and philosophical grounds. I won't defend this view in this book. For a wonderful defense of it with discussions of Aquinas, see Clarke (1993). I have applied this concept to ethics and torture; see Jeffreys (2008).

8 Philosopher Aurel Kolnai (1976) carefully develops a conception of dignity based on a person's bearing and response to her environment. For a recent discussion of dignity as a response to suffering, see Sedmak (2014).

9 Waldron (2012, 13–47) argues that modernity has extended aristocratic dignity to all human beings. Although I enjoy reading Waldron's work, I think he presents a weak account of the ontological basis of dignity.

10 I thank my colleague Greg Aldrete for helpful discussions about Cicero and dignity.

11 For good critiques of Pinker's arguments, see Griffiths (2008) and Meilaender (2009, 79–87).

12 Scheler is a complex thinker whose work presents readers with exegetical challenges. Generally, scholars divide his career into three periods, a pre-phenomenological period, his Christian period informed by phenomenology, and a post-Christian period in which he wrote extensively about the sociology of knowledge. I draw primarily from his Christian period, but also take material from his last period. In my work on Scheler, I have learned from the following sources: Staude (1967); Barber (1993); Blosser (1995); Deeken (1974); Frings (1965, 1997); Kelly (1977, 2011); Nota (1983); and Schneck (2002).

13 Phenomenologists call the bracketing of scientific and other knowledge the "phe-nomenological reduction." It is a complex concept that I do not discuss in this book. Husserl and Scheler also differ on how to employ it. Although Scheler was inspired by Husserl's work, he was never one of his disciples. The two thinkers differ on important topics, including the definition of philosophy and realism and idealism. For a discussion of their differences, see Frings (1997). In 1913, a group of Husserl's students broke with him, claiming that he had abandoned philosophical realism and endorsed idealism. Scheler sides with the "realist phenomenologists," and the realism/idealism debate remains a significant one among phenomenolo-gists. For discussions of it, see Mohanty (1995) and Ingarden (1975). In this book, I adopt the approach of the so-called realists, who include thinkers like Scheler, Adolph Reinach, Edith Stein, Roman Ingarden, John F. Crosby, and Barry Smith.

14 Contemporary analytic philosophers often distinguish between essential and accidental properties. Essential properties are those without which a being would not exist, while accidental properties can disappear while the being continues to exist. In these terms, dignity would be an essential property of the person, but hair color would be an accidental one. For an older, but well-known discussion of essential and accidental properties in analytic philosophy, see Plantinga (1979). Many analytic philosophers rely on possible worlds theory when discussing essential properties, but the phenomenologists I am drawing on in this book con-ceive of modality differently. In phenomenology, the search for essences is called an "eidetic method," and it relies on a complex conception of intuition. Analytic philosophers have often identified this approach with intuitionism, a movement in twentieth-century ethics. However, the phenomenological approach differs substantially from a simple appeal to an intuition of ethical truths. For a clear presentation of it, see Sokolowski (2000, 177–184). Husserl first fully defended this method in Husserl (2001a). He later linked eidetic intuition to complex issues in logic and modality; see Husserl (1973). Scheler explores eidetic intuition in several essays. For two good treatments of it, see Scheler (1973d) and Scheler (1973f).

15 How we classify values requires phenomenological work that I don't do in this book. Scheler devotes considerable attention to ordering of our values. For one of his discussions of rankings of values, see Scheler (1973a). In a well-known essay, he also discusses how love orders our values, developing the idea of an *ordo amoris*, or an order of love; see Scheler (1973c). Scheler's colleague Nicolai Hartmann strongly disagreed with him about how to rank values; see Hartmann

(1951, 44–71). Dietrich von Hildebrand differs from Scheler in drawing a distinction between the "subjectively satisfying" and the "important-in-itself." He refuses to say that pleasurable experiences like taking a warm bath involve values, and maintains that we experience values in a way that differs from these kinds of experiences of personal pleasure. For von Hildebrand's discussion, see von Hildebrand (1953, 23–65). In this book, I don't take a position on the issues dividing von Hildebrand and Scheler.

16 The strong influence of David Hume has shaped many attitudes toward ethics and the emotions. For one of Hume's discussion of sensations, see Hume (2000, bk. I, pt. 1, 116–121).

17 Of course, some twentieth-century thinkers in theology and philosophy rebelled against this trend in Anglo-American philosophy.

18 In Protestant ethics, James M. Gustafson has written extensively about the affections. For one example, see Gustafson (1975). He draws heavily on the American Protestant thinker Jonathan Edwards, who wrote a famous book about religious affections (see Edwards 2013). Von Hildebrand discusses the affections in many works, and I will be drawing on them throughout this book. For one clear discussion of the affective sphere using the language of "the heart," see von Hildebrand (2012). He makes careful distinctions between passions and affections, which I will not consider in this book.

19 Generally, philosophers have focused on intentionality and cognitive acts such as belief and knowledge. The concept of intentionality has roots in medieval Arabic and Christian philosophers. For an anthology examining its premodern uses, see Perler (2001). A neglected concept in much of modern philosophy, intentionality reappeared in the work of Franz Brentano; see Brentano (1973). Husserl made intentionality central to his thought, and those appropriating his work followed his lead. For Husserl's early use of the concept, see Husserl (2001b, 77–125). See also Sokolowski (2000, 8–16).

20 In contemporary classifications of the emotions, phenomenologists like Scheler and von Hildebrand would lie more in the direction of the "cognitivists," rather than the "non-cognitivists." Nussbaum is a cognitivist, while Jesse Prinz is a non-cognitivist. For a discussion of this distinction, see Prinz (2011, 56–82).

21 Phenomenologists agree in rejecting subjectivism, nominalism, and other approaches to values, but differ on the ontological status of values. Scheler mounts careful arguments against subjectivist theories of values that focus on mistaken or reductionist understandings of them. For one example, see Scheler (1973a, 86–100). The exact ontological status of values in Scheler is a matter of dispute. Some scholars maintain that he never really answers this question except to say that we don't create the values we experience. Others argue that he presents a clear ontology of values. For a good discussion of these issues, see Kelly (2011, 17–33, 61–81). Roman Ingarden wrote carefully about the ontological status of values. For some of his essays, see Ingarden (1983). I find Ingarden's essays particularly illuminating, and think he wrote more carefully on ontology than Scheler did.

22 For Scheler's important work on *ressentiment*, see Scheler (1972). Scheler discusses illusion and other distortions in "The Idols of Self-Knowledge" (Scheler 1973b).

23 Von Hildebrand discusses appropriate responses to value by using the concept of a "due response" to it. For the details of this complex and fascinating concept, see von Hildebrand (1953, 225–238).

24 Von Hildebrand discusses the will and self-transcendence in von Hildebrand (1953, 172–225).

25 In his book *The Nature of Love*, von Hildebrand carefully considers if transcendence comes at the expense of individuality and the person's subjectivity. He maintains that transcendence and subjectivity complement each other. For his discussion, see von Hildebrand (2009, 200–221).

26 Self-transcendence is not the only aspect of our nature that provides a ground for affirming inherent dignity. Elsewhere, I have discussed others like self-possession, communication without loss, and creativity; see Jeffreys (2008, 13–26) and Jeffreys (2013, 13–33).

27 For one example, see Scheler (1973a, 383).

28 Singer presents this argument in *Practical Ethics* (Singer 1993, 185–186).

29 Crosby uses the term "incommunicability" to describe that aspect of the person that does not participate in a universal or common nature. For his excellent discussion of this complex concept, see Crosby (1996, 41–81). Like Crosby, I have also found Jorge J. E. Gracia's work on individuality helpful; see Gracia (1988). In this paragraph, I draw heavily from Crosby's insights.

30 See Scheler (1973a, 489–494) and Scheler (1970, 121–125). For a good discussion of the issue of Scheler and personal individuality, see Crosby (2004b).

31 Scheler maintains that we cannot have knowledge of other persons and their value through analogy and inference. For his arguments, see Scheler (1970). For a similar argument in analytic philosophy in the 1960s, see Plantinga (1967, 187–245).

32 In the last two paragraphs, I rely on von Hildebrand's account of value perception. For his presentation, see von Hildebrand (1953, 211–225).

33 Thinkers who have written carefully and critically about the idea of social construction include John Searle and Sally Haslanger. For one of Searle's books on social construction, see Searle (1997). For Haslanger's work, see Haslanger (2012).

34 Jesse Prinz (2011) combines both a neuroscientific and a social agreement approach to values, particularly in his book *The Emotional Construction of Morals*. Prinz grounds many of his arguments in metaphysical naturalism. Like Husserl, Scheler, and von Hildebrand, I am not a metaphysical naturalist, and therefore find much of what Prinz writes unpersuasive. Additionally, I think he accepts the findings of psychology far too uncritically, ignoring the ontological, axiological, and social judgments of many psychologists. He shows little awareness of the extensive discussions of political, professional, and historical forces that shape psychological diagnoses. He never engages the work of thinkers like Foucault, Scull, Hacking, and many others who show how political views shape psychological

classification. Too often, he simply cites studies in psychology without recognizing their controversial nature. Finally, Prinz seeks to eliminate intentionality, but deals with it superficially and carelessly. For these and other reasons, I don't find his work helpful in exploring the emotions and dignity.

35 Husserl wrote an important dissent from naturalism in the last years of his life after the Nazis expelled him from German universities. Although it contains problematic ideas about European exceptionalism and the future of philosophy, it remains an important attack on naturalism that deserves careful attention today. For this work, see Husserl (1970). Dermot Moran has written a critical but appreciative study of this text that brings it into conversation with contemporary philosophy; see Moran (2012).

36 For just one example that contains good essays, see Gocke (2012).

37 I discussed this issue in a debate with Robert Kraynak; see Jeffreys (2004b) and Jeffreys (2004a).

38 I will return to this point in the next chapter when I discuss stigma.

39 For Scheler's discussion of autonomy, see Scheler (1973a, 494–501).

40 Jay Bernstein also considers this question when he explores Jean Hampton's work; see Bernstein (2015, 129–139).

41 I have explored dignity and torture in *Spirituality and the Ethics of Torture* (Jeffreys 2008). Drawing on the thought of the French thinker and survivor of the Nazi concentration camps Jean Améry, Jay Bernstein insightfully explores how torture undermines a person's trust in the world; see Bernstein (2015, 218–244).

42 Scheler recognizes this point; see Scheler (1970, 14).

43 I wrote about this phenomenon in *Spirituality and the Ethics of Torture* (Jeffreys 2008, 73–74). When I published this book, a few journalists and scholars had reported on this abuse. The role of psychologists in crafting torture policy was later confirmed in the 2014 Senate report on CIA torture; see Senate Select Committee on Intelligence (2014). For a discussion of a recent report on psychologists and the "war on terror," see Risen (2015).

44 For a discussion of how sexual relations with slaves reflect or don't reflect a sense of their humanity, see Davis (2014, 9–10, 21).

45 For an excellent account of Italian fascism, see Bosworth (2007).

46 For an assessment of the successes and failures of the PREA, see Bozelkoapril (2015) and Kaiser and Stannow (2012).

47 I am grateful to an anonymous reader from New York University Press who urged me to provide a more robust account of our failure to grasp the dignity of others. He or she offered a careful reading of an earlier version of this chapter that made me think long and hard about our distorted value perception.

CHAPTER 4. WHY DO WE STIGMATIZE INMATES?

1 Simon (2009, 6).

2 For some good discussions of the growth of background checks, see Bushway et al. (2007); Holzer, Raphael, and Stoll (2004); and Pager (2007).

3 In the next two paragraphs, I draw entirely on von Hildebrand's account of diverse kinds of value blindness; see von Hildebrand (1957, 11–38).

4 For one example, see Prinz (2011).

5 Prinz recognizes that intentionality presents problems for a naturalistic account of the emotions. For this reason, he tries to eliminate it altogether. Without intentionality, we encounter difficulties in differentiating between emotions, and Prinz tries to meet them. I don't find his arguments persuasive. For one of his discussions of these issues, see Prinz (2011, 60–68).

6 For discussions of the ambivalence and attractiveness of disgust, see Kolnai (2004a, 42–48), McGinn (2011, 41–65), and Nussbaum (2004, 87–99, 121).

7 For Kolnai's list of objects that elicit disgust, see Kolnai (2004a, 52–86). For McGinn's list, see McGinn (2011, 97–122). For Miller's list, see Miller (1998, 38). For Nussbaum's list, see Nussbaum (2004, 87–99). Kolnai's list contains idiosyncratic items that reflect 1920s Austrian society, and I don't share his moral assessment of practices such as homosexuality.

8 For Nussbaum's discussion of disgust and anti-Semitism, see Nussbaum (2004, 108–114). See also Bernstein (2015, 267–279).

9 I thank Michael Wreen for helpful conversations about disgust that helped me clarify my position. To account for certain forms of moral disgust, Nussbaum appeals to psychological laws of contagion and similarity to explain how we move from our disgust at core objects like feces to groups of people. She draws on psychologist Paul Rozin's work to make her case. I don't think these psychological "laws" exist, and therefore find Nussbaum's argument completely unpersuasive. For her argument, see Nussbaum (2004, 92–95).

10 Bernstein defends the idea that disgust can be a response to the destruction of human dignity; see Bernstein (2015, 279–286). He links disgust and our response to the human form in complex and interesting ways that I won't discuss in this book.

11 Ahmed adopts a philosophical framework that differs significantly from the phenomenological one I defend in this book, but I will not engage these differences in detail.

12 I have written extensively on this topic. For one example, see Jeffreys (2013, 108–110).

13 For an excellent early investigation of this torture, see Conroy (2001). For an archive of good articles on the Jon Burge case in the *Chicago Tribune*, see "Jon Burge" at http://articles.chicagotribune.com.

14 In 2016, the DOJ found a similar pattern of abuse in the Baltimore Police Department. Baltimore has long had problems with its jail, which had to close at one point because of violence and corruption. For the DOJ report on the Baltimore Police Department, see U.S. Department of Justice, Civil Rights Division (2016).

15 John Conroy writes eloquently about how we don't believe victims of torture because they often come from segments of society that the public devalues; see Conroy (2001, 242–257).

16 I have taken the details of this case from "Rikers Island Death" (2015). On April 17, 2016, the news show *CBS 60 Minutes* obtained disturbing footage of Bradley Bal-

lard in Rikers. It showed staff members walking past his cell, and people apparently reacting in disgust to the conditions of his cell; see "Rikers Island" (2016).

17 For the details of this case, I have relied on "Officer at Rikers Island Is Charged" (2014).

18 See "Parents Say Jailers' Denial of Meds Killed Son" (2016).

19 Marie Gottschalk chronicles the dynamics I discuss in this paragraph; see Gottschalk (2006, 2016). She writes about the role victims' rights groups have played in designing policies that contribute to mass incarceration. I have learned a lot from reading her work.

20 In this paragraph, all references are to Vera Institute of Justice (2015, 29).

21 For a detailed discussion of bail and jail population, see Clark (2010).

22 Researchers began noticing these unfair outcomes at least as far back as the 1960s, when the Vera Institute conducted its famous Manhattan Bail Study in New York City. On this topic, I have found the following sources useful: Williams (2003) and Velázquez, Neal, and Bradford (2012).

23 Private phone companies charge excessive fees to inmates in jails. For a report on this phenomenon, see Prison Policy Initiative (2013). The organization's website (www.prisonpolicy.org) contains other blogs and posts related to the issue of the phone industry in jails and prisons.

24 For Feeley's book, see Feeley (1992).

25 For an excellent study of how New York City punishes misdemeanor offenders without convicting them, see Kohler-Hausmann (2014). Kohler-Hausmann uses the term "managerial justice" instead of "actuarial justice." She focuses on how officials use misdemeanor arrests and records to affect the behavior of hundreds of thousands of people in New York City.

26 Willie Horton was an inmate in Massachusetts who committed crimes while on furlough from prison, and became the subject of an infamous Republican attack advertisement during the 1988 presidential election.

CHAPTER 5. WHAT CAN WE DO?

1 Chicago Community Trust (1922, 23).

2 For Foucault's famous discussion, see Foucault (1985, 195–231). Critics debate the historical accuracy and philosophical merit of Foucault's interpretation of Bentham. I think Foucault significantly ignores how physical torture has been part of the history of jails and prisons since their inception. I also reject his philosophical approach to the person and values. For these reasons, I have avoided using Foucault's work in this book. For an excellent book that discusses Foucault's interpretation of Bentham and Bentham's historical context, see Semple (1993). Semple considers the contradictions in Bentham's thought. On one hand, his proposals for the Panopticon reflect a totalitarian vision. On the other hand, he had a deep interest in political liberty. The tension between these aspects of his thought has puzzled Bentham scholars for a long time.

3 For a helpful discussion of bonding and funding for county jails, see Petteruti and Walsh (2008, 18–21).

4 Liat Ben-Moshe has written thoughtfully about the tension between reformist and radical approaches to coercive institutions, and I have learned from her work. For one of her essays, see Ben-Moshe (2013).

5 The U.S. federal government counts seventy-nine jails in "Indian Country"; see Minton (2015). We are only beginning to get good information about what happens in these institutions.

6 The *Washington Post* did excellent reporting on this case. For an editorial on this cases, see "In a Virginia jail, a Young Man Wasted Away and Died" (2016). For similar cases in my state where families gained little information about why their loved ones died in custody, see "Unanswered Questions Surround Deaths" (2014).

7 I am grateful to Michael Mushlin for helpful correspondence about jail monitoring.

8 For one example, see "Lincoln Hills Officials Failed to Oversee Rape Investigations" (2016). For an example of the *New York Times* coverage of the Clinton Prison abuses, see "An Inmate Dies and No One Is Punished" (2015).

9 The ACLU maintains a website with a docket of its ongoing cases. It is available at www.aclu.org. In 2006 in my state of Wisconsin, the ACLU brought a lawsuit against the woman's prison, the Taycheedah Correctional Facility. It revealed a host of degrading conditions, and a complete failure to dispense psychiatric medications properly. The ACLU settled the lawsuit with the state, and conditions have improved at Taycheedah. I thank Amy Fettig of the ACLU's National Prison Project for a helpful conversation about how the ACLU takes its cases.

10 For references, see chapter 2, note 6.

11 Several decades ago, John J. Dilulio strongly condemned judicial interventions in penal systems, arguing that they were counterproductive and inefficient; see Dilulio (1990). For a more balanced and in my view more convincing assessment of judicial intervention, see Feeley and Rubin (1998). Some of the debate about judicial intervention focuses on the Texas prison system. For one good discussion of this debate, see Perkinson (2010, 251–286). Recently, Jonathan Simon has written insightfully and eloquently about the possibility of new judicial interventions based on Supreme Court decisions; see Simon (2014, 133–173). I will return to Simon's work in the conclusion.

12 The use-of-force recommendations I discuss in the next few paragraphs appear in many DOJ documents. They seem to be standard suggestions for reducing excessive force in jails and prisons. For one good example, see the DOJ Consent Decree with the Miami-Dade County Jail, which has often experienced difficulties with excessive force (U.S. Department of Justice, Civil Rights Division 2013b, sec. III, A, 5–6). See also Human Rights Watch (2015).

13 The general recommendations I discuss in this section also appear in many DOJ documents. The DOJ Consent Agreement with the Cook County Jail provides one

good example; see *United States of America v. Cook County, Illinois, Agreed Order*, no. 10 C 2946 (N.D. Ill., May 13, 2010), www.justice.gov.

14 For a website with resources about CIT training, see CIT International, www.citinternational.org.

15 In his survey work, E. Fuller Torrey often defines "serious" and "severe" psychiatric illness as "schizophrenia, schizoaffective disorder, bipolar disorder, and major depression with psychotic features" (Torrey et al. 2014, 26).

16 For discussions of the failures of community treatment in mental health care, see Grob (1991). Public opposition to halfway houses and community corrections was often fierce in the late 1970s and early 1980s. Those proposing to revive community corrections and mental health initiatives need to explain how they will overcome this kind of opposition in an era that shows little tolerance for marginalized people.

17 Examples of this kind of narrative include Torrey (2013) and Johnson (1990).

18 Willowbrook was a giant state mental hospital on Staten Island in New York City. It held more than five thousand people in filthy conditions where they were physically and sexually abused. In the 1950s and early 1960s, Dr. Saul Krugman performed hepatitis experiments on children at Willowbrook that including feeding them feces-laden milk. For a discussion of Willowbrook, see Rothman and Rothman (2005). The Pennhurst State School was a giant mental institution in Pennsylvania where thousands of patients lived in squalor. For a good discussion of Pennhurst, see Beitiks (2012). The Camarillo State Hospital in Camarillo, California, was the largest state mental hospital west of the Mississippi. It had a long history of abusing and neglecting its patients. Although it held over seven thousand inmates in the 1950s, scholarship on Camarillo seems thin, and I've been unable to locate anything more than memoirs about it.

19 The literature on coerced sterilization in the United States is substantial. Randell Hansen and Desmond King offer a good bibliography; see Hansen and King (2013). Hansen and King estimate that sixty-three thousand Americans were coercively sterilized in the twentieth century. This is a conservative estimate, and the number is probably higher given the number of illegal sterilizations that occurred in state mental institutions. Many of them never kept records of those they sterilized.

20 Elliot S. Valenstein chronicles the disturbing history of psychosurgery in the United States; see Valenstein (1986). In a fascinating study of treatments for those with mental illness in the early part of the twentieth century, Andrew Scull details the experiments of Henry Cotton in New Jersey. Cotton removed all the teeth of his patients at the Trenton State Hospital in New Jersey because he held that chronic infections caused mental illness; see Scull (2007).

21 For a further discussion of this topic, see Harcourt (2007).

22 For one good account of approaches to risk assessment, see Justice Policy Institute (2012).

23 I am grateful to Marie VanNostrand for corresponding with me about the PSA. She has been one of the main researchers developing it with the Arnold Foundation.

24 I thank Bernard Harcourt for helping me to gain clarity about this point.

25 I am grateful to Cliff Keenan, Director of Pretrial Services for the District of Columbia, for a helpful conversation and correspondence about the District of Columbia's Pretrial Services.

26 Bernard Harcourt makes this point about statistical arguments and crime in many of his writings; see Harcourt (2006, 2011). I have learned much from reading his work.

27 In this paragraph, I draw heavily on Constitution Project (2015).

28 *Rothgery v. Gillespie County*, 554 U.S. 191 (2008).

29 *Rothgery v. Gillespie County*, 554 U.S. 191 (2008), 2.

30 Marie Gottschalk has written insightfully about the excessive power of prosecutors in the United States. For her discussions, see Gottschalk (2006, 77–115) and Gottschalk (2016, 258–283). John F. Pfaff has also written an excellent book arguing that U.S. prosecutors have too much power; see Pfaff (2017, 127–159). The literature on policing and arrests is large. For one discussion of it that focuses on misdemeanor arrests and includes references to articles on "broken windows" and "stop and frisk" policing, see Kohler-Hausmann (2014).

CONCLUSION

1 Dostoyevsky (2004, 19–20).

2 For example, Elizabeth Hinton does an excellent job of exploring how modern American liberalism contributed to mass incarceration. However, she displays a remarkable confidence that history could have moved in a different direction if people had only made choices she believes they should have made. At the end of her book, she states that today's incidents of police brutality and killings of African Americans "could have been avoided entirely had federal policymakers decided to respond in a different way to the civil rights movement and the enlightened protest of the 1960s" (Hinton 2016, 339–340). I don't share this confidence that the history of our penal system could have been different had we only followed the lead of enlightened people.

3 *Hudson et al. v. Preckwinkle et al.*, no. 13cv8752 (N.D. Ill., February 27, 2014), sec. 4, http://uplcchicago.org.

4 For one example of this kind of work, see the Justice Policy Institute website, www.justicepolicy.org, which provides access to numerous reports aimed at reforming the jail while providing for public safety.

5 For a recent study of Cook County's efforts that evaluates them positively, see Reidel et al. (2016). For an excellent discussion of misdemeanor arrests in New York City, see Kohler-Hausmann (2014).

6 An older but still good look at jails in the nineteenth century is Jordan (1970a). Jordan also penned a fascinating essay about how Western territories and states punished horse thieves through a combination of flogging, lynching, vigilante committees, and prisons; see Jordan (1970b). Timothy J. Gilfoyle paints an extraordinary picture of the corruption, brutality, and squalor of New York City's

famous Tombs Jail; see Gilfoyle (2003). I learned of these sources from Melanie D. Newport, who keeps a blog about the history of the jail that I have found useful; see Newport (n.d.).

7 Hernàndez has also published a fine book where she shows how throughout its history, Los Angeles used its jail to control the lives of Native Americans, Chinese and Mexican immigrants, and African Americans; see Hernàndez (2017).

8 I have participated in a restorative justice workshop at the Green Bay Correctional Institution. It is a powerful experience that can bring about important changes in people. However, I don't think it can entirely replace other forms of justice. It requires the voluntary participation of offenders, and some are unwilling to cooperate.

9 Nicolas Carrier and Justin Piché have written insightfully about the nuances and complexities of the abolitionist movement; see Carrier and Piché (2015a, 2015b). I have learned much from these articles, and I thank Nicolas Carrier for corresponding with me about his work.

10 For a fascinating account of debates about punishment in nineteenth-century America, see Glenn (1984). Stephen J. Leonard tells a horrifying story of lynching in Colorado before the state began using jails and prisons as its primary means of punishment; see Leonard (2002). For an examination of how local authorities and mobs used lynching to support white supremacy, see Wood (2009).

11 Scholars often discuss why Scandinavian countries avoid some of the problems we find in penal institutions in the United States and elsewhere. The "Scandinavian exception" has been a subject of considerable scholarly attention. For a good article on this topic, see Ugerlvik (2016).

12 Robert Ferguson and James Q. Whitman have both written intriguing studies of why Americans have remained more punitive than their European counterparts. For these books, see Ferguson (2014) and Whitman (2003).

13 Although I don't always think it's particularly applicable to the United States, I have learned from the tradition of criminology in Norway. I find Nils Christie's work thoughtful and challenging; see Christie (2007).

14 For the debate about the origins of penal institutions in the United States, see McKelvey (1977), Rothman (1990), and Meranze (2012). One book that details the torture that occurred in New York State prisons is William David Lewis's history; see Lewis (1965).

15 The Stanford prison experiment, conducted by social psychologist Philip Zimbardo in 1971, involved placing Stanford students in a mock prison where some were assigned the role of guards and others the role of inmates. After a few days, Zimbardo halted the study because the "guards" engaged in abusive behavior. I am highly critical of this experiment, primarily because I think it failed to provide adequate informed consent for its participants. Recently, Zimbardo applied the results of his experiments to the Abu Ghraib prisoner scandal in Iraq, and provided a full reprisal and reflection on his experiment. For this work, see Zimbardo (2008).

16 Discussions of this concept appear in many articles on prison abolitionism. For
    two examples, see Carrier and Piché (2015a) and McLeod (2015).
17 James Q. Whitman provides a useful discussion of degradation in punishment,
    distinguishing between punishment that degrades and punishment that incapaci-
    tates; see Whitman (2003, 19–39).
18 The literature on "broken windows" policing is large. The theory originally ap-
    peared in the writings of James Q. Wilson and George L. Kelling; see Wilson
    and Kelling (1982). For a highly critical examination of this theory, see Harcourt
    (2005).
19 One of the most extensive studies that relates school policy, police behavior, and
    juvenile justice is Fabelo et al. (2011). In this and other studies, African Ameri-
    cans, Latinos, and students with disabilities are disproportionally represented
    among those students arrested by police authorities at school. The Center for
    Public Integrity has done a great deal of work on this issue under the rubric of
    "Juvenile Justice." For its website with useful links, see www.publicintegrity.org.
20 For good discussions of this issue, see McLeod (2016), Miller (2004), and Stefan
    and Winick (2005).
21 A good recent example of the kind of approach I note in this paragraph is the
    report of the Independent Commission on New York City Criminal Justice and
    Incarceration Reform (2017). This document outlines a plan to close Rikers Island
    and replace it with smaller jails throughout New York City. In many ways, this
    is a remarkable document, with many important policy prescriptions and a call
    to close one of the worst jails in the county. However, it fails to explore some key
    questions about what might replace the jail, particularly for those who suffer from
    mental illness. Instead, it makes vague recommendations for "community-based
    services."

BIBLIOGRAPHY

Ahmed, Sara. 2014. *The Cultural Politics of Emotion.* 2nd ed. New York: Routledge.

Alexander, Michelle. 2012. *The New Jim Crow: Mass Incarceration in the Era of Color-blindness.* New York: New Press.

———. 2016. "Following Horrific Violence, Something More Is Required of Us: We Need a Profound Shift in Our Collective Consciousness in Order to Challenge an Entrenched System of Racial and Social Control—and Build a New America." *Moyers and Company,* July 9. http://billmoyers.com.

American Civil Liberties Union. 2006. "Abandoned and Abused: Orleans Parish Prisoners in the Wake of Hurricane Katrina." August. www.aclu.org.

———. 2009. "Immigration Officials Sued for Holding Detainees in Appalling Conditions at L.A. Detention Facility." April 2. www.aclu.org.

———. 2010. "In for a Penny: The Rise of America's New Debtors' Prisons." October. www.aclu.org.

———. 2011. "Cruel and Usual Punishment: How a Savage Gang of Deputies Controls Los Angeles Jails." September. www.aclu.org.

———. 2012. "Joint Statement by Passaic County, the Seton Hall Law School Center for Social Justice and the American Civil Liberties Union of New Jersey regarding Colon, et al. v. Passaic County, et al." February. www.aclu-nj.org.

———. 2015. "Locked in the Past: Montana's Jails in Crisis." February. http://aclumontana.org.

———. N.d. "National Prison Project." www.aclu.org.

American Psychiatric Association. 2004. "Mental Illness and the Criminal Justice System: Redirecting Resources toward Treatment, Not Containment, Resource Document." May 2. www.floridatac.com.

Arnold Foundation. 2013. "Developing a National Model for Pretrial Risk Assessment." November. www.arnoldfoundation.org.

"As City Jail Death Rates Rise, Will Reforms Help?" 2015. *Philadelphia Daily News,* November 3. www.philly.com.

"At Rikers Island, Union Chief's Clout Is a Roadblock to Reform." 2014. *New York Times,* December 14. www.nytimes.com.

Baradaran, Shima, and Frank McIntyre. 2011. "Predicting Violence." *Texas Law Review* 90: 497–570. http://ssrn.com.

Barber, Michael D. 1993. *Guardian of Dialogue: Max Scheler's Sociology of Knowledge and Philosophy of Love.* Lewisburg, PA: Bucknell University Press.

Bazelon, Emily. 2017. "Department of Justification." *New York Times Magazine*, February 28. www.nytimes.com.

Beitiks, Emily Smith. 2012. "The Ghosts of Institutionalization at Pennhurst's Haunted Asylum." *Hastings Center Report* 42 (1): 22–24.

Ben-Moshe, Liat. 2013. "The Tension between Abolition and Reform." In *The End of Prisons: Reflections from the Decarceration Movement*, edited by Mechthild E. Nagel and Anthony J. Nocella II, 83–93. Amsterdam, Netherlands: Rodopi.

———. 2017. "The Institution Yet to Come: Analyzing Incarceration through Disability Lens." In *The Disability Studies Reader*, 5th ed., edited by Leonard J. Davis, 119–130. New York: Routledge.

Bentham, Jeremy. 2011. *The Panopticon Writings (Radical Thinkers)*. Edited by Miron Bizovic. Brooklyn, NY: Verso.

Bernstein, Jay M. 2015. *Torture and Democracy: An Essay on Moral Inquiry*. Chicago: University of Chicago Press.

"Beyond Punishment: A Miami-Herald I-team Investigation of Lowell Correctional Institution." 2015. *Miami Herald*, December 13–20. http://miami-herald.com.

Blackmon, Douglas A. 2008. *Slavery by Another Name: The Re-enslavement of Black People in America from the Civil War to World War II*. New York: Doubleday.

Blosser, Philip. 1995. *Scheler's Critique of Kant's Ethics*. Athens: Ohio University Press.

Blue, Ethan. 2012. *Doing Time in the Depression: Everyday Life in Texas and California Prisons*. New York: New York University Press.

Boonin, David. 2008. *The Problem of Punishment*. Cambridge: Cambridge University Press.

Bosworth, R. J. B. 2007. *Mussolini's Italy: Life under the Fascist Dictatorship, 1915–1945*. New York: Penguin.

Bozelkoapril, Chandra. 2015. "Why We Let Prison Rape Go On." *New York Times*, April 17. www.nytimes.com.

Brentano, Franz. 1973. *Psychology from an Empirical Standpoint*. Edited by Oskar Kraus. Translated by Antos C. Rancurello, D. B. Terrell, and Linda L. McAlister. New York: Humanities Press.

Bushway, Shawn, Shauna Brigg, Faye Taxman, Meredith Thanner, and Michelle Van Brakle. 2007. "Private Providers of Criminal History Records: Do You Get What You Pay For?" In *Barriers to Reentry? The Labor Market for Released Prisoners in Post-industrial America*, edited by Shawn Bushway, Michael A. Stoll, and David F. Weiman, 174–200. New York: Russell Sage Foundation.

Cameron, Edwin. 2014. "Dignity and Disgrace: Moral Citizenship and Constitutional Protection." In McCrudden, *Understanding Human Dignity*, 467–483.

Caputo, Angela. 2013. "Charges Dismissed." *Chicago Reporter*, November 4. http://chicagoreporter.com.

Carrier, Nicolas, and Justin Piché. 2015a. "Blind Spots of Abolitionist Thought in Academia: On Longstanding and Emerging Challenges." *Champ pénal/Penal Field* 12. http://champpenal.revues.org.

———. 2015b. "The State of Abolitionism." *Champ pénal/Penal Field* 12. http://champ-penal.revues.org.

Carson, Bethany, and Eliana Diaz. 2015. "Payoff: How Congress Ensures Private Prison Profit with an Immigrant Detention Quota." Grassroots Leadership, April. http://grassrootsleadership.org.

Chicago Appleseed Fund for Justice. 2013. "Pre-trial Delay and Length of Stay in Cook County Jail: Observations and Recommendations from the Chicago Appleseed Fund for Justice." October. www.chicagoappleseed.org.

Chicago Community Trust. 1922. *The Cook County Jail Survey*. Chicago: Chicago Community Trust.

"Chicago Inmate Gouges Out His Eyes: The Cost of Not Caring." 2014. *USA Today*, July 21. www.usatoday.com.

Christie, Nils. 2007. *Limits to Pain: The Role of Punishment in Penal Policy*. Eugene, OR: Wipf and Stock.

Cicero. 2000. *On Obligations*. Translated with an introduction and notes by P. G. Walsh. Oxford: Oxford University Press.

Clark, John. 2010. "The Impact of Money Bail on Jail Bed Usage." *American Jails*, July/August: 47–54. www.readperiodicals.com.

Clarke, W. Norris, S.J. 1993. *Person and Being*. Milwaukee: Marquette University Press.

———. 1996. "Living on the Edge: The Human Person as 'Frontier Being' and Micro-cosm." *International Philosophical Quarterly* 36 (2): 183–199.

———. 2001. *The One and the Many: A Contemporary Thomistic Metaphysics*. South Bend, IN: University of Notre Dame Press.

Conroy, John. 2001. *Unspeakable Acts, Ordinary People: The Dynamics of Torture. An Examination of the Practice of Torture in Three Democracies*. Oakland: University of California Press.

Constitution Project. 2015. "Don't I Need a Lawyer? Pretrial Justice and the Right to Counsel at First Judicial Bail Hearing." March. www.constitutionproject.org.

"Cook County Department of Corrections, Cermak Health Services, Cook County, Health and Hospital Systems." N.d. http://hmprg.org.

Costa, Jean-Paul. 2014. "Human Dignity in the Jurisprudence of the European Court of Human Rights." In McCrudden, *Understanding Human Dignity*, 393–403.

"County Jail Exits Federal Oversight of 40 Years." 2017. *Chicago Tribune*, June 12. www.chicagotribune.com.

Crosby, John F. 1996. *The Selfhood of the Human Person*. Washington, DC: Catholic University of America Press.

———. 2004a. "A Neglected Source of Human Dignity." In *Personalist Papers*, 3–33. Washington, DC: Catholic University of America Press.

———. 2004b. "Max Scheler on Personal Individuality." In *Personalist Papers*, 145–173. Washington, DC: Catholic University of America Press.

Cummins, Eric. 1994. *The Rise and Fall of California's Radical Prison Movement*. Stanford, CA: Stanford University Press.

Cusac, Anne-Marie. 2009. *Cruel and Unusual: The Culture of Punishment in America.* New Haven, CT: Yale University Press.

Davis, Angela Y. 2003. *Are Prisons Obsolete?* New York: Seven Stories Press.

Davis, David Brion. 2014. *The Problem of Slavery in the Age of Emancipation.* New York: Knopf.

Davis, Zachary. 2014. "Scheler and Human Dignity." In McCrudden, *Understanding Human Dignity*, 268–275.

Debs, Eugene V. 2000. *Walls and Bars: Prison and Prison Life in the "Land of the Free."* Introduction by David Dellinger. Chicago: Charles H. Kerr.

Deeken, Alfons, S.J. 1974. *Process and Permanence in Ethics: Max Scheler's Moral Philosophy.* New York: Paulist Press.

Deitch, Michelle. 2010. "Independent Correctional Oversight Mechanisms across the United States: A 50-State Inventory." *Pace Law Review* 30: 1754–1929. http://digitalcommons.pace.edu.

"Deplorable Conditions on Display at Wayne County Jails." 2015. *Detroit Free Press*, August 17. www.freep.com.

De Waal, Frans. 2016. *Are We Smart Enough to Know How Smart Animals Are?* New York: Norton.

Dickerson, John. 2007. "Inhumanity Has a Price." *Phoenix New Times*, December 20. www.phoenixnewtimes.com.

Dilulio, John J. 1990. *Governing Prisons: A Comparative Study of Correctional Management.* New York: Free Press.

Dostoyevsky, Fyodor. 2004. *House of the Dead* and *Poor Folk*. Introduction by Joseph Frank. Translated by Constance Garnett. New York: Barnes & Noble.

Drier, Horst. 2014. "Human Dignity in German Law." In Düwell et al., *Cambridge Handbook of Human Dignity*, 375–385.

Dubler, Joshua. 2014. *Down in the Chapel: Religious Life in an American Prison.* New York: Farrar, Straus and Giroux.

Duff, R. A. 1986. *Trials and Punishments.* Cambridge: Cambridge University Press.

Dumke, Mike. 2013. "Do We Have the Right People Locked Up? How a Medieval Court System Is Costing You Money—and Compromising Safety." *Chicago Reader*, October 16. www.chicagoreader.com.

Dupré, Catherine. 2014. "Constructing the Meaning of Human Dignity: Four Questions." In McCrudden, *Understanding Human Dignity*, 113–123.

Düwell, Marcus, Jens Braarvig, Roger Brownsword, and Dietmar Mieth, eds. 2014. *The Cambridge Handbook of Human Dignity: Interdisciplinary Perspectives.* Cambridge: Cambridge University Press.

Dworkin, Ronald. 1978. *Taking Rights Seriously.* Cambridge, MA: Harvard University Press.

Edwards, Jonathan. 2013. *The Religious Affections.* Reprint ed. Mineola, NY: Dover Publications.

"18 Current, Former L.A. County Sheriff's Deputies Face Federal Charges." 2013. *Los Angeles Times*, December 9. www.latimes.com.

English, Clarence Richard. 2007. *Jail Barn Boss: Memoir of a Former Jail Warden*. Kearney, NH: Morris.

Evans, Timothy C. 2017. "General Order No. 18.8A. Procedures for Bail Hearings and Pretrial Release." Circuit Court of Cook County, Illinois, July 17. www.cookcountycourt.org.

Fabelo, Tony, Michael D. Thompson, Martha Plotkin, Dottie Carmichael, Minor P. Marchbanks III, and Eric A. Booth. 2011. *Breaking School Rules: A Statewide Study of How School Discipline Relates to Students' Success and Juvenile Justice Involvement*. New York: Justice Center, Council on State Governments, July. http://csgjusticecenter.org.

Feeley, Malcolm M. 1992. *The Process Is the Punishment*. New York: Russell Sage Foundation.

Feeley, Malcolm M., and Edward L. Rubin. 1998. *Judicial Policy Making and the Modern State: How the Courts Reformed America's Prisons*. New York: Cambridge University Press.

Feeley, Malcolm M., and Jonathan Simon. 1992. "The New Penology: Notes on the Emerging Strategy of Corrections and Its Implications." *Criminology* 30: 449–474. http://scholarship.law.berkeley.edu.

Ferguson, Robert A. 2014. *Inferno: An Anatomy of American Punishment*. Cambridge, MA: Harvard University Press.

Foucault, Michel. 1985. *Discipline and Punish: The Birth of the Prison*. Translated by Alan Sheridan. New York: Vintage Books.

Frings, Manfred S. 1965. *Max Scheler: A Concise Introduction to the World of a Great Thinker*. Pittsburgh, PA: Duquesne University Press.

———. 1997. *The Mind of Max Scheler*. Milwaukee: Marquette University Press.

Gilfoyle, Timothy J. 2003. "'America's Greatest Criminal Barracks': The Tombs and the Experience of Criminal Justice in New York City, 1838–1897." *Journal of Urban History* 29 (5): 525–554.

Glenn, Myra C. 1984. *Campaigns Against Corporal Punishment: Prisoners, Sailors, Women, and Children in Antebellum America*. Albany: State University of New York Press.

Gocke, Benedikt Paul, ed. 2012. *After Physicalism*. South Bend, IN: University of Notre Dame Press.

Goffman, Alice. 2014. *On the Run: Fugitive Life in an American City*. Chicago: University of Chicago Press.

Goffman, Erving. 1986. *Stigma: Note on the Management of a Spoiled Identity*. New York: Touchstone Books.

———. 2007. *Asylums: Essays on the Social Situation of Mental Patients and Other Inmates*. Piscataway, NJ: Transaction.

Gottschalk, Marie. 2006. *The Prison and Gallows: The Politics of Mass Incarceration in America*. Cambridge: Cambridge University Press.

———. 2012. "The Carceral State and the Politics of Punishment." In *Handbook of Punishment and Society*, edited by Jonathan Simon and Richard Sparks, 205–241. Newbury Park, CA: Sage.

———. 2016. *Caught: The Prison State and the Lockdown of American Politics.* Princeton, NJ: Princeton University Press.

"Gov. Hogan Announces 'Immediate' Closure of Baltimore Jail." 2015. *Baltimore Sun*, July 30. www.baltimoresun.com.

Gracia, Jorge J. E. 1988. *Individuality: An Essay on the Foundations of Metaphysics.* Albany: State University of New York Press.

Griffin, Donald R. 2001. *Animal Minds: From Cognition to Consciousness.* Chicago: University of Chicago Press.

Griffiths, Paul J. 2008. "The Very Autonomous Stephen Pinker." *First Things*, August. www.firstthings.com.

Grim, Dieter. 2014. "Dignity in a Legal Context: Dignity as an Absolute Right." In McCrudden, *Understanding Human Dignity*, 381–391.

Grob, Gerald N. 1991. *From Asylum to Community: Mental Health Policy in Modern America.* Princeton, NJ: Princeton University Press.

———. 2011. *Mad among Us: A History of the Care of the Mentally Ill.* New York: Free Press.

Guenther, Lisa. 2013. *Solitary Confinement: Social Death and Its Afterlives.* Minneapolis: University of Minnesota Press.

Gushee, David P. 2014. "A Christian Theological Account of Human Worth." In McCrudden, *Understanding Human Dignity*, 275–288.

Gustafson, James M. 1975. *Can Ethics Be Christian?* Chicago: University of Chicago Press.

Hacking, Ian. 2000. *The Social Construction of What?* Cambridge, MA: Harvard University Press.

Hansen, Randell, and Desmond King. 2013. *Sterilized by the State: Eugenics, Race, and the Population Scare in Twentieth-Century North America.* Cambridge: Cambridge University Press.

Harcourt, Bernard. 2003. "The Shaping of Chance: Actuarial Models and Criminal Profiling at the Turn of the Twenty-First Century." *University of Chicago Law Review* 70: 105–127.

———. 2005. *Illusions of Order: The False Promise of Broken Windows Theory.* Cambridge, MA: Harvard University Press.

———. 2006. "From the Asylum to the Prison: Rethinking the Incarceration Revolution." *University of Texas Law Review* 84: 1751–1786.

———. 2007. *Against Prediction: Profiling, Policing and Punishing in an Actuarial Age.* Chicago: University of Chicago Press.

———. 2011. "An Institutionalization Effect: The Impact of Mental Hospitalization and Imprisonment on Homicide in the United States, 1934–2001." *Journal of Legal Studies* 40: 39–83.

Hartmann, Nicolai. 1951. *Ethics.* Vol. 2, *Moral Values.* Translated by Stanton Coit. Introduction by J. H. Muirhead. London: George Allen & Unwin.

Haslanger, Sally. 2012. *Resisting Reality: Social Construction and Social Critique.* Oxford: Oxford University Press.

Hernàndez, Kelly Lytle. 2014. "Hobos in Heaven: Race, Incarceration, and the Rise of Los Angeles, 1880–1910." *Pacific Historical Review* 3: 410–447.

———. 2017. *City of Inmates: Conquest, Rebellion, and the Rise of Human Caging in Los Angeles, 1771–1965*. Chapel Hill: University of North Carolina Press.

Hill, Thomas E. 2014. "Kantian Perspectives on the Rational Basis of Human Dignity." In Düwell et al., *Cambridge Handbook of Human Dignity*, 215–222.

Hinton, Elizabeth. 2016. *From the War on Poverty to the War on Crime: The Making of Mass Incarceration in America*. Cambridge, MA: Harvard University Press.

Hobbes, Stephen. 2016. "Death on Their Own Watch." *Sun-Sentinel*, December 1. http://projects.sun-sentinel.com.

Holzer, Harry, Stephen J. Raphael, and Michael A. Stoll. 2004. "Will Employers Hire Former Offenders? Employer Preferences, Background Checks, and Their Determinants." In *Imprisoning America: The Social Effects of Mass Incarceration*, edited by Mary Pattillo, David F. Weiman, and Bruce Western, 205–244. New York: Russell Sage Foundation.

Hounmenau, Charles. 2010. "Standards for Monitoring Human Rights of People in Police Lockups." Jane Addams College of Social Work, University of Illinois at Chicago, July. www.uic.edu.

Human Rights Watch. 2010. "The Price of Freedom: Bail and Pretrial Detention of Low Income Nonfelony Defendants in New York City." December. www.hrw.org.

———. 2013. "Profiting from Probation: America's 'Offender-Funded' Probation Industry." February. www.hrw.org.

———. 2015. "Callous and Cruel: Use of Force Against Inmates with Disabilities in U.S. Jails and Prisons." May 12. www.hrw.org.

Hume, David. 2000. *A Treatise of Human Nature*. Edited by David Fate Norton. Oxford: Oxford University Press.

Husserl, Edmund. 1970. *The Crisis of the European Sciences and Transcendental Philosophy: An Introduction to Phenomenological Philosophy*. Translated by David Carr. Evanston, IL: Northwestern University Press.

———. 1973. *Experience and Judgment: Investigations in a Genealogy of Logic*. Translated by James S. Churchill and Karl Ameriks. London: Routledge and Kegan Paul.

———. 2001a. *Logical Investigations*. Vol. 1. Translated by J. N. Findley. Preface by Michael Dummett. Edited by Dermot Moran. London: Routledge.

———. 2001b. *Logical Investigations*. Vol. 2. Translated by J. N. Findlay. Edited by Dermot Moran. London: Brill.

Illinois Bar Association. 2014. "Cook County Justice System Leaders to Tour DC Area Courts." June 14. http://iln.isba.org.

Illinois General Assembly. 2015. "730 ILCS 169/. Accelerated Resolution Court Act." July 1. www.ilga.gov.

Illinois Supreme Court, Administrative Office of the Illinois Courts. 2014. "Circuit Court of Cook County Pretrial Operational Review." March. www.illinoiscourts.gov.

"In a Virginia Jail, a Young Man Wasted Away and Died—and No One Bothered to Notice." 2016. *Washington Post*, June 10. www.washingtonpost.com.

Independent Commission on New York City Criminal Justice and Incarceration Reform. 2017. "A More Just New York City." April 2. www.safetyandjusticechallenge.org.

Ingarden, Roman. 1975. *On the Motives Which Led Husserl to Transcendental Idealism.* Translated by Arnor Hannibalsson. The Hague: Martinus Nijohff.

———. 1983. *Man and Value.* Translated by Arthur Szylewicz. Washington, DC: Catholic University Press of America.

"Inmate Tony Purrell Dies after Jail Fight." 2014. *Chicago Sun-Times*, February 20. www.suntimes.com.

"An Inmate Dies and No One Is Punished." 2015. *New York Times*, December 13. www.nytimes.com.

"In S.F. Debate, Both Sides Point to Humane Treatment." 2015. *San Francisco Chronicle*, December 15.

Irwin, John. 1985/2013. *The Jail: Managing the Underclass in American Society.* Foreword by Jonathan Simon. Berkeley: University of California Press.

Isaac, Rael Jean, and Virginia C. Armat. 1991. *Madness in the Streets: How Psychiatry and the Law Abandoned the Mentally Ill.* New York: Free Press.

Jackson, George. 1994. *Soledad Brother: The Prison Letters of George Jackson.* Introduction by Jean Genet. Foreword by Jonathan Jackson, Jr. Chicago: Lawrence Hill Books.

"Jailhouse Jeopardy: Guards Often Brutalize and Neglect Inmates in Harris County Jail, Records Show." 2015. *Houston Chronicle*, October 3. www.houstonchronicle.com.

James, Doris J., and Laurent Glaze. 2006. "Mental Health Problems of Prison and Jail Inmates." U.S. Department of Justice, Bureau of Justice Statistics, December 14.

Jaravsky, Ben. 2012. "Dumping Responsibility: The Case Against Closing CDPH Mental Health Clinics." Mental Health Movement, January. www.stopchicago.org.

———. 2013. "Before the Schools, Mayor Emmanuel Closed the Clinics." *Chicago Reader*, March 26. www.chicagoreader.com.

Jeffreys, Derek S. 2004a. "Ignoring Thomistic Metaphysics: A Reply to Robert Kraynak." *Journal of Markets and Morality* 7 (2): 527–531.

———. 2004b. "Personalists Are Not Kantians: Robert Kraynak and the Value of the Person." *Journal of Markets and Morality* 7 (2): 507–516.

———. 2008. *Spirituality and the Ethics of Torture.* New York: Palgrave Macmillan.

———. 2013. *Spirituality in Dark Places: The Ethics of Solitary Confinement.* New York: Palgrave Macmillan.

Johnson, Ann Braden. 1990. *Out of Bedlam: The Truth about Deinstitutionalization.* New York: Basic Books.

Jordan, Philip D. 1970a. "The Close and Stinking Jail." In *Frontier Law and Order: Ten Essays*, 140–155. Lincoln: University of Nebraska Press.

———. 1970b. "Gimmie a Hoss I Kin Ride!" In *Frontier Law and Order: Ten Essays*, 81–99. Lincoln: University of Nebraska Press.

"Judge: Sheriff Gusman 'Relinquishing Operational Control' over Troubled Orleans Jail." 2016. *New Orleans Times-Picayune*, June 21. www.nola.com.

Justice Policy Institute. 2012. "Bail Fail: Why the U.S. Should End the Practice of Using Money for Bail." September. www.justicepolicy.org.

Kaiser, David, and Lovisa Stannow. 2011. "Prison Rape and the Government." *New York Review of Books*, March 24. www.nybooks.com.

———. 2012. "Prison Rape: Obama's Program to Stop it." *New York Review of Books*, October 11. www.nybooks.com.

Kant, Immanuel. 2012. *Groundwork of the Metaphysics of Morals*. Translated by Mary Gregor and Jens Timmerman. Introduction by Christine M. Korsgaard. Cambridge: Cambridge University Press.

Kass, Leon R. 1997. "The Wisdom of Repugnance." *New Republic* 216 (22): 17–26.

Keenan, Cliff. 2015. "The Pretrial Services of the District of Columbia: A Leader in the Field." Washington, DC: Pretrial Services for the District of Columbia, April.

Kelly, Eugene. 1977. *Max Scheler*. Boston: Twayne.

———. 2011. *Material Ethics of Value: Max Scheler and Nicolai Hartmann*. London: Spring.

Kerstein, Samuel J. 2014. "Kantian Dignity: A Critique." In Düwell et al., *Cambridge Handbook of Human Dignity*, 222–230.

Kohler-Hausmann, Issa. 2014. "Managerial Justice and Mass Misdemeanors." *Stanford Law Review* 66 (3): 611–683.

Kolnai, Aurel. 1976. "Dignity." *Philosophy* 51 (197): 251–271.

———. 2004a. "Disgust." In Smith and Korsmeyer, *On Disgust*, 29–93.

———. 2004b. "The Standard Modes of Aversion: Fear, Disgust and Hatred." In Smith and Korsmeyer, *On Disgust*, 93–108.

"Lawsuit Accuses Cook County of Allowing 'Sadistic Culture' at Jail." 2014. *Chicago Tribune*, February 27. www.chicagotribune.com.

Leonard, Stephen J. 2002. *Lynching in Colorado, 1859–1919*. Boulder: University of Colorado Press.

Lewis, William David. 1965. *From Newgate to Donnemora: The Rise of the Penitentiary in New York, 1796–1848*. Ithaca, NY: Cornell University Press.

"Lincoln Hills Officials Failed to Oversee Rape Investigations." 2016. *Milwaukee Journal Sentinel*, June 26. http://archive.jsonline.com.

Lowenkamp, Christopher T., and Marie VanNostrand. 2013. "Assessing Pretrial Risk without a Defendant Interview." Arnold Foundation, November. www.pretrial.org.

Lowenkamp, Christopher T., Marie VanNostrand, and Alexander Holsinger. 2013. "Investigating the Impact of Pretrial Detention on Sentencing Outcomes." Arnold Foundation, November. www.arnoldfoundation.org.

Macallair, Daniel E. 2015. *After the Doors Were Locked: A History of Youth Corrections in California and the Origins of Twenty-First Century Reform*. Lanham, MD: Rowman & Littlefield.

Macklin, Ruth. 2003. "Dignity Is a Useless Concept: It Means No More Than Respect for Persons or Their Autonomy." *British Medical Journal* 327 (7429): 1419–1420.

Mamalian, Cynthia A. 2011. "State of the Science of Pretrial Risk Assessment." Pretrial Justice Institute, March. www.pretrial.org.

"Many Identities of New York Officers' Killer in a Life of Wrong Turns." 2015. *New York Times*, January 2. www.nytimes.com.

Maritain, Jacques. 1956. *The Existence and the Existent*. Translated by Lewis Glantiere and Gerald Phelan. New York: Doubleday.

Markowitz, Eric. 2015. "Report: Private Prison Lobbyists Spend Millions to Keep Immigrants Locked Up." *International Business Times*, April 19. www.ibtimes.com.

Marlin, Toni. 1998. "Strip Search." *Chicago Reader*, March 5. www.chicagoreader.com.

Martin, Steve J., and Sheldon Ekland-Olson. 1987. *Texas Prisons: The Walls Came Tumbling Down*. Foreword by Harry M. Whittington. Austin: Texas Monthly Press.

Martinson, Robert. 1974. "What Works?—Questions and Answers about Prison Reform." *Public Interest* 10: 22–54.

Mathiesen, Thomas. 2006. *Prisons on Trial*. 3rd ed. Foreword by Andrew Rutherford. Sherfield-on-Loddon: Waterside Press.

Mattick, Hans W., and Ronald P. Sweet. 1970. *Illinois Jails: Challenge and Opportunity for the 1970s*. Chicago: Illinois Law Enforcement Commission.

McConville, Sean. 1995. "Local Justice." In *The Oxford History of the Prison: The Practice of Punishment in Western Society*, edited by Norval Morris and David J. Rothman, 297–327. New York: Oxford.

McCrudden, Christopher, ed. 2014. *Understanding Human Dignity*. Oxford: Oxford University Press.

McGinn, Colin. 2011. *The Meaning of Disgust*. Oxford: Oxford University Press.

McKelvey, Blake. 1977. *American Prisons: A History of Good Intentions*. Montclair, NJ: Patterson Smith.

McLeod, Allegra M. 2015. "Prison Abolition and Grounded Justice." *UCLA Law Review* 62: 1156–1239.

———. 2016. "Decarceration Courts." In *Sentencing Law and Policy*, edited by John Plaff, 680–691. Saint Paul, MN: West Academic.

Meilaender, Gilbert. 2009. *Neither Beast nor God: The Dignity of the Human Person*. Jackson, TN: Encounter Books.

Meranze, Michael. 2012. *Laboratories of Virtue: Punishment, Revolution, and Authority in Philadelphia, 1760–1835*. Chapel Hill: University of North Carolina Press.

Miller, Eric J. 2004. "Drug Courts and Judicial Interventionism." *Ohio State Law Journal* 65: 1483–1569.

Miller, Vivien M. L. 2012. *Hard Labor and Hard Time: Florida's "Sunshine Prison" and Chain Gangs*. Gainesville: University Press of Florida.

Miller, William Ian. 1998. *The Anatomy of Disgust*. Cambridge, MA: Harvard University Press.

Minton, Todd D. 2015. "Jails in Indian Country, 2014." Bureau of Justice Statistics, October 25. www.bjs.gov.

Minton, Todd D., and Daniella Goloinelli. 2014. "Jail Inmates at Mid-year 2013—Statistical Tables." U.S. Department of Justice, Office of Justice Programs, Bureau of Justice Statistics, August 12. www.bjs.gov.

Mire, Bridget. 2014. "Justice Department Says Juvenile Detention Center Is Safe." *Houmatoday*, November 19. www.houmatoday.com.

Mitchell, Don. 2003. *The Right to the City: Social Justice and the Fight for Public Space.* New York: Guilford.

Mitford, Jessica. 1973. *Kind and Usual Punishment: The Prison Business.* New York: Knopf.

Mohanty, J. N. 1995. "The Development of Husserl's Thought." In *The Cambridge Companion to Husserl,* edited by Barry Smith and David Woodruff Smith, 45–78. Cambridge: Cambridge University Press.

Moran, Dermot. 2012. *Husserl's Crisis of the European Sciences and Transcendental Phenomenology: An Introduction.* Cambridge: Cambridge University Press.

Moyn, Samuel. 2014. "The Secret History of Constitutional Dignity." *Yale Human Rights and Development Journal* 17 (1): 39–73. http://digitalcommons.law.yale.edu.

Murphy, Jeffrie G. 1994. *Punishment and Rehabilitation.* Independence, KY: Wadsworth.

Mushlin, Michael B., and Michelle Deitch. 2016. "What's Going On in Our Prisons?" *New York Times,* January 4. www.nytimes.com.

Nagel, Thomas. 2012. *Mind and Cosmos: Why the Materialist Neo-Darwinian Conception of Nature Is Almost Certainly False.* Oxford: Oxford University Press.

National Coalition for the Homeless. 2016. "No Safe Street: A Survey of Hate Crimes and Violence Committed Against Homeless People in 2014 and 2015." July. http://nationalhomeless.org.

National Coalition for the Homeless and National Law Center on Homelessness and Poverty. 2006. "A Dream Denied: The Criminalization of Homelessness in the U.S." January. http://nationalhomeless.org.

———. 2009. "Homes Not Handcuffs: The Criminalization of Homelessness in U.S. Cities." http://nationalhomeless.org.

National Institute of Corrections. 2013. "Corrections Statistics by State." http://nicic.gov.

Newport, Melanie D. 2016. "Jail America: The Reformist Origins of the Carceral State." Ph.D. dissertation, Temple University.

———. N.d. "Exploring the History of the Jail Crisis." http://melanienewport.com.

"New York Officers' Killer, Adrift and Ill, Had a Plan." 2014. *New York Times,* December 21. www.nytimes.com.

Niebuhr, Reinhold. 1960. *Moral Man and Immoral Society: A Study in Ethics and Politics.* New York: Charles Scribner's Sons.

Nietzsche, Friedrich. 1969. *On the Genealogy of Morals.* Translated by Walter Kaufmann and R. J. Hollingdale. Edited by Walter Kaufman. New York: Vintage Books.

"N.J. Will Eliminate Cash Bail, Speed Up Criminal Trials in 2017." 2016. *Newsworks,* December 22. www.newsworks.org.

Nota, John H., S.J. 1983. *Max Scheler: The Man and His Work.* Translated by Theodore Plantinga and John H. Nota, S.J. Chicago: Franciscan Herald Press.

Nussbaum, Martha C. 2003. *Upheavals of Thought: The Intelligence of the Emotions.* Cambridge: Cambridge University Press.

———. 2006. *Hiding from Humanity: Disgust, Shame, and the Law*. Princeton, NJ: Princeton University Press.

Ober, Joshua. 2014. "Meritocratic and Civic Dignity in Greco-Roman Antiquity." In Düwell et al., *Cambridge Handbook of Human Dignity*, 53–64.

"Officer at Rikers Island Is Charged with Lying in Inmate's Death." 2014. *New York Times*, December 8. www.nytimes.com.

Olson, David E. 2012. "Characteristics of Inmates in the Cook County Jail." Criminal Justice and Criminology: Faculty Publications and Other Works, Paper 4. http://ecommons.luc.edu.

Olson, David E., and Koert Huddle. 2013. "An Examination of Admissions, Discharges and the Population of the Cook County Jail." *Cook County Sheriff's Reentry Council Research Bulletin*, March. http://works.bepress.com.

Oshinsky, David. 1997. *Worse Than Slavery: Parchman Farm and the Ordeal of Jim Crow Justice*. Princeton, NJ: Princeton University Press.

Pager, Devah. 2007. *Marked: Race, Crime, and Finding Work in an Era of Mass Incarceration*. Chicago: University of Chicago Press.

"Parents Say Jailers' Denial of Meds Killed Son." 2016. *Courthouse New Service*, March 15. www.courthousenews.com.

Pawasarat, John, and Lois M. Quinn. 2013. *Wisconsin's Mass Incarceration of African American Males: Workforce Challenges for 2013*. www.fusmadison.org.

Perkinson, Robert. 2010. *Texas Tough: The Rise of America's Prison Empire*. New York: Metropolitan Books/Henry Holt.

Perler, Dominik. 2001. *Ancient and Medieval Theories of Intentionality*. Leiden: Brill.

Petteruti, Amanda, and Nastassia Walsh. 2008. "Jailing Communities: The Impact of Jail Expansion and Effective Public Safety Strategies." Justice Policy Institute, April. www.justicepolicy.org.

Pfaff, John F. 2017. *Locked In: The True Causes of Mass Incarceration and How to Achieve Real Reform*. New York: Basic Books.

Pico della Mirandola, Giovanni. 1998. *On the Dignity of Man*. Indianapolis: Hackett.

Pinker, Stephen. 2008. "The Stupidity of Dignity." *New Republic*, May 28. http://pinker.wjh.harvard.edu.

Pisciotta, Alexander W. 1996. *Benevolent Repression: Social Control and the American Reformatory-Prison Movement*. New York: New York University Press.

Plantinga, Alvin. 1967. *God and Other Minds: A Study in the Rational Justification of Belief in God*. Ithaca, NY: Cornell University Press.

———. 1979. *The Nature of Necessity*. Oxford: Clarendon.

Police Accountability Task Force. 2016. "Recommendations for Reform: Restoring Trust between the Chicago Police and the Communities They Serve." April. http://chicagopatf.org.

"President Preckwinkle Opens Medical Facility at the Cook County Department of Corrections." 2014. Cook County Economic Development, June 4. http://blog.cookcountyil.gov.

Prinz, Jesse. 2011. *The Emotional Construction of Morals*. Oxford: Oxford University Press.

Prison Policy Initiative. 2013. "Please Deposit All of Your Money: Kickbacks, Rates, and Hidden Fees in the Jail Phone Industry." May. www.prisonpolicy.org.

———. 2017. "Whole Pie Initiative." March 14. www.prisonpolicy.org.

Radkoff, Jed S. 2014. "Why Innocent People Plead Guilty." *New York Review of Books*, November 20. www.nybooks.com.

Rantala, Ramona R., Jessica Rexroat, and Allen J. Beck. 2014. "Survey of Sexual Violence in Adult Correctional Facilities, 2009–11—Statistical Tables." U.S. Department of Justice, Office of Justice Programs, Bureau of Justice Statistics. www.bjs.gov.

Ray, Tyler. 2012. "President Obama: Close the Ten Worst Immigration Detention Facilities." *ACLU Blog*, November 29. www.aclu.org.

Reidel, Lauren E., Colleen L. Barry, Emma E. McGinty, Sanchini N. Bandara, Daniel W. Webster, Robert E. Toone, and Haiden A. Huskamp. 2016. "Improving Health Care Linkages for Criminal Justice-Involved Persons: The Cook County Jail Medicaid Enrollment Initiative." *Journal of Correctional Health Care* 22: 189–199.

Rejali, Darius. 2009. *Torture and Democracy*. Princeton, NJ: Princeton University Press.

Reutter, David M. 2007. "Pennsylvania County Jail System Overcrowded, Under-Regulated." *Prison Legal News*, December 15. www.prisonlegalnews.org.

———. 2015. "Second Federal Lawsuit Filed over Abuses at Pennsylvania County Prison." *Prison Legal News*, November 3. www.prisonlegalnews.org.

"Rikers Island." 2016. *CBS 60 Minutes*, April 17. www.cbsnews.com.

"Rikers Island Death." 2015. *New York Times*, January 22. www.nytimes.com.

"Rikers Island Fight Club." 2008. *Village Voice*, April 8. www.villagevoice.com.

Risen, James. 2015. "Psychologists Shielded U.S. Torture Program, Report Finds." *New York Times*, July 10. www.nytimes.com.

Rosen, Michael. 2012. *Dignity: Its History and Meaning*. Cambridge, MA: Harvard University Press.

———. 2014. "Dignity: The Case Against." In McCrudden, *Understanding Human Dignity*, 143–154.

Rosenberg, Tina. 2015. "Out of Debtors' Prison, with Law as Key." *New York Times*, March 27. http://opinionator.blogs.nytimes.com.

Rothman, David J. 1978. "The State as Parent: Social Policy in the Progressive Era." In *Doing Good: The Limits of Benevolence*, edited by Willard Gaylin, Ira Glasser, Steven Marcus, and David J. Rothman, 67–97. New York: Pantheon Books.

———. 1990. *The Discovery of the Asylum: Social Order and Disorder in the New Republic*. Boston: Little, Brown.

———. 2002. *Conscience and Convenience: The Asylum and Its Alternatives in Progressive America*. New York: Aldine de Gruyter.

Rothman, David J., and Sheila M. Rothman. 2005. *The Willowbrook Wars: Bringing the Mentally Disabled into the Community*. Livingston, NJ: Aldine Transaction.

Scheler, Max. 1970. *The Nature of Sympathy*. Translated by Peter Heath. Hamden, CT: Archon Books.

———. 1972. *Ressentiment*. Translated by Lewis Coser and William W. Holdheim. Introduction by Manfred S. Frings. Milwaukee: Marquette University Press.

———. 1973a. *Formalism in Ethics and Non-formal Ethics of Values. A New Attempt toward the Foundation of an Ethical Personalism*. Translated by Manfred S. Frings and Roger L. Funk. Evanston, IL: Northwestern University Press.

———. 1973b. "The Idols of Self-Knowledge." In Scheler, *Selected Philosophical Essays*, 3–98.

———. 1973c. "Ordo Amoris." In Scheler, *Selected Philosophical Essays*, 98–136.

———. 1973d. "Phenomenology and the Theory of Cognition." In Scheler, *Selected Philosophical Essays*, 136–202.

———. 1973e. *Selected Philosophical Essays*. Translated by David R. Lachterman. Evanston, IL: Northwestern University Press.

———. 1973f. "The Theory of Three Facts." In Scheler, *Selected Philosophical Essays*, 202–288.

———. 1987. *Person and Self-Value: Three Essays*. Translated and Edited by Manfred Frings. Dordrecht: Martinus Nijhoff.

———. 2009. *The Human's Place in the Cosmos*. Translated by Manfred S. Frings. Evanston, IL: Northwestern University Press.

Schept, Judah. 2015. *Progressive Punishment: Job Loss, Jail Growth, and the Neoliberal Logic of Carceral Expansion*. New York: New York University Press.

Schnacke, Timothy R., Michael R. Jones, and Claire M. Brooker. 2010. "The History of Bail and Pretrial Release." Pretrial Justice Institute, September. www.pretrial.org.

Schneck, Stephen, ed. 2002. *Max Scheler's Acting Persons: New Perspectives*. Amsterdam: Rodopi.

Scull, Andrew. 1977. *Deincarceration: Community Treatment and the Deviant*. Englewood Cliffs, NJ: Prentice Hall.

———. 2007. *Madhouse: A Tale of Megalomania and Modern Medicine*. New Haven, CT: Yale University Press.

———. 2016. *The Insanity of Place/The Place of Insanity: Essays on the History of Psychiatry*. New York: Routledge.

Searle, John. 1997. *The Construction of Social Reality*. New York: Free Press.

Sedmak, Clemons. 2014. "Human Dignity, Interiority, and Poverty." In McCrudden, *Understanding Human Dignity*, 559–571.

Semple, Janet. 1993. *Bentham's Prison: A Study of the Panopticon Penitentiary*. Oxford: Oxford University Press.

Senate Select Committee on Intelligence. 2014. "Committee Study of the Central Intelligence Agency's Detention and Interrogation Program." December 3. https://fas.org.

"Shocking Jail Video Shows Guard and Dog Attacking Prisoner." 2015. *NBC News*, April 30. www.nbcnews.com.

Simon, Jonathan. 2005. "Reversal of Fortune: The Resurgence of Individual Risk Assessment in Criminal Justice." *Annual Review of Law and Social Science* 1: 397–421.

———. 2009. *Governing through Crime*. New York: Oxford University Press.

———. 2014. *Mass Incarceration on Trial: A Remarkable Court Decision and the Future of Prisons in America*. New York: New Press.

Singer, Peter. 1993. *Practical Ethics*. Cambridge: Cambridge University Press.

"Six Year Sentence for Guard in Rikers Island Beatings." 2010. *New York Times*, August 6. www.nytimes.com.

Smith, Barry, and Carolyn Korsmeyer, eds. 2004. *On Disgust*. Chicago: Open Court.

Sokolowski, Robert. 2000. *Introduction to Phenomenology*. Cambridge: Cambridge University Press.

Spiegelberg, Herbert. 1986. "Human Dignity: A Challenge to Contemporary Philosophy." In *Steppingstones toward an Ethics for Fellow Existers*, 175–198. Dordrecht: Martinus Nijhoff.

Spillane, Joseph E. 2014. *Coxsackie: The Life and Death of Prison Reform*. Baltimore: Johns Hopkins University Press.

Staude, John Raphael. 1967. *Max Scheler, 1874–1928: An Intellectual Portrait*. New York: Free Press.

Steadman, Henry J., Fred C. Osher, Pamela Clark Robbins, Brian Case, and Stevens Samuels. 2009. "Prevalence of Serious Mental Illness among Jail Inmates." *Psychiatric Services* 60 (6): 761–765. http://csgjusticecenter.org.

Steenbakkers, Piet. 2014. "Human Dignity in Renaissance Humanism." In Düwell et al., *Cambridge Handbook of Human Dignity*, 85–94.

Stefan, Susan, and Bruce J. Winick. 2005. "A Dialogue on Mental Health Courts." *Psychology, Public Policy and Law* 11: 507–526.

Stillman, Sarah. 2014. "Get Out of Jail, Inc.: Does the Alternative-to-Incarceration Industry Profit from Injustice?" *New Yorker*, June 23. www.newyorker.com.

"Suit: Overcrowding, Inattentive Guards Led to Inmate's Beating Death." 2015. *Chicago Sun-Times*, February 10. http://chicago.suntimes.com.

Tompkins, Silvan S. 2008. *Affect Imagery Consciousness I: The Positive Effects*. New York: Springer.

Torrey, E. Fuller. 2013. *American Psychosis: How the Federal Government Destroyed the Mental Illness Treatment System*. New York: Oxford University Press.

Torrey, E. Fuller, Mary T. Zdanowicz, Aaron D. Kennard, Richard H. Lamb, Donald F. Eslinger, Michael C. Biasotti, and Doris A. Fuller. 2014. "Treatment of Persons with Mental Illness in Prisons and Jails." Treatment Advocacy Center, April 8. http://tacreports.org.

"Tribune Coverage: Illinois Budget." 2017. *Chicago Tribune*, July 6. www.chicagotribune.com.

Trotter, Greg. 2015. "Cook County Jail Trying to Attract Psychiatrists for Mentally Ill Inmates." *Chicago Tribune*, July 9. www.chicagotribune.com.

Tyson, Sarah. 2015. "Prison Abolition and a Culture of Sexual Difference." In *Death and Other Penalties: Philosophy in a Time of Mass Incarceration*, edited by Geoffrey Adelsberg, Lisa Guenther, and Scott Zeman, 210–224. New York: Fordham University Press.

Tyson, Sarah, and Joshua M. Hall, eds. 2014. *Philosophy Imprisoned: The Love of Wisdom in the Age of Mass Incarceration*. Lanham, MD: Lexington Books.

Ugerlvik, Thomas. 2016. "Prisons as Welfare Institutions? Punishment and the Nordic Model." In *Handbook on Prisons*, 2nd ed., edited by Yvonne Jewkes, Jamie Bennett, and Ben Crewe, 375–388. London: Routledge.

"Unanswered Questions Surround Deaths in Detention in Milwaukee County." 2014. *Milwaukee Journal Sentinel*, February 1. www.jsonline.com.

United Nations. 1948. "The Universal Declaration of Human Rights." www.un.org.

U.S. Attorney's Office, Northern District of Illinois. 2017. "Investigation of the Chicago Police Department." January 13. www.justice.gov.

U.S. Attorney's Office, Southern District of New York. 2014. "Manhattan U.S. Attorney Finds Pattern and Practice of Excessive Force and Violence at NYC Jails on Rikers Island That Violates the Constitutional Rights of Adolescent Male Inmates." August. www.justice.gov.

U.S. Department of Justice, Civil Rights Division. 2005. "Grant County Detention Center." May 18. www.justice.gov.

———. 2006a. "Dallas County Jail, Dallas, Texas." December 8. www.justice.gov.

———. 2006b. "Sebastian County Adult Detention, Fort Smith, Arkansas." May 9. www.justice.gov.

———. 2007. "Oahu Community Correctional Center." March 14. www.justice.gov.

———. 2008a. "Investigation of Civil Rights Division and the United States Attorney's Office into Conditions at the Cook County Jail." July 11. www.justice.gov.

———. 2008b. "Investigation of the Oklahoma County Jail and Jail Annex, Oklahoma City, Oklahoma." July 31. www.justice.gov.

———. 2009a. "CRIPA Investigation of the Westchester County Jail, Valhalla, New York." November 19. www.justice.gov.

———. 2009b. "Investigation of the Lake County Jail." December 7. www.justice.gov.

———. 2009c. "Mobile County Metro Jail." January 15. www.justice.gov.

———. 2009d. "Orleans Parish Prison System, New Orleans, Louisiana." September 11. www.justice.gov.

———. 2011a. "Investigation of the Leflore County Juvenile Detention Center." March 31. www.justice.gov.

———. 2011b. "Investigation of the Miami-Dade County Jail." August 24. www.justice.gov.

———. 2011c. "Investigation of Robertson County Detention Center." August 26. www.justice.gov.

———. 2011d. "Terrebonne Parish Juvenile Detention Center, Houma, Louisiana," January 18. www.justice.gov.

———. 2012a. "Investigation of Piedmont Regional Jail, Pursuant to the Civil Rights of Institutionalized Persons Act, 42 U, S.C. § 1997, and the Religious Land Use and Institutionalized Persons Act of 2000 ('RLUIP A')." September 6. www.justice.gov.

———. 2012b. "Update to Letter of Findings, United States Civil Rights Investigation of the Orleans Parish Prison." April 23. www.justice.gov.

———. 2013a. "Investigation of the Escambia County Jail." May 22. www.justice.gov.

———. 2013b. "Miami-Dade County Jail Settlement Agreement." April 30. www. justice.org.

———. 2015a. "Investigation of the Ferguson Police Department." March 4. www. justice.gov.

———. 2015b. "Joint Settlement Agreement Regarding the Los Angeles County Jails and Stipulated [Proposed] Order of Resolution." August 5. www.justice.gov.

———. 2016. "Investigation of the Baltimore Police Department." August 10. www. justice.gov.

———. 2017. "For Immediate Release, Former Oklahoma Jail Superintendent and Assistant Superintendent Sentenced for Using Excessive Force." February 17. www. justice.gov.

U.S. District Court for Illinois. 2015. "*United States v. Cook County, Illinois.* Corrections Monitor Susan W. McCampbell's Report No. 10, May 27, 2015." www.justice.gov.

Valenstein, Elliot S. 1986. *Great and Desperate Cures: The Rise and Decline of Psychosurgery and Other Radical Treatments for Mental Illness.* New York: Basic Books.

Velázquez, Tracey, Melissa Neal, and Spike Bradford. 2012. "Bailing on Justice: The Dysfunctional System of Using Money to Buy Pretrial Freedom." *Prison Legal News,* November. www.prisonlegalnews.org.

Vera Institute of Justice. 2015. "Incarceration's Front Door: The Misuse of Jails in America." August 29. www.vera.org.

von Hildebrand, Dietrich. 1953. *Christian Ethics.* New York: David McKay.

———. 1957. *Graven Images: Substitutes for True Morality.* With Alice Jordain. New York: David McKay.

———. 1991. *What Is Philosophy?* Introduction by Joseph Seifert. New York: Routledge.

———. 2009. *The Nature of Love.* Translated by John F. Crosby with John Henry Crosby. Introduction by John F. Crosby. Preface by Kenneth L. Schmitz. South Bend, IN: St. Augustine's Press.

———. 2012. *The Heart: An Analysis of Human and Divine Affection.* Introduction by John F. Crosby. Preface by John Haldane. South Bend, IN: St. Augustine's Press.

Waldron, Jeremy. 2012. *Dignity, Rank, and Rights.* Commentaries by Wai Chef Dimock, Don Herzog, and Michael Rosen. Edited by Meir Dan-Cohen. Oxford: Oxford University Press.

Walsh, John P. 2013. *The Culture of Urban Control: Jail Overcrowding in the Crime Control Era.* Lanham, MD: Lexington Books.

Whitman, James Q. 2003. *Harsh Justice: Criminal Justice and the Widening Gap between America and Europe.* Oxford: Oxford University Press.

Williams, Marian R. 2003. "The Effects of Pretrial Detention on Imprisonment Decisions." *Criminal Justice Review* 28 (2): 299–311.

Wilson, James Q. 1975. *Thinking about Crime.* New York: Basic Books.

Wilson, James Q., and George L. Kelling. 1982. "Broken Windows: The Police and Neighborhood Safety." *Atlantic,* March, 29–38.

Wines, E. C., and Theodore W. Dwight. 1867. *Report on the Prisons and Reformatories of the United States and Canada Made to the Legislature of New York, January 1867.* Albany, NY: Van Ben Thuysen and Sons.

Wisconsin Department of Justice. 2014. "Wisconsin Domestic Abuse Incident Report for the Period of January 1, 2012–December 31, 2012." www.doj.state.wi.us.

Wolter, Allen B., O.M., ed. 1987. *Duns Scotus: Philosophical Writings.* Indianapolis: Hackett.

Wood, Amy Louise. 2009. *Lynching and Spectacle: Witnessing Racial Violence in America, 1890–1940.* Chapel Hill: University of North Carolina Press.

Zagzebski, Linda. 2001. "The Uniqueness of Persons." *Journal of Religious Ethics* 29 (3): 401–423.

Zimbardo, Philip. 2008. *The Lucifer Effect: Understanding How Good People Turn Evil.* New York: Random House.

INDEX

abolitionism, 11, 129, 156, 166–168, 180, 181n11

Accelerated Resolution Court Act, 160

actuarial justice, 117–118, 194n25

affective response, 71, 80–82, 84, 86, 97, 99, 103–104, 116, 124, 125, 126, 129, 135, 136, 149–151, 156, 168–169, 171, 176

Affordable Care Act, 162

Ahmed, Sara, 8, 79, 106–107, 193n11

Alexander, Michelle, 166, 181n5

American Civil Liberties Union (ACLU), 13, 39, 42, 43, 44, 45, 59, 60, 61, 63, 69–70, 187n41, 195n9

Aquinas, Thomas, 72, 78, 188n7

Arnold Foundation, 58, 122, 142, 143, 186n38, 196n23

Auburn Prison (New York), 168

Ballard, Bradley, 115

Baltimore County Jail (Maryland), 49, 185n20

Ben-Moshe, Liat, 139, 173, 195n4

Bentham, Jeremy: and "Inspection Principle," 127–128; and Panopticon, 127–128, 194n2

Bernstein, Jay M., 106, 188n5, 192nn40, 41, 193n8, 193n10

Blue, Ethan, 187n45

Boonin, David, 185n2, 187–188n46

Brentano, Franz, 190n19

Brinsley, Ismaaiyl, 1–2, 182n2

Broward County Jail (Florida), 186n31

Brown County (Wisconsin), 57, 121, 170, 179

Brown County Jail (Wisconsin), 140

Brown v. Plata, 174

Burge, Jon, 112, 193n13

Bush, George W., 75; and torture, 92

Camarillo State Hospital (California), 139, 196n18

Cameron, Edwin, 76, 188n5

Carrier, Nicolas, 182n12, 198n9, 199n16

Chicago, City of, 4, 24, 25, 26, 35, 162; and mental health clinics, 31

Chicago Community Trust, 127, 164–165

Chicago Police Department: and arrests, 111–113; and racism, 113

Clinton Correctional Facility (New York), 133, 195n8

Cicero, and dignity, 71, 74, 78, 188n3, 188n10

Christie, Nils, 182n11, 198n13

Clarke, W. Norris, S.J., 188n7

Cook County Jail (Illinois), 4, 15–36, 56, 60, 67, 176–177; reforms in, 31–32, 159–166

Conroy, John, 193n13, 193n15

Constitution Project, 147–148

contempt, 9, 69, 168; deadly consequences of, 114–116; elimination of, 149–151, 176; in jails, 109–116; nature of, 103–104, 108–109, 125, 126

Corrections Corporation of America (CCA), 69

Crisis Intervention Training (CIT), 137

Crosby, John F., 83, 180, 189n13, 191nn29–30

Cummins, Eric, 187n46

ABOUT THE AUTHOR

Derek S. Jeffreys is Professor of Humanities and Religion at the University of Wisconsin, Green Bay. His work focuses on ethics and violence, and he has written books on ethics and solitary confinement, and ethics and torture.